TOEFL SKILLS
FOR TOP SCORES

Patricia Noble Sullivan
Grace Yi Qiu Zhong

11 - YS 165

-YS 166

May -19

ARCO

NEW YORK

ARCO

Simon & Schuster, Inc.
Gulf + Western Building
One Gulf + Western Plaza
New York, NY 10023

DISTRIBUTED BY PRENTICE HALL TRADE

Manufactured in the United States of America

1 2 3 4 5 6 7 8 9 10

Library of Congress Cataloging-in-Publication Data

Sullivan, Patricia, 1942–
    TOEFL skills for top scores.

    1. English language—Textbooks for foreign
speakers. 2. English language—Examinations,
questions, etc. I. Zhong, Grace. II. Title.
PE1128.S94 1988   428.2′4′076   88–7870
ISBN 0–13–467762–5

TO MICK AND JOHN
FOR THEIR ENCOURAGEMENT
AND SUPPORT

CONTENTS

WHY THIS BOOK WAS WRITTEN   IX

ACKNOWLEDGMENTS   XI

HOW TO USE THIS BOOK   XIII

TWENTY-ONE SECRETS
TO HELP YOU PREPARE FOR THE TEST   1

    Secret One: Plan Your Time Well   1
    Secret Two: Notice Differences in Testing Dates   2
    Secret Three: Learn to Concentrate   4
    Secret Four: Practice, Practice, Practice   4
    Secret Five: Identify the Testing Point   8
    Secret Six: Use Available Study Material   11
    Secret Seven: Make It Hard on Yourself   12
    Secret Eight: Prepare for the Rhythm of TOEFL   14
    Secret Nine: Be Aware of Your Physical Limitations   14
    Secret Ten: Train Your Mind to Shift
       Quickly from One Task to Another   15
    Secret Eleven: Work Quickly and Steadily   17
    Secret Twelve: Make Every Second Count   18
    Secret Thirteen: Mark Your Answer Sheet Efficiently   19
    Secret Fourteen: Don't Be Afraid to Guess   20
    Secret Fifteen: Know the Difference
       between Raw Scores and Converted Scores   20
    Secret Sixteen: Get a Double Benefit   25
    Secret Seventeen: Recognize Your Strengths and Use Them   26
    Secret Eighteen: Understand the Inverted V Pattern   27
    Secret Nineteen: Let Your Test-Day Excitement Help   28
    Secret Twenty: Expect the Unexpected   29
    Secret Twenty-One: Get a Head Start with Mental Warm-ups   30

EXERCISE WORKBOOK   33
Listening Comprehension   33
Structure and Written Expression   48
Vocabulary and Reading Comprehension   80
Writing the TOEFL Essay   94
Overall Hints and Strategies for Taking the TOEFL   107

PRACTICE TEST 1   111
Section 1   111
Section 2   119
Section 3   125

PRACTICE TEST 2   137
Section 1   137
Section 2   145
Section 3   151

ANSWERS TO WORKBOOK EXERCISES   163
Practice Test 1—Answer Key   175
Practice Test 2—Answer Key   176

EXPLANATORY ANSWERS FOR PRACTICE TEST 1   177

LISTENING COMPREHENSION TAPESCRIPTS   233
Exercise Workbook   233
Practice Test 1   239
Practice Test 2   243

ANSWER SHEETS   249

WHY THIS BOOK WAS WRITTEN

There are many TOEFL books for sale. Most of them give you practice tests, vocabulary lists, and grammar exercises. These are all important, of course. But—they aren't enough. This book, besides giving you practice tests and exercises, gives you another look at the TOEFL, the inside look.

In this book you will learn how to answer such common questions as:

- What study techniques can help me pass the test?
- Why do some people who can speak, read, and understand English still get a low score?
- How can I reduce my fear of taking the test?
- How can I work well under such great pressure?
- How can I increase my speed in answering the questions?
- What can I do if I hear the tape and understand the speakers, but don't have enough time to choose the correct answer?
- How can I learn the immense amount of vocabulary on the test?
- How can I understand the American cultural questions on the test if I haven't lived in the USA?
- How can I finish in time if I am a very slow reader?

The Chinese author of this book was once in just your situation. When she arrived in the United States, she had to take the TOEFL in order to be admitted to the university. She felt, however, that her background in English was not good enough. She took several practice tests, and studied hard. But she was still afraid of the test. When she finally did take it, she did not get a score high enough to enter the university. She looked around at other students and wondered why some of them did well on the test and some did poorly, even though they all seemed to know English quite well. Then she changed her study habits and began working on test-taking skills. As a result, she did pass the TOEFL, and was accepted as a graduate student. In the process of preparing again and again for the TOEFL, she learned many things about test-taking. You could probably learn these things if you took the test many times, but that takes a lot of time and money, and it is often difficult to arrange. By following the advice and exercises in this book, you will learn about test-taking skills that will help you improve your score as you prepare for the TOEFL.

We see three major areas that help determine how well you do on the test. They are:

1. your knowledge of the English language (vocabulary, reading, structure, and listening comprehension)
2. your skills at taking a standarized timed test
3. the amount of anxiety you have when you take the test

This book prepares you to answer the TOEFL questions not only by increasing your knowledge of English, but also by increasing your knowledge of test-taking skills and strategies. By learning to analyze the questions and the testing points, you will become more confident in your test-taking skills. Your anxiety will lessen as you learn more about the test. We suggest that you prepare for the TOEFL as you might prepare for a competitive game or sport. Practice the skills of the game, but also become familiar with the rules of the game. For the TOEFL, the "rules of the game" include knowledge of test-taking skills.

As people with two very different backgrounds, we bring together two approaches to studying for the TOEFL. One of us has been an instructor of English and TOEFL techniques for many years in many countries; the other has been a student of English and a taker of the TOEFL many times. We both want you to pass the TOEFL. We want you to be able to do your best. We would also like to hear about either problems or successes you have with this book. You can write to us at Arco Books, One Gulf + Western Plaza, New York, NY 10023. We hope to hear from you.

Patricia N. Sullivan
Grace Yi Qiu Zhong

ACKNOWLEDGMENTS

Several people have helped us in the development of this book. We would especially like to thank John Wang and Adam Sullivan for their graphs and illustrations. Barbara Franklin and Gerry Rosina Craver made valuable comments on the early stages of the book. Pat Noble spent many hours reading and correcting the manuscript. Thanks also to the students at Cabrillo College and the University of California at Santa Cruz who took practice tests and did exercises over a two-year period.

HOW TO USE THIS BOOK

Each part of this book has a different purpose. The parts can be used in any order, but we suggest the following:

TWENTY-ONE SECRETS TO PREPARE FOR THE TEST

Read through Secrets One through Fourteen and do all the suggested exercises. After reading Secret Fourteen, take Practice Test 1. Correct it, using the answer key and the explanatory answers. Then go back and read Secrets Fifteen through Twenty-one. At the same time, begin the Exercise Workbook.

EXERCISE WORKBOOK

Do the exercises in the Exercise Workbook after you have taken Practice Test 1 and corrected it. Do the exercises in any order. You may do all of them or choose only the ones that help you the most. While you are doing this part of the book, continue reading Secrets Fifteen through Twenty-one to prepare you for the day you take the real test. The Exercise Workbook also contains a TOEFL essay section. Read and practice the exercises in this part any time.

TOEFL ESSAY

Read and practice the exercises in this part any time.

PRACTICE TESTS

Take Practice Test 1 after you have read Secrets One through Fourteen. Correct your test and make notes about the errors you made. Then turn back to the Exercise Workbook, and do the exercises in the areas that you need to work on. Take Practice Test 2 whenever you feel you are ready. Don't write your answers on the test. Write your answers only on the answer sheets in the back of the book. By doing this, you can take the Practice Tests again. Even though you may remember some of the answers, the process of taking the test will help you improve your test-taking skills. Each time you take the Practice Tests, you can try to answer the questions more quickly.

N O T E

The listening comprehension exercises and practice tests in this book are recorded on a cassette tape. To order your tape, fill out the order blank at the back of the book and mail it to the address indicated.

TOEFL SKILLS FOR TOP SCORES

TWENTY-ONE SECRETS TO HELP YOU PREPARE FOR THE TEST

The word "secret" is usually used for information shared by only a few people. The secrets on the next pages, however, are known by many good test-takers. Now they can be part of your knowledge, too.

SECRET ONE: PLAN YOUR TIME WELL

Studying for the TOEFL is hard. There may be many other things that you would rather do. But in order to do well on the exam, you must make extra time for studying. You must organize your time.

ORGANIZE YOUR TIME

You are adding something new to your daily schedule. You need to figure out the best time for a regular study period. First of all, write the answers to these questions:

What day do you plan to take the TOEFL? _____

How much time is there until that day? _____

Now figure out the best time of the day for you to study. Answer these questions:

What time do you usually get up? _____

What do you do in the morning? _____

What time do you have lunch? _____

What is your afternoon schedule? _____

What time do you eat dinner? _____

What do you usually do after dinner?_____

Look at your daily schedule and figure out the best time for you to plan on a regular time for studying.

The best time for me to study for the TOEFL is from _____
                                                                                                TIME

to _____ on _____.
         TIME   **DAYS**

SECRET TWO: NOTICE DIFFERENCES IN TESTING DATES

Even though the TOEFL tests are basically the same on every test date, there are some differences. You should be aware of some possible differences so that they won't surprise you while you are taking the test. You can also use your knowledge of testing date differences to help you decide on the best date for you to take the test.

First of all, if there are any major changes, they will be announced in the Bulletin of Information for the TOEFL that you use for registration. Be sure to read that booklet carefully.

The Format of the Answer Sheet: There are two different ways that TOEFL test answer sheets are organized:

horizontally Ⓐ Ⓑ Ⓒ Ⓓ   or vertically Ⓐ
                                                                                        Ⓑ
                                                                                        Ⓒ
                                                                                        Ⓓ

You won't know which form is used until you see the test. And when you begin the test, you have only a few seconds to choose and mark each answer. You don't want to waste even one second by wondering where to mark your answers. You need to save all possible time for concentrating on choosing the answers. In the back of this book, you will find both styles of answer sheets. Use a different one for each practice test so that you are familiar with both styles.

The Length of the Test: In the description of the TOEFL test sections in this book, you will read about the standard number of questions (Listening Comprehension = 50; Structure and Written Expression = 40; Vocabulary and Reading Comprehension = 60. Total number of questions = 150).

On some test dates, however, you might find more questions and more time for marking your answers. When you are allowed to open your test booklet for each section, look quickly ahead to see how many questions there are. Then you can plan your time better. On some past dates there have been 80 Listening Comprehension questions, 60 Structure and Written Expression questions, and 90 Vocabulary and Reading Comprehension questions. If you get this long form, don't be worried. All tests vary a little. This is the reason for converted scores (see Secret Fifteen). Your raw score will be adjusted so that the value of the tests is equal, no matter how many questions you have or how hard they are.

Keeping Your Test Booklet: On certain days that are announced in the Bulletin, you will be allowed to keep your test booklet. Check your Bulletin for information on how you can receive it. If the test booklet is mailed, you must bring a 6-inch (15.3 cm) by 9-inch (22.8 cm) self-addressed, stamped envelope to the test center. Having the test booklet can be helpful. You can also buy the tape and your own answer sheet for a short period of time after you take the test.

Test of Written English (TWE): The Test of Written English is not given on every test day. In the past, it has been given four times a year, but this may change each year. On the days it is given, you are required to write a short essay. Check the current Bulletin to see which specific test days offer the writing test. Many universities want to see your essay score.

Cost: There are international test dates (usually on Saturdays) and special test dates (usually on Fridays). The special test days cost more. Try to plan your schedule so that you can take the cheaper test.

N O T E

Always read the most recent Bulletin of Information carefully so that you can take advantage of all the options in choosing a test date. The standard (shorter) test form, the TWE, and the chance to receive your own test booklet usually happen on the same test-taking day. Look for the stars (*) beside the dates in the Bulletin of Information.

SECRET THREE: LEARN TO CONCENTRATE

Now that you have figured out what test to take and the best time for you to study, you need to be sure to use your time well. You are probably a busy person. By using your time well and concentrating, you will get more done in a shorter amount of time. Do the following:

1. Choose a place to study that has a desk or table with a comfortable chair and a good light.
2. Get all your study materials together on your desk (books, pencils, paper, tape recorder).
3. Tell the people you live with that you do not want to be interrupted.
4. Sit down and allow yourself two minutes to calm down. Relax your body. Breathe deeply. Clear your mind of all the other things you have been thinking about.
5. Check the time that you are beginning to study, and decide how long you will concentrate.
6. Begin your work and don't stop until your break time.

Concentrating means that you think about only one thing (your TOEFL study material). If this is very difficult for you, then start slowly. You might get a timer and set it for fifteen minutes at first. Put your timer where you can't see it while you are studying. Concentrate until the timer goes off. Then take a short break, and let yourself think about anything you want. Stand up and walk around. Talk to someone if you want. But in a few minutes, sit down and set the timer again. Continue this procedure, each time setting the timer for a longer period of time. Continue this over several days or study periods until you can concentrate for an hour.

SECRET FOUR: PRACTICE, PRACTICE, PRACTICE

A person can study all the rules of driving a car, and still be a poor driver. Knowing the rules is not enough. Actual practice is essential. It takes time to develop good skills, no matter what you are learning.

SAMPLE TESTS

Taking a test is a skilled activity. In addition to studying vocabulary and grammar, you must practice the skills of taking the test itself. As you take the practice tests, your test-taking skills get better. This book gives you two practice tests. When you apply to take the TOEFL test, you can also order the TOEFL test kit, which will give you more practice tests. Because of the time limit on the test, you must be efficient. The more you practice, the more efficient you become.

The best practice is under conditions similar to those you will have in the testing situation. Force yourself to stay within the time limitation. Your skills will develop slowly, but will become more reliable with time. Passing the test requires more than saying, "I understand the question." It requires that you respond correctly on paper under stress. It requires a quick, automatic reaction. Many people feel that they have studied enough when they can understand the general question and also the details in the questions. They haven't. There is one more necessary step. You must be able to respond quickly and automatically. If you still need a lot of time to "think over" or "process" what you have heard or read, then you need more practice.

Pay attention to the simple rules and the easy tasks. You will use these simple rules to help you answer complicated questions. Remember, you need to *use* those rules, not just say that you understand them.

LISTENING COMPREHENSION

Many students consider the listening section of the TOEFL to be the most difficult part of the test. This is true for many because:

1. It comes first on the test.
2. The spoken parts are not repeated.
3. There is only a short time to respond to each question.
4. It is sometimes hard to get good listening practice material.

This book comes with a tape for listening comprehension. (See the order form on page 253.) You should listen to your tape again and again. Spend an hour a day or even two hours a day listening to the tape, especially during the two weeks before you take the test. There are four levels in the development of your listening comprehension skills:

1. You can understand some words, but not the complete sentence.
2. You can understand the complete sentence.

3. You can understand the complete sentence and also figure out the main point that you are being tested on.
4. You can figure out the main testing point and its relationship to the possible answers.

As you practice again and again on the same tape, you will progress through the four levels. As you practice on new tapes, you will also notice your comprehension level getting better. When you reach the fourth level, you will know that you have a reliable listening skill and are ready for the real test. (See Secret Four for more about figuring out the testing point.)

STRUCTURE

One good way to practice and to test yourself on the application of rules is to make your own personal summary of rules. When you work on the practice exercises, do more than just try to get the right answer. Try to think actively of what the rule is, and how to apply that rule to the grammar exercise question. Follow the steps below to make your own personalized rule summary.

Personal Rule Summary

STEP 1: Carefully study the rules, explanations, and examples in the Structure section of this book or of any other grammar book. Then, write each of the rules again in your own words, and write your own example sentence for each rule. The examples in text books are written to help you understand the rules, but you don't need to remember those particular sentences. You do, however, have to know the rules, and writing your own sentences will help you remember the rules. Write a sentence that is true, and that uses the name of someone you know.

> EXAMPLE: You want to remember the rule for using "for" and "since." First, write the rule from your grammar book. Then write your own personal true sentence.
> Your sentence might be:
>
> "I have been studying for the TOEFL test since March." *or*
> "I have been studying for the TOEFL test for two months." *or*
> "My brother can stand on his head for two minutes."

This step will help you change your thick grammar book into a thin, simple, meaningful collection of information. Begin slowly. Get a separate notebook just for your rule summary. Write a few rules and examples in it each day. Slowly your rule summary will grow.

STEP 2: Take a practice TOEFL test, trying to remember and apply the rules from Step 1. Then correct your practice test and find the mistakes you made. Classify those mistakes into two categories:

1. Mistakes you made because you forgot the rule.
2. Mistakes you made because you did not know the rule.

STEP 3: Change your rule summary, adding the information from Step 2 to your summary. If you made a mistake because you forgot the rule, then make a note about that beside the rule. If you didn't know the rule, then add it to your list of rules.

> EXAMPLE 1: In your rule summary you may have a rule like this:
>
> When words are written in a series, and connected by "and," they must have parallel structure. (They must all be nouns, or gerunds, or infinitives.)
>
> But in your practice test, you miss a question like this:
>
> "The men gave all their time, their money, and energy."
>
> You need to add a note to your summary that says you also need to keep pronouns parallel. (The correct sentence is "The men gave all their time, their money, and their energy.")
>
> EXAMPLE 2: You may have this rule in your summary:
>
> Some verbs, like "agree," "decide," and "fail," need an infinitive after them (not a gerund).
>
> But you miss a question that looks like this:
> "He promised taking me to the store."
>
> Then you must add to your summary that the word "promise" also needs an infinitive after it. (The correct sentence is "He promised to take me to the store.")

If you follow these three steps and keep your rule summary up-to-date,* you will have an excellent personalized study guide. It may seem too time-consuming in the beginning, but actually it will save you time in the end. You will understand the reasons for your mistakes. You will build on your

---

D E F I N I T I O N

*To keep something up-to-date:** to add new information to a file or notebook as soon as your information changes.

own knowledge, and you will be able to apply the rules to new sentences. Then, when the time comes for you to take the real test, all you have to do for the grammar section is review your own list and notes.

Remember, it takes a lot of time and practice to learn a new skill. Whether you are learning to drive a car, ride a bike, swim, or take a test, the more you practice, the better you will be.

SECRET FIVE: IDENTIFY THE TESTING POINT

When you look at a cow, you see an animal with four legs, but when a skillful butcher looks at that cow, he may see a combination of muscle, fat, and bone. By looking at the "inside" of the cow, the butcher has more knowledge about the cow and can do a skillful job. In a similar way, you can do a more skillful job of test-taking if you look at the "inside" of the TOEFL test.

When preparing for the TOEFL, you are probably studying the general rules of the test and answering practice test questions. These are the "outside" of the test. We suggest you add one more step to your study: look for the underlying testing points.

What is a testing point? A testing point is the information that the examiner is testing for. There are many different kinds of testing points. The examiner might be testing you on a particular grammatical rule, or the meaning of a word, or the mood of the speaker. When you look for the testing point, you are asking yourself, "What kind of knowledge is the question asking me to demonstrate?"

Why is it important to identify the testing point? It is important because it saves you time on the test. If you know the testing point you can concentrate on only one part of a test question. Look at the following example of a structure test question:

> TEST SENTENCE: My friend Jean, who is a virtuoso with castanets, are performing at the university theater tonight.
>
> > *Testing Point:* agreement of main subject and verb. If you can recognize the testing point, you can see that the error is with the main verb.

Extra Information: The meaning of the words "virtuoso" and "castanets" in the adjective clause are unnecessary for the testing point in this question. You don't have to waste time trying to figure them out.

Confusing Information: The examiner is trying to confuse you by using a plural word ("castanets") before the verb ("are").

Correction: The correct sentence should be: "My friend Jean . . . is performing. . . ."

R E M E M B E R

Your goal on the TOEFL exam is to get the correct answers quickly; it is not always necessary to understand every word in each question.

If you practice answering test questions without thinking of testing points, you might have a misleading score. There are hundreds of questions that have been used in previous TOEFL tests, and hundreds more that will be used on future tests. You cannot learn all the questions that will be on future tests.

- By forcing yourself to think of the testing point, you will be learning about a category of language. The categories will be repeated on future tests. Test questions are developed to reflect certain testing points.
- By teaching yourself to identify testing points, you are helping yourself to combine a knowledge of rules with possible ways to apply those rules.
- It takes time to learn to identify testing points, but that study time is important. As you practice determining the testing points, you get faster at it. You will be able to find the testing points quickly, and that will help you to work faster and more precisely on the test.

We suggest that you use the following system for your independent study and your practice tests so that by the time you take the real test, you can quickly identify testing points.

1. Read the question.
2. Think: What is the testing point?
3. Search your mind: What are the rules of the testing point?
4. Use your experience: What is the best answer?
5. Choose the answer in the test booklet.

If you are like most people, you are probably aware of only doing Steps 1 and 5 above (read the question and choose the answer). Steps 2 and 3 may seem to take too much time. But actually you probably do Steps 2 and 3 without realizing it for the questions you know. Try this same process for the difficult questions. It will become easier for you as you continue to look for categories of testing points. You will begin to recognize testing points quickly. It will save you time later when you take the real test.

When you study grammar, you should be making your own personal rule summary (see page 6). As you add rules and personal example sentences, your book will become thick. This "thick book" is important because it is thorough and detailed. The next step is to outline the rules and look for testing points. This second step turns your "thick book" into a "thin book." Both steps are important. Without the "thick book," your study is not thorough; without the "thin book" your knowledge is not in order and it difficult to apply your knowledge to test questions quickly.

Below are listed a few grammar testing points. See how many more you can list as you are studying.

STRUCTURE

Adjective Clause: The man who lost his wallet called the police station.

Superlative: One of the most exciting times of my life was boarding the plane to cross the ocean.

Parallel Construction: His singing and dancing thrilled the audience.

Noun Clause as Subject: What the teacher said was astonishing.

LISTENING COMPREHENSION

Reference: Larry took his brother's car to work. (Possible question: Who went to work?)

Comparative: Sue gets less exercise than she should. (Possible question: Does Sue get enough exercise?)

Negative: They have hardly any money. (Possible question: Do they have a lot of money?)

Conditional: If he had asked her, she would have gone with him. (Possible question: Did he ask her to go?)

EXERCISE 1

Sample Testing Points

DIRECTIONS: For each sentence below, write one possible grammatical testing point. (On a real test, there could be other testing points.) Use the sample sentences on this page as a guide. The first one has been done for you. The answers are on page 163.

Testing Point

1. If you don't hurry, you'll miss the bus.   *conditional*

2. Carlos didn't have to go to work today.

3. My uncle is the most reasonable man I know.

4. Maria gave her mother a scarf for her birthday.

5. Mei Ling is good at swimming, drawing, and singing.

SECRET SIX: USE AVAILABLE STUDY MATERIAL

You probably have English books; you may already have a TOEFL exercise book. These are essential. But there are other sources of English language study material that can help you improve your English and study for the TOEFL exam. Remember that the TOEFL exam is testing your general language knowledge. And your general language knowledge will improve as you use a variety of study material.

Look around you. Even if you are not in the United States, you can probably find some places where English is used. Are there any radio programs in English? Are there any English language newspapers? Is there a program in English on television? Can you find any advertisements in English? Do you know any Americans you can talk to? All of these are sources for your personal study. If you are in the United States already, you have a big selection of material.

Here are some things you can do:

1. Find an English language program on the radio. Listen for the news. (An American speaker is best since you will hear an American accent on the

TOEFL tape.) If you are in the United States, then listen to any news program.

2. Get a tape recorder and tape the news program as you listen to it. Once you have it taped, you can listen to it again and again until you understand most of it. Try to understand the meanings of the new words by guessing. After listening several times, write down the new words (guess at the spelling), and look them up in your dictionary or ask a friend for the meaning. You already know something about the words because of what you know about the news story.

3. Find an English language newspaper and look for an article about the same topic that you have just been listening to. Your reading comprehension will be greatly improved because you already know something about the story. Now you will see some of the same words that you learned by listening to the tape.

4. Talk to a friend in English about this same news story. In this way you are combining the skills of listening, reading, and speaking. You are increasing your vocabulary. The new words will be easy to remember because you keep repeating them and they are a part of one story that is in the news. You are increasing your English skills and also learning something interesting.

SECRET SEVEN: MAKE IT HARD ON YOURSELF

The best place to concentrate is in a quiet room where you can relax and focus on your study material. You should use your study materials, follow the directions exactly, and gain familiarity with the format of the test. This will definitely help you, and this is the way you should usually study.

Always practicing in optimum conditions, however, is not realistic. Taking the actual test is not like studying quietly at your own desk in your own room. Even if you can get a score of 550 on the practice tests while you are in a relaxed and comfortable environment, you could still get a much lower score on the same test under a real test situation. Why? You will have more pressure, and probably more anxiety, so the test may seem more difficult. Small disturbances, like supervisors walking around or doors opening and closing, could easily distract you.

How can you prepare for this anxiety? This pressure?

One way to overcome this test-taking stress is to make your studying more difficult. Compensate for your relaxed surroundings. Make it hard on yourself. Here are several ways to increase the level of difficulty when you study:

1. Read articles that are more difficult than your TOEFL material. Read the most difficult articles you can.*
2. Lessen the amount of time given for an easy-to-read article.
3. Try concentrating on your study material while there is interference in the room (like people talking on the telephone, doors opening and closing, noise outside, etc.).
4. Ask a friend to remind you to work harder.
5. Concentrate for a longer time than you usually do.

Don't study like this all the time, but try these techniques occasionally. You might begin with one condition, and then later combine several as you become more proficient.

N O T E

*Other sources for reading material are practice books for the Scholastic Aptitude Test (SAT), the Graduate Record Exam (GRE), and the Law School Admission Test (LSAT). They all have short reading passages with comprehension questions. Look in a bookstore near you or ask at a college or university.

Techniques like this are often used in sports. When runners are warming up they may add weights to their legs. When baseball players practice swinging, they hold two bats instead of one. They are making their practice hard so that the real game will seem easier. You can do the same thing.

R E M E M B E R

Don't study like this all the time. Just try it occasionally. The ability to work well under stress is a tool that can help you during the test. Practice it before you take the test. If you can study under extra hard conditions, it will make the test seem easier and that will give you confidence.

SECRET EIGHT: PREPARE FOR THE RHYTHM OF THE TOEFL

The word "rhythm" is usually used when talking about music or dance, but it can mean any regular pattern. We live in rhythms. We have regular sleeping and eating times. During the day we alternate between opposite activities such as sitting down and moving around. In studying, it also helps to keep a rhythm. After a period of concentration, you need a period of relaxation. Even while continuing to study, you can change the rhythm by changing from listening, to working on grammar, to reading or vocabulary development. You can also change the rhythm of your studying by varying your reading material from easy to hard, or from intensive (in-depth study on one topic) to extensive (a wide selection of topics). Some people can concentrate better if they exercise for ten or fifteen minutes before studying. When you get tired of studying, stop. Do some physical exercises, take a walk, or have something to eat.

While studying for the TOEFL, you need to prepare for the rhythm of the test. During the actual TOEFL test, you have between twenty-five and sixty-five minutes for each section. Get used to this rhythm. Concentrate heavily for about a half hour on one topic, and then change to another topic. When you get close to the day of the test, be sure that you can work easily for three-hour time periods. By preparing for three hours as you study for the TOEFL, you will be getting ready to work within the rhythm of the test.

N O T E

While you are taking the TOEFL exam, you may not be allowed to get up out of your chair or leave the room for about three hours. There is no break.

SECRET NINE: BE AWARE OF YOUR PHYSICAL LIMITATIONS

Your body has limits. You get tired. Sometimes when you are working hard toward a goal, you forget to listen to your body. You continue to push yourself more and more. You work later and longer than you should, and you find it difficult to concentrate. Your anxiety increases as you get tired and make mistakes. At this point you are pushing yourself too much. You have gone to the point of diminishing return.* It's not helping you to study more at this point.

You need to be aware of this physical limitation. Be aware of the point of diminishing return. When you feel yourself slowing down or see that you are missing the answers you feel you should know, then take a break. Change subjects. Change activities. Or lie down and go to sleep. Try to relax. You will feel more refreshed and more productive later.

DEFINITION

*The point of diminishing return: getting less and less in return for the time or energy you are putting into something.

SECRET TEN: TRAIN YOUR MIND TO SHIFT QUICKLY FROM ONE TASK TO ANOTHER

Taking the TOEFL exam is different from studying for it. When you take it, you are demonstrating your knowledge. In a very limited amount of time, you need to demonstrate as much as you can. You must work efficiently. You don't have the luxury of reading slowly over questions you don't understand.

Efficiency and speed are very important in taking a timed test. But, unfortunately, sometimes you may feel that you can't work as quickly as you want to. Your natural tendency* is to stay with a problem until you solve it. But the timing on the test forces you to move ahead. You must move on to the next question. If your mind stays on an unsolved problem, you lose the concentration you need for the next question.

DEFINITION

*Natural tendency: the way you want to think or act.

Shifting your mind quickly is especially difficult during the listening comprehension part of the test. Think of the number of steps you go through to answer a single question:

1. You read the possible answers.
2. You listen to the tape.
3. You read the answers again.
4. You choose the correct answer.
5. You mark your answer sheet.

Your brain is quickly shifting from reading to listening to reading to choosing to marking. You must be efficient; you must concentrate. Practice keeping up a rhythm of shifting your mind during the timed practice tests. Even if you don't know the answer, keep up the rhythm. Shift your mind to be ready to listen to and concentrate on the next taped question.

Here are the complete steps you should work on for the listening section of the TOEFL:

1. Pre-read the four choices before the tape comes on.
2. Try to figure out the testing point by analyzing the answer choices. For instance, if the four choices are:

> At the airport
> At a bank
> At the post office
> At a restaurant

then you know you must listen for *where* something happened. But if the four choices are:

> Mr. Jones served the chairman.
> Mr. Jones replaced the last chairman.
> Mr. Jones is no longer the chairman.
> Mr. Jones was manager of the apartment.

then you know you must listen for *what* Mr. Jones did.
3. Shift your mind to be ready to listen to the tape. This timing is hard to judge, but it gets easier as you practice and get used to the time allowed on the tape for answering.
4. Listen discriminately to the tape to answer the questions: *Who?, What?, When?, Where?, Why?*
5. Read the four answer choices again.
6. Make a decision.
7. Mark your answer sheet.
8. Immediately begin reading the answer choices on the next question.

Your mind is shifting all the time—reading . . . analyzing . . . listening . . . analyzing . . . choosing . . . marking.

You need to practice this rhythm. You need to practice concentrating on one task, and then switching completely to another task.

Practice conscientiously. Keep the rhythm carefully. You will gain confidence, and you will enhance your ability to demonstrate your knowledge.

N O T E

A thought from China: "It is better to break one finger than to injure all your fingers."

How does this saying relate to Secret Ten?

SECRET ELEVEN: WORK QUICKLY AND STEADILY

When you begin working through the questions in the TOEFL, you will see that some of them are easy for you, and some of them are hard. If you are not sure of the answer to a question, don't spend too much time puzzling over* it. It is better to get through all the questions, and then go back over the ones you are not sure of. In this way, you will gain time for checking over your answers and not be worried that you haven't finished yet. Here is one way to do it:

1. Read and answer the questions at a steady pace.
2. When you come to a question that is very hard, eliminate as many answers as you can, and then guess the best answer. Answer it, but put another light pencil mark in the margin beside that question in your answer book. Making this small mark will not only remind you where to check back, it will also help your mind to leave that unsolved problem and move onto the next problem.
3. After you have finished all the questions in the section, then go back to the ones with a pencil mark, and read them again. If you change an answer, be sure to erase your first mark completely so that the computer doesn't think you answered twice.

D E F I N I T I O N

*To puzzle over: to wonder, to try to understand.

This technique is good for several reasons:

1. When you go back a second time, you won't feel anxious wondering how many more questions you have, or what they are. You will have already gone to the end of the section, so you will know what questions are there.
2. Sometimes the questions seem clearer when you see them a second time. It seems as though your brain thinks about them even though you are working on other problems.
3. By being a little more relaxed, the answer might be more obvious.

N O T E

There are different answering strategies for different types of questions. Many people find that for Listening Comprehension and Structure, their first immediate response is the best; but for Reading, your second answer (after reading the passage again) might be better.

SECRET TWELVE: MAKE EVERY SECOND COUNT

While taking a timed test, you must be as efficient as you can. Especially in the listening comprehension section, you don't want to waste time by searching for the right place on the answer sheet to mark your answer. Be sure to get used to using an answer sheet by practicing with one whenever you take a practice test. Here are two suggestions for maximizing your time.

Use your pencil to hold your place on the answer sheet. You must be absolutely sure that you are marking your answer in the correct place. When your eyes are moving back and forth from the test book to the answer sheet, it is sometimes easy to lose your place. You waste time if you have to search for the correct place when you are ready to mark your answer. Every second counts. Try this technique:

1. Place your pencil on the right line on your answer sheet.
2. Continue to hold your pencil in that place while you read the questions in your test book. Use your other hand to keep your place in your test book.

3. Mark your answer, then move your pencil to the next line before you read the next question in your test book. Always keep your pencil in place on the answer sheet.

SECRET THIRTEEN: MARK YOUR ANSWER SHEET EFFICIENTLY

Hold your pencil perpendicular to the paper. When you write, you probably hold your pencil at a slant as shown in Figure 1. But when you are marking an answer sheet, you are not writing. You are only making an oval mark. It is easier for you to make this mark on your answer sheet if you hold your pencil straight up and down (perpendicular). Try holding your pencil as shown in Figure 2. You will be able to see the mark you make more easily, and also hold your place on the answer sheet.

When you begin filling out the form at the test center, you should begin with a sharp pencil. By the time you have finished all the personal forms (name, address, etc.), the point on your pencil will be more flat. That's good. You don't need a sharp point to fill in the answer space on the test. If the point is flat, it is much easier and quicker to fill in the oval space. In addition, the point won't break very easily.

Don't spend very much time filling in the oval space. Do it quickly and move your pencil to the next line. Remember to use a number two pencil. Bring at least two pencils in case one breaks.

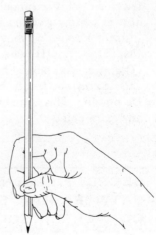

Figure 1. The correct way to hold your pencil for writing (slanted)

Figure 2. The best way to hold your pencil for marking answer sheets (straight up and down)

SECRET FOURTEEN: DON'T BE AFRAID TO GUESS

Sometimes people work steadily through the test questions without checking to see how much time they have left. When they finally look at the clock, they realize that there are only a few minutes left. What if that happens to you and you still have a lot of questions to answer? What is the best thing to do?

The following list describes five things you can do. They are in the order of *best* to *worst*.

1. If you are working on the Vocabulary and Reading Comprehension section and you have only about five minutes left, try to answer the questions without reading the paragraph. Read quickly through the questions to see if you have enough background knowledge to make a logical guess. If you are working on the Structure and Written Expression section, don't read all of each sentence. Read only the main clause, and look quickly for one type of common error (possibly an error in subject/verb agreement).

2. Even if you have no background knowledge for the Vocabulary and Reading Comprehension questions, read them quickly and guess at the answers. Do the same thing for the grammar questions.

3. If you really have only one minute left, pick one letter ("B" possibly), and mark all remaining ovals with the same letter. This is better than leaving everything blank, and you have a random chance of getting a few right. This technique is only good as a last chance. First try to answer whatever you can quickly with your own knowledge.

4. Instead of doing (3) above, some people randomly mark any answer, (A), (B), (C), or (D) when they are out of time. This is not as good as (3) above. You have a better chance of getting a few correct if you choose only one letter.

5. Do nothing. This is the worst choice. You have no chance of getting any extra points.

SECRET FIFTEEN: KNOW THE DIFFERENCE BETWEEN RAW SCORES AND CONVERTED SCORES

When you take the practice tests, you check your answers and count the number correct. This is your "raw score" (raw score = number correct). When you take the real test, your correct answers are counted, and the total equals your raw score. But, in addition, you are given a "converted score." The converted score is based on a table that changes with each test depending on the difficulty of that particular test. It allows all the TOEFL scores to stay equal in value even though one test may be harder or easier than another.

Look at the example of the TOEFL converted score ranges for a TOEFL exam given in 1985 (Table 1).

Table 1. TOEFL Converted Score Ranges

Number Correct (Raw Score)	Listening Comprehension (Section 1)	Structure and Written Expression (Section 2)	Vocabulary and Reading Comprehension (Section 3)
60			
57–59			66–67
54–56			62–64
51–53			60–61
48–50	65–68		57–59
45–47	62–64		55–56
42–44	59–61		53–54
39–41	56–58		51–53
36–38	54–55	62–68	50–51
33–35	52–53	57–60	48–49
30–32	50–51	54–56	46–47
27–29	48–50	51–53	44–45
24–26	47–48	48–50	42–43
21–23	45–46	45–47	40–41
18–20	43–44	42–44	37–39
15–17	41–43	39–41	35–36
12–14	39–40	36–38	31–33
09–11	35–38	33–35	28–30
06–08	31–34	29–32	26–27
03–05	28–30	25–28	23–25
00–02	25–27	21–24	21–22

You can figure out your sample score by counting your raw score and looking at the table to get your converted score. For example:

	Your raw score	Your converted score
Section 1	24	47
Section 2	20	44
Section 3	38	51

To get a sample total score, you multiply each score by 10, add the scores and then divide by 3:

$$47 = 470$$
$$44 = 440$$
$$51 = 510$$

Total = 1420 ÷ 3 = 473 total score

R E M E M B E R

This table is not the same for every TOEFL test, and this score is only an approximation of your real score.

Now, examine the converted score table more closely. You can see that for most of the questions, if you get one more correct in your raw score, you will also get one more point in your converted score. But this is not always true. For some questions, you can get one more correct in your raw score, but your converted score remains the same. For others, if you get one more correct in your raw score, you will get more than one point in your converted score. Look at the converted score table (Figure 3) to see where the value of the points changes.

In Section 1, if you get 17 in your raw score, your converted score is 43. But even if you get one more correct (18), your converted score stays the same (43). If you get a raw score of 35 in Section 2, Structure and Written Expression, your converted score is 60. And with only one more raw score point (36), your converted score jumps to 62. There are other places where the converted score either stays the same or jumps more than one point. Find them in Figure 3.

Let's see how this converted score table can change your score.

EXAMPLE: You take a practice test and get the following scores:

	Raw Score	Converted Score	Total Score
Section 1	24	47 = 470	
Section 2	24	48 = 480	
Section 3	36	50 = 500	
		1450 ÷ 3 =	483

Now you study more and improve each of your scores by 11 points.

	Raw Score	Converted Score	Total Score
Section 1	35	53 = 530	
Section 2	35	60 = 600	
Section 3	47	56 = 560	
		1690 ÷ 3 =	563

Your total score has jumped 80 points (from 483 to 563). Even though your raw score increased an equal amount in each section (11 points), your converted score had a different amount of increase in each section. Your Listening Comprehension score and your Vocabulary and Reading Comprehension score increased 60 points (from 470 to 530 and from 500 to 560), but your Structure and Written Expression score increased 120 points (from 480 to 600). That can make a big difference in your total score. (Remember that this data was based only on the table in Figure 3. Other converted score tables, however, have similar results.)

If you have information that includes other converted scales, study them. Look to see where there is a jump of one or two points, or of no points. Use this information to help you plan your study time. *Put your effort into increasing your score where the answers have the most value.*

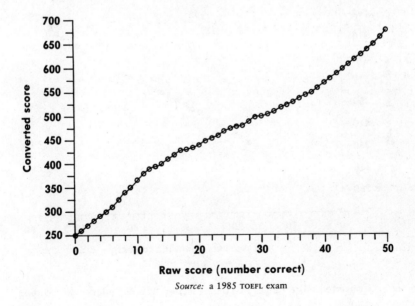

Source: a 1985 TOEFL exam

Figure 3. Converted score ranges of TOEFL (Section 1: Listening Comprehension)

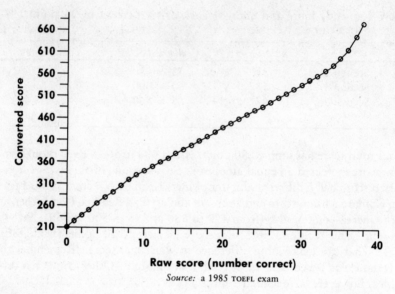

Figure 4. Converted score ranges of TOEFL (Section 2: Structure and Written Expression)

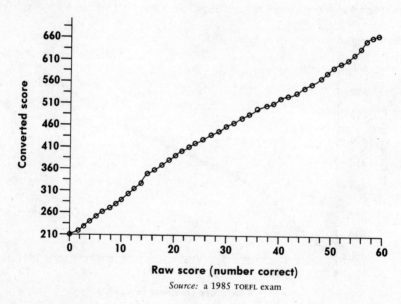

Figure 5. Converted score ranges of TOEFL (Section 3: Vocabulary and Reading Comprehension)

Figures 3, 4, and 5 show the relationship between raw scores and converted scores for each section of the TOEFL. Look for the places where the lines go up more steeply, or where the lines don't go up at all. Remember, a difference of one point in your converted score is multiplied by 10 to get your total score.

SECRET SIXTEEN: GET A DOUBLE BENEFIT

By now you have been practicing, practicing, practicing. You are probably tired of it. You may be getting discouraged and wonder what you are learning. You might think it would be more useful to spend your time studying your own field of interest.

But wait! Studying for the TOEFL is not a waste of your time, even if the vocabulary in your field of interest is very different from the vocabulary you are studying for the TOEFL. There are some long-term benefits to TOEFL preparation, and there is a double benefit to the time you spend practicing now.

All this time that you spend studying for the TOEFL, you are learning more than just English language skills. You are also practicing study skills that will help you succeed in an American college.

You are developing the ability to:

1. understand native speakers
2. be a more efficient reader
3. work under pressure
4. concentrate
5. perform well, even with a time limit
6. generalize ideas from specific information

All of these skills are necessary in any college for everyone, including native English speakers. In college, you want to be able to succeed along with American students. You will have to read, to write, and to take tests whether your major is computer science, engineering, biology, or literature. By developing these study skills, you are helping yourself to succeed in American college life.

Try to think of the TOEFL as a game. You are learning to play this game. It is not a punishment. You are gaining knowledge and improving your skills in many areas. On the test day, you may even feel eager to demonstrate your ability and improvement. That kind of attitude will help you relax and get a good score.

SECRET SEVENTEEN: RECOGNIZE YOUR STRENGTHS AND USE THEM

What are your strong areas in English? Are you better at grammar than listening comprehension? Are your reading skills better than your grammar skills? What academic strengths do you have?

Look at your test scores, and analyze your strong areas. Then plan on how you can use those strengths to help you in your weaker areas.

Read about what Malia and Leonardo did to use their strengths to improve their test scores.

Malia

Malia was worried about the Listening Comprehension section of the test because she had trouble understanding fast American speech. However, she was very good at reading and grammar. She decided to use her reading skills to help her understand the tape. As she prepared for the test, she practiced reading the answer choices in the test booklet before she listened to the tape. When she took the real test, she was able to continue this skill. By looking at the answer choices quickly, she got an idea of the topic that she would later hear on the tape. She was then better prepared, and more able to understand the speakers. By using her reading skills, she improved her score on the Listening Comprehension test.

Leonardo

Leonardo was worried about his Vocabulary and Reading Comprehension score. He felt that he read too slowly. He was, however, good at grammar, and he was also a very logical thinker. He tried to speed up his reading by using his knowledge of grammar. He looked for relationships between words in the paragraph. He practiced looking quickly for words like "but," "however," or "on the contrary" to be prepared for a contrast. He looked for words like "in addition" and "moreover" to let him know that more important information would be coming next. He also read the first sentence and the last sentence of the paragraph slowly in order to get the main idea. Then he used this main idea and the general organization of the paragraph to help him summarize the paragraph. By using his knowledge of grammar and his organizational skills, he was able to improve his reading comprehension and his reading speed.

SECRET EIGHTEEN: UNDERSTAND THE INVERTED V PATTERN (/\ )

Finally, the day of the test is here. You feel nervous. In fact, you feel so nervous that you think you have forgotten everything you learned. But you haven't. Think of the "inverted V pattern."

The inverted V pattern is a phenomonon experienced by athletes before competition. The athlete who is getting ready to run a race, compete in gymnastics, or play a team sport experiences an increase in his or her anxiety level. This anxiety level increases to its highest point just before the competition, and then decreases once the competition begins (see Figure 6).

You may feel this same anxiety when you are getting ready to give a speech, take a test, or perform in class. Your hands feel sweaty and your heart beats fast. You feel very nervous. But as soon as you begin the activity, your fear goes away. You are able to concentrate. You forget about your nervousness and your hands stop sweating. You do all right.

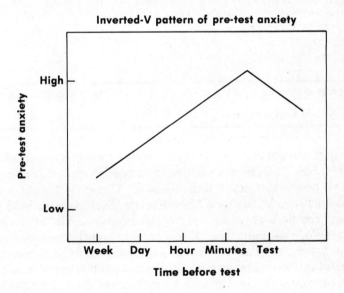

Figure 6. Anxiety rises as test time approaches, then drops as test begins.

Now that you know this, you should feel less anxious. You know that you are normal. Everybody feels like you do. As soon as you begin working on the test, you will be able to concentrate. You will be able to do your best. Remember that you are prepared. You have done the following:

1. You have practiced the language skills that will be on the test.
2. Your practicing has helped you to imagine the test situation in your mind.
3. You have identified many different testing points. (Secret Five)
4. You have practiced under many different conditions. (Secret Seven)
5. You have trained your mind to concentrate and shift. (Secret Ten)

But what if you still feel nervous, what can you do?

First of all, expect the anxiety. Understand it. Remember that it usually goes away, or at least lessens.

Second, if your muscles feel tight, if your hands feel sweaty, if your heart is beating fast, then relax your body. Take a few deep breaths, hold your breath for a second, then let it out slowly. This will help you relax. Now, imagine yourself taking the test and doing well on it.

Third, don't be rushed getting to the test center. Get up early after a good night's sleep. Have a good breakfast. If possible, find out where the test room is before the day of the test. Get there ten minutes early. (If you arrive too early, you may get more nervous while you wait a long time.)

Fourth, while you are waiting for the doors to be opened and the test to be passed out, you can begin getting ready to take the test. (Read more about this in Secret Twenty-One.)

SECRET NINETEEN: LET YOUR TEST—DAY EXCITEMENT HELP YOU

On the day of the test you may notice another feeling: a feeling of excitement. You have prepared for this day. You hope to do well. You may feel something like "butterflies in your stomach." This feeling of excitement is different from anxiety. Anxiety is a feeling of fear. Excitement is a feeling of anticipation. You think about the test in a positive way, not in a negative way.

In psychology the word "arousal" refers to the body becoming more alert. In common use, "to arouse" means to wake someone up. It is important to understand that there are physical changes in your body when you become aroused or excited. Your sense awareness (hearing, feeling, seeing) may be greater; you may hear sounds more clearly. This can be both good and bad. On one hand, with an increase in arousal, your body will be more alert and you will be more able to concentrate on one task (the TOEFL). That's good. On the other hand, if your arousal level is too high, you might be easily distracted by sounds (like a clock ticking, a door opening, or someone coughing), or movements (like an examiner walking around the test room).

The best level of arousal changes with different tasks. For some things, it is better to have a high level of arousal, and for others, it helps to have a lower level of arousal. The best level for each task changes with the difficulty of the task and with the differences in each person. If the task is easy, and if you are very skilled, you need a high arousal level to perform well. But if the skill is more difficult, and if you are less skilled, you do better with a lower arousal level. For a difficult task like taking the TOEFL, it's better if you have a low level of arousal.

You can probably think of some examples of this principle in your own life. Think about something you did very well. It could be when you kicked a goal playing soccer, or when you played a difficult piece of music well, or when you discussed something in English without thinking of the language. Now think of how you felt just before that time when you did well. Were you nervous? Or were you feeling relaxed and calm? What were you thinking about? It may have been a situation where the results were not too important, where no one was judging you, but where you felt excited and pleased with what you were doing. That is the level of arousal that is best for the TOEFL exam. Most people do their best when they are alert but calm, when they are excited, but not anxious.

Everyone needs some arousal to do well. If you have a very, very low arousal level, you are not alert enough to do anything. You may even go to sleep! For most TOEFL students, this is not a problem! If there is any problem at all, it is with an arousal level that is too high, not too low. If you feel that your arousal level is too high, then you may be too anxious. Read back over Secret Eighteen. Try to relax and concentrate on your test preparation.

Remember as you go in to take the exam: your excitement can help you. Your arousal level can work for you to help you to be alert and to concentrate so that you can do your best.

SECRET TWENTY: EXPECT THE UNEXPECTED

Everybody wants the test-taking day to be perfect. We plan to eat well the day before, get plenty of sleep, and be well prepared. We want everything to go well after preparing for all this time.

But what happens if things do not go well? What happens if your relatives suddenly come to visit you the night before the test? Or if you have to move out of your house on the day before you take the test? Or if you feel sick and are getting a cold? You cannot control these things.

Sometimes there are problems inside the test room, too. There may be noise outside, or noise in the room. Maybe you will miss hearing some of the test questions on the tape. (Refer back to Secret Seven for some ideas on how to deal with these problems.)

What can you do?

One thing you can do is expect that some problems might occur. You cannot control everything in your life. It is easier to deal with problems if you anticipate that you might have some, than it is if you insist that nothing will go wrong.

If an unexpected situation comes up, there may be nothing you can do about it. Try to *accept* the situation as it is.

Even if nothing unexpected has happened, but you still feel that you aren't ready for the test, don't worry about it. Maybe you feel that you need more time to study. That's okay. Many people feel that they never have enough time to study. You are not alone.

Say these sentences to yourself several times:

> "I will do my best on this test. I will do my best with the situation as it is right now. I will not get frustrated or angry about things that I cannot control."

If you have no unexpected problems, then you are very lucky. You can feel fortunate!

N O T E

Get a good night's sleep before the exam. Get up early and eat a good breakfast. Eat plenty of protein to give yourself energy, and don't drink too much coffee or tea. Get to the test center about ten minutes early.

SECRET TWENTY-ONE: GET A HEAD START WITH MENTAL WARM-UPS

It's the day of the test. You are at the test center waiting to begin. You feel nervous. Stop. Don't think of your nervousness. Take a few deep breaths. Relax your muscles, and think about Secret Eighteen, the "Inverted V Pattern." Remember your nervousness should go away in a few minutes. Now, get a head start.*

If you were going to run a race in a few minutes, you wouldn't just stand around waiting and getting nervous. You would bend and stretch your body to prepare yourself physically. You can do the same with your mind. Begin mental warm-ups.

You can do the following things:

1. Keep your mind busy. Concentrate on your language skills, not on yourself. Look over your notes and your vocabulary words. Glance at your rule summary (see Secret Four). Practice concentrating totally on one thing and then shifting your mind to another topic (see Secret Ten).

2. As soon as you get your test booklet, and are allowed to open it, begin reading. Read ahead in the listening comprehension section. Look at the four answer choices and try to imagine the situation that you will hear on the tape. Try to figure out the testing point (see Secret Five). Keep reading ahead until the examiner asks you to focus on the sample questions, then switch your mind quickly back (see Secret Nine) and concentrate totally on the examiner's voice. You will be ready to understand the first statements on the tape. Your mind will be warmed-up and ready to go.

3. *Do not* try to break the seal and open your test booklet before you are allowed to. For one thing, it will probably not help you. For another thing, it is against the rules and may disqualify you from taking the test. Don't risk it!

DEFINITION

*To get a head start: to have an advantage over other competitors.

EXERCISE WORKBOOK

LISTENING COMPREHENSION

There are three parts to the Listening Comprehension section of the TOEFL. In each of them you will hear the taped conversation or sentence only once. You will have about thirteen seconds to answer each question. When you practice for the test, use any TOEFL practice tape or record. Don't stop the tape while you are taking the practice test. Answer the questions quickly to give yourself time to read the next answers before the tape comes on again. (See Secret Ten.)

Each part of the Listening Comprehension test is different, so your strategies for studying should be different. Here are the major differences in each part:

Part A: You hear a short sentence spoken once. In your test booklet you see four sentences. You must choose the sentence that is closest in meaning to the spoken sentence.

Part B: You hear a short conversation between two people. Then you hear a question about the conversation. In your test booklet, you read four answers, and choose the correct answer to the question.

Part C: You hear a short talk or conversation. At the end of the talk, you are asked a few questions about the talk. You choose the best answer for each question.

This workbook section gives you exercises for practicing listening comprehension skills. The exercises are on the tape that accompanies this book.

Each of these parts of the Listening Comprehension section requires different listening skills. For Part A, you are listening for a restatement of a sentence. You are listening for detailed information and specific words. In Part B, you need to listen in a more general way. It often helps to know where the conversation takes place and what the relationship is between the two speakers. For Part C, you need to remember the information for a longer time. You should practice remembering the general ideas. Knowing about American culture will help you to understand questions in all parts of the exam.

PREPARING FOR PART A

In most of the sentences for Part A, you are being tested on two or more different testing points. (See Secret Five for information on testing points.) One of the testing points is often the specific meaning of one or two of the words in the spoken sentence. Another testing point might be grammar or discrimination between sounds. The answer choices may have sentences with words that sound like the spoken words, but that do not have the same meanings.

In Secret Four (page 5), the listening comprehension skill is divided into four levels. If you are at Level 1, it means that you can understand only some of the words in the recorded sentence. At Level 2, you can understand the complete sentence. When you are at Level 3, you can not only understand the complete sentence, but also figure out the main testing point. (See Secret Five for information about the testing point.) At Level 4, you can figure out the testing point and also figure out how the answer relates to the testing point.

Even if you are at Level 1 in listening comprehension, you can practice skills for Part A of the TOEFL. Even if you don't understand the whole sentence, you can work on improving your ability to discriminate between specific sounds and words. You need to focus on listening discrimination. You also need to work on increasing your vocabulary by learning synonyms. (A "synonym" is a word which has almost the same meaning as another word, i.e., "home" and "house," or "car" and "automobile.") The following exercises will help you with both of these skills.

EXERCISE 2   HAVE TAPE READY

Discrimination between Similar-Sounding Words

DIRECTIONS: On the tape, you will hear a sentence spoken just one time. As you listen to the speaker, read the sentences below. The sentences you hear will not be the same as the ones you read, but one sentence will have a similar meaning. Put a check by the sentence that is closest in meaning to the one you hear. When you are finished, check your answers in the answer key on page 163. Now listen to the first sentence as an example:

On the tape you hear:_____ *It was Thursday.*_____

In the book you read:

_____ The speaker is talking about a day.

_____ The speaker is talking about drinking.

You should have checked, "The speaker is talking about a day." If you checked, "The speaker is talking about drinking," it probably means that you heard the word "thirsty" instead of "Thursday." Now continue with the examples as you listen to the tape.

N O T E

Most workbook exercises for Listening Comprehension require spoken testing material, which is included on the tape that accompanies this book. This is indicated by the words "HAVE TAPE READY" to the right of the exercise number. For the benefit of readers who may not have the tape, the tapescripts are also included in this book, beginning on page 233.

---

1. _____ He left his job.

   _____ He wrote his name.

2. _____ The people working on the ship were nice.

   _____ We had a good time on the ship.

3. _____ He didn't like the wet air.

   _____ He didn't like the animal.

4. _____ The company began the school.

   _____ The company gave money to the school.

5. _____ He did something wrong.

   _____ They ate beef.

6. _____ It costs too much.

   _____ It's not a good gift.

7. _____ The speaker is talking about one person.

   _____ The speaker is talking about several people.

8. _____ Where is the animal park?

   _____ Where is the woman?

9. _____ He answered fifty.

_____ He answered fifteen.

10. _____ Are you getting something clean?

_____ Are you looking at something?

EXERCISE 3   HAVE TAPE READY

Synonyms

This exercise is on the tape. In Part A of the Listening Comprehension section of the TOEFL, you will hear single, unrelated sentences similar to the ones below. In order to choose the correct restatement, you will have to understand many idioms and other vocabulary words. This exercise contains sentences similar to those on TOEFL Listening Comprehension tests.

DIRECTIONS: In Exercise 3, you will hear sentences spoken just one time. After you listen to each sentence, turn off the tape and write another sentence that means the same thing, but uses some different words. When you have finished, check your sentences with the answer key on page 163. Remember that the answer key has only sample sentences. There may be more than one correct restatement of each sentence that you hear.

EXAMPLE: On the tape you hear: "I can't stand it."

Turn off the tape and write a sentence that means the same thing as "I can't stand it."

_____

After you write the sentence, turn on the tape again to hear the next sentence. Continue writing restatements for each sentence you hear.

1. _____

2. _____

3. _____

4. _____

5. _____

6. _____

7. _____

8. _____

9. _____

10. _____

11. _____

12. _____

13. _____

14. _____

15. _____

DETERMINING THE TESTING POINTS

The sentences spoken in Part A of the Listening Comprehension section have several testing points. One testing point might be understanding the meaning of a word or phrase. Another testing point can be discrimination between two words that sound similar. A third testing point might be grammatical structure. While you are working in your TOEFL study book on Part A of the Listening Comprehension section, do more than just find the correct answers. Also try to figure out the main testing points. It might take you a little bit longer when you practice, but you will gain knowledge, and it will help you work faster when you take the real test. For a general discussion of testing points, see page 8.

Look at the following two examples of TOEFL test questions.

EXAMPLE 1

You hear: "George ate too much."
You see: (A) Two friends ate with him.
          (B) George overate.
          (C) George is late to lunch.
          (D) He was late too often.

The correct answer is (B), George overate.

Let's analyze this question. What information do you need in order to answer it correctly? You need to know that "overate" means "ate too much." The answer choices also test you on:

the difference between "too," "two," and "to"
discrimination between "much," "lunch" and "ate," "late"

The main testing point for this question is vocabulary:

Synonym: "ate too much" means "overate"

EXAMPLE 2

You hear: "My aunt made a terrible mistake!"
You see: (A) An error was made.
         (B) My aunt burned the steak.
         (C) She doesn't like making mistakes.
         (D) It was terrible that she took the wrong thing.

The correct answer is (A), An error was made.

The main testing points are vocabulary and grammar.

Synonym: "mistake" means "error"
Grammar: passive voice

The answer choices also test "mistake" and "steak."

EXERCISE 4   HAVE TAPE READY

Determining the Testing Points

In Exercise 4, you will hear several sentences. After you listen to each
sentence, stop the tape and write the answers to the questions about that
sentence. When you have finished, check your answers in the answer key on
page 164.

A. *You hear:* _____

   You see: (A) This book has the newest information.
            (B) This book has the right date.
            (C) Today is the due date.
            (D) Your book is very late.

   1. What spoken and written words are synonyms? _____
      _____

   2. What words sound similar, but have different meanings?
      _____*due date*_____ and _____
      _____*late*_____ and _____

   3. What is the correct answer? _____

B. *You hear:* _____

   You see: (A) She threw away the door.
            (B) She walked through the door.

    (C) She danced for him.
    (D) She looked at him.

1. What spoken and written words are synonyms? _____

_____

2. What words sound similar, but have different meanings?

_____*danced*_____ and_____

_____*threw*_____ and_____

3. What is the correct answer? _____

C. *You hear:* _____

    You see: (A) Don't put it in the oven.
              (B) Be sure to cover the pudding while it cooks.
              (C) Don't cook the pudding too long.
              (D) You should cook it on top of the stove.

1. What spoken and written words are synonyms? _____

2. What words sound similar (listening discrimination)?

_____*put it*_____ and_____

3. What is the correct answer? _____

D. *You hear:* _____

    You see: (A) Would you rather rent a room on a higher floor?
              (B) I think this place is too expensive.
              (C) I'd rather pay more.
              (D) I don't think it's a high-rent area.

1. What spoken and written words are synonyms? _____

_____

2. What words sound similar (listening discrimination)?

_____*I'd rather*_____ and_____

_____*don't think*_____ and_____

3. What is implied in this sentence? _____

E. *You hear:* _____

    You see: (A) He jumped higher than anyone else.
              (B) He broke the most popular record.
              (C) The jumper said, "Hi."
              (D) It's the biggest record in the world.

    1. What are the different meanings of the following words?

            (A) a record = _____

            (B) a record = _____

            (C) broke the record = _____

            (D) broke the record = _____

    2. What is the answer? _____

F. *You hear:* _____

    You see: (A) You can't eat it.
              (B) Be sure to take enough.
              (C) I can take more.
              (D) Don't take too much.

    1. Which words have a similar meaning?
      ____*Don't take*_____and_____

      _____*more than*_____and_____

    2. Which words sound like "can't eat?" _____

    3. What is the correct answer? _____

G. *You hear:* _____

    You see: (A) Jim forgot what he did.
              (B) I can't remember what Jim did.
              (C) What Jim did was important to me.
              (D) Jim didn't do very much.

In this kind of question, you must understand the complete meaning of each sentence. Look at each of the answer choices:

(A) "Jim forgot what he did." = unknown information, unnecessary
(B) "I can't remember what Jim did." = the opposite is true
(D) "Jim didn't do very much." = the opposite is true

    1. What is implied in answer (C)? _____

H. *You hear:* _____

    You see: (A) No one was home when the man knocked.
              (B) The delivery man left the door open.
              (C) The door was delivered even though no one answered the message.
              (D) The man went home after he locked the door.

For this type of question, you must understand each sentence as a whole.

    1. What is the correct answer? _____

    2. What is the inference in this question? _____

PREPARING FOR PART B

In Part B of the Listening Comprehension section, you need to practice more general listening skills than in Part A. You need to listen for a general idea about where the conversation takes place. You need to think about the relationship between the two speakers. Even if the question does not specifically ask you where the speakers are, it helps you understand the question better if you know where the conversation takes place and who the speakers are.
    There might be a question like this:

Man: Will that be cash or charge?
Woman: I'd like to charge this dress.
Question: Where does this conversation probably take place?

(A) At a store
(B) At a bank
(C) At a post office
(D) At your address

The answer is (A), "At a store."
    Many of the questions in this section are difficult because of the cultural information about life in the United States. Often the questions and the correct answers use words that are related to one topic in American life. In the above example, the question, "Will that be cash or charge" is a very common question asked by a cashier in almost any store.
    When you study new vocabulary, it helps you to remember the new words if you learn them in word groups. Do the following as you study:

    1. Learn the words that belong together at the same time.
    2. As you study each word group, concentrate on the situation. Imagine the place in your mind. Think of who would say these words. What

might be the relationship between people using these words? What is the particular use of each word in this situation? (Some words will have different meanings in other situations.)

The words in the next exercise are common in American life. If you are not sure of the meanings of these words, ask your teacher or an American friend. You can also use your dictionary, but it will help you to get more information about American culture if you ask an American. It also helps your listening comprehension.

EXERCISE 5   HAVE TAPE READY

Word Groups

DIRECTIONS: For Exercise 5, you will hear groups of words on the tape that belong in categories. The words in each group represent one place. After you hear each category, stop the tape and write the name of the place where you would be most likely to hear the words spoken. The answers are in the answer key, page 164.

Word Groups

1. _____   6. _____

2. _____   7. _____

3. _____   8. _____

4. _____   9. _____

5. _____   10. _____

EXERCISE 6   HAVE TAPE READY

Word Categories

DIRECTIONS: This exercise uses the same word groups as Exercise 5. For this exercise, you will hear several words spoken on the tape. Each time you hear a word, write it next to the correct place listed below. The words are not given in order. When you are finished, you will have more than one word on some lines. Do not stop the tape for this exercise. Work as fast as you can. The first word is written for you. Check your answers in the answer key, page 165. Here are the words.

at a bank _____

at a graduation _____

at a wedding _____

at a dentist's office _____

at a performance _____

in a hospital _____

at a beauty parlor _____*curl*_____

at a drugstore _____

at a university _____

at a restaurant _____

EXERCISE 7   HAVE TAPE READY

Place and Speaker (Inference)

DIRECTIONS: In Part B of the TOEFL exam, you can figure out the answer more easily if you know where the conversation takes place and the relationship between the speakers. In Exercise 7 you will hear sentences from situations that might be used in TOEFL exams. As you listen to the tape, imagine where each sentence would most likely be spoken. Write the name of the place and the possible speaker on the lines. When you have finished, check your answers in the answer key, page 165. There may be other possible answers.

In what place would you probably hear the following sentences? Who would probably say them?

	Place	Speaker
1.	_____	_____
2.	_____	_____
3.	_____	_____
4.	_____	_____
5.	_____	_____
6.	_____	_____
7.	_____	_____
8.	_____	_____

9. _____   _____

10. _____   _____

PREPARING FOR PART C

In Part C of the Listening Comprehension Test, you will hear two or three short talks or conversations. You must listen and remember the main information for a longer time than in either Part A or Part B. After each talk or conversation, there will be some questions. Some talks might have as few as three or four questions, while others might have eight or more. You will be asked general questions about the talk.

EXERCISE 8

Using Logical Skills: Guess the Question

It can help you to look at the answer choices before you hear the tape. In Part C, you have very little time to read ahead, but there is a little time while the speaker on the tape is reading the directions. This exercise helps you develop your logical thinking skills. Even though there is no mini-talk for this exercise, see if you can guess what the questions might be. This exercise is not on the tape.

DIRECTIONS: Look at the topic of the mini-talk and the answer choices below. Then answer the questions. (This is a guessing and logical thinking exercise only. There is really no mini-talk for this exercise!)

Topic: Lecture on an American Poet

1. From the above topic, which two of the answers below are the best choices for answering the question? (You are just guessing; you don't know the question.) Why aren't the others good choices?

   (A) The poems of Walt Whitman
   (B) The poems of Emily Dickinson
   (C) A critique of eighteenth-century poets
   (D) A comparison of American and British poets

   _____

   _____

2. Read the following answer choices:

   (A) She seldom left her home.
   (B) She published poems more frequently.
   (C) She couldn't write because of personal problems.
   (D) She published less than any other period.

   What do the answer choices in question 2 tell you about your answer to question 1?

   _____

3. What kind of a question might be asked for number 2? Write a sample question.

   _____

4. Read the following answer choices:

   (A) In her twenties
   (B) In her thirties
   (C) In her fifties
   (D) In her eighties

   What type of question might be asked for number 4? Write a sample question.

   _____

5. Read the following answer choices:

   (A) Hear a lecture on other poets.
   (B) Discuss one of Emily Dickinson's poems.
   (C) Discuss one of Walt Whitman's poems.
   (D) Write original poems.

   What type of question might go with number 5? Write a sample question.

   _____

Mini-Talk Practice: Guess the Answer

In Part C, the mini-talk part of the TOEFL, the questions are usually asked in the same order that you hear the information on the tape. Sometimes you can guess which answer choice will be correct by following the answers as you listen to the tape. It is not easy to listen and read at the same time, but this exercise gives you a chance to practice this skill.

For the exercise below, there are no questions. You are only guessing what the questions might be. As you listen to the mini-talk on tape, follow the answer choices, making a very light dot beside the ones that might relate to what you are hearing. Sometimes you will need to make two or even three dots. Listen for words that you hear that are repeated below and mark them. You should be able to guess one or two of the answers below that might be asked later.

EXERCISE 9   **HAVE TAPE READY**

Practice for the Mini-Talk: Guess the Answer

DIRECTIONS: As you listen to the following talk, look at the answer choices on pages 46–47. You see five sets of answer choices. You do not know the questions, only the possible answers. First, look briefly at the groups of answers to get an idea of what types of questions might be asked. (For instance, the question for number 1 might be, "Who is talking?") Second, as you listen to the tape, mark the answers that you think will answer the questions. Then read the actual questions, listed in the answer key on page 166, and choose your answers again. You should have been able to eliminate one or two of the answer choices before you even read the questions.

Mini-Talk Answer Choices

Mark possible answers as you listen to the tape.

1. (A) Professor Smith
   (B) A teaching assistant
   (C) A specialist in chemistry
   (D) A university technician

2. (A) At the beginning
   (B) In the middle
   (C) At the end
   (D) Before the final exam

3. (A) To explain the grading procedures
   (B) To demonstate an experiment
   (C) To tell students what safety equipment to buy
   (D) To teach important safety precautions

4. (A) Loose scarves
   (B) Open sandals
   (C) Long necklaces
   (D) Eyeglasses

5. (A) Wash their lab equipment
   (B) Do an experiment
   (C) Buy a notebook
   (D) Put waste in the proper container

GENERAL ADVICE FOR LISTENING COMPREHENSION

Rhythm Is Important

Secret Ten discusses shifting your mind in order to be ready to listen to the speaker on the tape. This is absolutely necessary. Since the tape comes on at regular intervals, you must also keep a regular rhythm. Even if you miss a problem, you must leave it, and go on to the next one. You must be willing even to miss a question in order to keep the rhythm. If you feel you don't quite understand the question, then mark any answer and switch your mind back to be ready to listen to the next question on tape. Even when you are taking the practice tests, **don't stop the tape.** You must always practice the rhythm of the speaker on the tape. (Look back to the note on page 17.)

Remember these things:

1. Skim the possible answers before the tape comes on. Look for the similarities and differences in the answer choices. (Secret Ten, page 15)
2. Shift your attention to the speaker on the tape as he or she begins to speak. (Secret Ten, page 15)
3. Use two hands: one to hold your place on the answer sheet; the other to hold your place in the test booklet. (Secret Twelve, page 18)

Easy or Hard?

Some problems look easy and some problems look hard. Don't be fooled by them. An "easy" question may have complicated answer choices. And a complicated statement or mini-talk may have easy answer choices. Think carefully about all questions, even the ones that look easy. Don't be careless with your answers. You don't want to lose points for "easy mistakes."

Also, if a question sounds hard, don't be afraid. Sometimes the answers are easier to figure out than the question.

Not Enough Time (see Secret Fourteen)

If the answer choices are long and you run out of time, then read only the main words in each answer choice. Look for words that you heard the speaker say and mark the answer choice that contains those words.

STRUCTURE AND WRITTEN EXPRESSION

There are forty questions and two parts in Section 2, Structure and Written Expression. You have twenty-five minutes to answer the questions in this section of the TOEFL.

The First Part: Completion

In the first part, you will see a part of a sentence and four choices for completing that sentence. The four choices can be single words, or longer phrases. Most of the choices are grammatically correct by themselves, but only one of them will complete the sentence correctly. To find the correct answer, you must understand the meaning of the whole sentence.

There are fifteen completion sentences in this part. The questions will look like this:

EXAMPLE 1: Completion

A butterfly is not a spider _____ an insect.

    (A) any
    (B) yet
    (C) for
    (D) but

EXAMPLE 2: Completion

_____ last season is evident by the marks of mud on the trees.

    (A) There was a flood
    (B) That there was a flood
    (C) A flood
    (D) Having a flood

The answer to Example 1 is (D). The word "but" introduces a contrasting phrase. The answer to Example 2 is (B). "That there was a flood" is a noun clause used as a subject. The flood was last season, but the main verb of the sentence is "is." (It is evident now that there was a flood last season.)

The Second Part: Error Identification

In the second part, you will see a sentence with four words or phrases underlined. One of them shows an error. You must mark the letter of the error in the sentence. Do not try to change other parts of the sentence. The error is always underlined. You do not need to correct the error, so don't waste time trying to think of how to correct the answer.

There are twenty-five questions in this part. They will look like this:

EXAMPLE 1: Error Identification

After <u>ran</u> the <u>race</u>, the winners <u>all</u> received their <u>prizes</u>.
    A   B   C   D

EXAMPLE 2: Error Identification

The medicine <u>certainly</u> made <u>him</u> feel <u>wonderfully</u> by <u>the</u> end of the day.
         A   B   C   D

The answer to Example 1 is (A). After a preposition you use a gerund. The phrase should be "After running the race . . . .")

The answer to Example 2 is (C). The word "wonderfully" is an adverb that describes the sense of feeling; that is, how well he is able to feel something while touching it. (He could not feel anything very well while wearing heavy gloves.) In the above sentence, the correct word would be "wonderful," an adjective describing the man's health.

Practice Exercises

This exercise section is divided into four parts:

Frequency List of Structures from Past Exams with Sentence Examples of Each Structure
Exercises with the Twelve Most Common Structures
Finding the Main Subject and Verb of a Sentence
General Advice

FREQUENCY OF STRUCTURES TAKEN FROM 200 QUESTIONS IN SECTION 2 OF TOEFL TESTS FROM 1984, 1985, AND 1986

The TOEFL test is very broad in its testing of grammatical structures. It covers a wide range of material. The following list will give you an overall idea of which structures have been tested on in recent exams. It is a general guide to help you in distributing your study time.

The grammatical structures below were taken from a sample of five TOEFL exams given in 1984, 1985, and 1986. The structures are from Section 2 (Structure and Written Expression). They are arranged according to how often they appeared as part of a test question. Only one grammatical structure was listed for each TOEFL question, even though the question actually could have tested more than one structure. In each TOEFL test there are forty questions in Section 2, making a total of 200 items in this frequency list. A list of example sentences follows the frequency list.

This list is for your self-study. You should be familiar with each of the grammar points below. You should be able to write correct sentences, and to correct incorrect sentences. The grammar points at the beginning of the list are the ones that have been tested on most frequently during the past tests. A list like this does not predict what will be on future tests; instead, it gives you information about past tests that can help you to estimate problems on future tests, and guide you in your choice of study topics.

Grammatical Structure	*Frequency (Out of 200 Questions)*
1. Parallel Construction	25
2. Noun, Adjective, Verb, Adverb	17
3. Singular or Plural Noun	11
4. Noun Clause as Subject or Object	9
5. Preposition Following a Verb or Adjective	9
6. Adjective or Adverb Clause Beginning with a "wh" Word	9
7. Adjective or Adverb Phrase	9
8. Prepositional Phrase after a Noun or Adjective	8
9. Verb Tense	8
10. Comparatives/Proportional Statements: more than, the more . . . the more	7
11. Superlative: the most, the . . . est, one of the . . . est	7
12. Word Order/Subject/Verb	6
13. Double Subject/ Unnecessary Repetition	5
14. Pronouns: Singular/Plural; Subject/Object	5
15. So, so that, such, such a, such as	5
16. A, an, the	4
17. Like, alike, the same, dislike, unlike	4
18. Both, either . . . or, neither . . . nor	4
19. Take, make, do	4
20. Plural or Singular Verb	4
21. Gerund/Infinitive	3

| | Frequency (Out of 200 |
Grammatical Structure	Questions)
22. As, as . . . as, by . . . as	3
23. Indefinites: everyone, everything, whatever	3
24. Passive Voice	3
25. Not only . . . but also, not only . . . as well, is not . . . but	3
26. No, not, none	2
27. Vocabulary Referring to People: . . . -ist, . . . -or	2
28. Conditional: real, unreal, past	2
29. Other, others, another	2
30. Compound Sentence	2
31. Because, because of	1
32. Little, few, small	1
33. Separate, apart	1
34. Rather, rather than	1
35. That, those, this	1
36. Rarely, seldom	1
37. Too, enough	1
38. And, or	1
39. Expletive: there	1
40. Not until . . . did	1
41. Have long had	1
42. Much, many	1
43. Since, for	1
44. Each, every, all	1
45. Big, great	1
46. Instead of	1

Frequency of Structures: Example Sentences

The following sentences are correct examples of the structures in the frequency list. The sentences are similar to sentences used in TOEFL exams.

1. Parallel Construction (25 times)

> Many people say that Hong Kong is the major center of banking, trade, and commerce in Asia.
> Sleeping, resting, and drinking fluids are the best ways to cure a cold.
> Because of its availability and price, wood is often used in building homes in the United States.

2. Noun, Adjective, Verb, Adverb (17 times)

> The seasonal changes of weather cause color changes in the leaves of deciduous trees.
> Some skunks can walk briefly on their hind legs.
> Carrots that are grown too closely together in poor soil will not form properly.

3. Singular or Plural Noun (11 times)

> Many herbs are grown in home gardens.
> The government is responsible to the people.
> Many diverse people make up the population of the United States.

4. Noun Clause as Subject or Object (9 times)

> That she was a popular woman was evident by her high standing in the polls.
> The results of the interview show that more than half of the people are in favor of building the new city school.
> How he got home last night is still a mystery to me.
> What would be very difficult for others was easy for Einstein.

5. Preposition Following a Verb or Adjective (9 times)

> He is capable of doing better than he does.
> The tax form was prepared by a tax consultant.
> The walnut shell is resistant to many diseases.
> Excessive absenteeism results in problems for the schools.

6. Adjective or Adverb Clause Beginning with a "wh" Word (9 times)

> Franklin Delano Roosevelt, who was confined to a wheelchair, was a very popular and succesful U.S. president.
> When Columbus left Europe in 1492, he was unaware of the the changes that would occur as a result of his discovery.
> The conditions which are necessary for the completion of this project have not been met.

7. Adjective or Adverb Phrase (9 times)

> The founder of the Peace Corps, John F. Kennedy, was president of the U.S. from 1961 to 1963.
> Regardless of its size, a city park is meant for all people to enjoy.
> Seen through a telescope, the planets take on a new appearance.

8. Prepositional Phrase after a Noun or Adjective (8 times)

> New York is a major center of banking.
> There was a mark of elegance in the King's dress.
> Underground oil is found between cracks of buried rock.

9. Verb Tense (8 times)

   In 1776, when the Declaration of Independence was signed, the United States became a new country.

   How many of us have not become frustrated over complete changes in the law!

   Some desert plants that have been without water for six years can still bloom when watered.

10. Comparatives/Proportional Statements: more than, the more . . . the more (7 times)

    The greater the increase in population, the harder it is for people to find adequate housing.

    Incorrect: This test is difficulter than the last one.

    Correct: This test is more difficult than the last one.

11. Superlatives: the most, the . . . -est, one of the . . . -est (7 times)

    Of all the national parks in the United States, Yellowstone is one of the most visited.

12. Word Order/Subject/Verb (6 times)

    Earthquakes result from the movement of continental plates beneath the surface of the earth.

    The bee fly larva feeds on insects.

13. Double Subject/Unnecessary Repetition (5 times)

    Incorrect: The Senate it is the law-making arm of the U.S. government.

    Correct: The Senate is the law-making arm of the U.S. government.

    Incorrect: The information received from the Viking spacecraft extremely greatly expanded our knowledge of our solar system.

    Correct: The information received from the Viking spacecraft greatly expanded our knowledge of our solar system.

14. Pronouns: Singular/Plural; Subject/Object (5 times)

    Incorrect: Scientists say that the color of the lake is a result of his unusual algae.

    Correct: Scientists say that the color of the lake is a result of its unusual algae.

15. So, so that, such, such a, such as (5 times)

    It was such a long way home that I took a cab.

    The day was so hot that people swarmed to the beach.

    Things that are hard for me in school, such as writing essays, take up a lot of my time.

16. A, an, the (4 times)

> The "ivy league" colleges are all in the eastern part of the United States.
> An orange is a citrus fruit.

17. Like, alike, the same, unlike (4 times)

> Unlike public schools, private schools charge tuition.
> The twins are alike in every way except for their preference in sports.
> Your perfume smells like roses.

18. Both, either . . . or, neither . . . nor (4 times)

> Both plants and animals need oxygen to survive.
> Neither plants nor animals can survive without oxygen.
> Animals can survive in either a dry climate or a humid one.

19. Take, make, do (4 times)

> While driving in rainy weather, you should take extra precaution to drive carefully.
> The Rockefeller family made a fortune in the oil industry.

20. Plural or Singular Verb (4 times)

> One function of local taxes is to provide for the repair of city streets.

21. Gerund/Infinitive (3 times)

> The purpose of this test is to determine how well you know English grammar.
> Impressionist artists tended to consider imagination and light more important than faithful reproduction of objects.

22. As, as . . . as, by . . . as (3 times)

> Few trains can go as fast as the Toyko high-speed Bullet train.
> Football as an observer's sport is very popular in the U.S.A.
> People are not affected as much by physical change as they are by emotional change.

23. Indefinites: everyone, everything, whatever (3 times)

> I ate everything I saw; he ate none of it.
> Whatever you want to do is fine with me.

24. Passive Voice (3 times)

> New laws should be written to accommodate changes in society.

25. Not only . . . but also, not only . . . as well, is not . . . but (3 times)

> Not only was the test long, it was also hard.
> Not only was the test long, it was hard as well.
> A hamburger is not made from ham, but from beef.

26. No, not, none (2 times)

> No two fingerprints are identical.

27. Vocabulary referring to people: . . . -ist, . . . -or (2 times)

> Edward R. Murrow was a well-known journalist during World War II.

28. Conditional: real, unreal, past (2 times)

> Had it not been for the drought, the farmers in the midwest might have been able to break even financially this year.

29. Other, others, another (2 times)

> Unlike most other schools, the University of California has nine separate campuses.
> Our university has three campuses; the others in our state have only one.
> My pencil is broken. Do you have another one?

30. Compound Sentence (2 times)

> Oak is a hard wood and pine is a soft wood.

31. Because, because of (1 time)

> Few people live in Alaska because of its cold weather.
> Few people live in Alaska because it has cold weather.

32. Little, few, small (1 time)

> In the United States, there are few small farms.
> Bartering home-grown vegetables has little importance in U.S. agriculture.

33. Separate, apart (1 time)

> Collections of paintings by French impressionists are held in separate museums all over the country.
> When the paintings were moved, they were held apart by padding to protect them from damage.

34. Rather, rather than (1 time)

> Optimism, rather than pessimism, is the outlook for next year's economy.

I don't want to go dancing tonight; rather, let's go to a movie.
I'd rather go to a movie than go dancing.
It's rather hot in here. (Meaning: It's somewhat hot.)

35. That, those, this (1 time)

> The amount of rice grown in California is greater than that in any other state in the United States.
> Mountains in the western part of the United States are higher than those in the eastern part.

36. Rarely, seldom (1 time)

> Rarely do I go out at night during the school week.

37. Too, enough (1 time)

> Many packaged foods in the U.S. have too much sugar and not enough nutrients.

38. And, or (1 time)

> The flute and the trumpet are both wind instruments.
> I can't play the flute or the trumpet.

39. Expletive: there (1 time)

> There have been times in history when remarkable events have occurred in a relatively short time.

40. Not until . . . did (1 time)

> Not until after World War II did airplanes become a common way to travel.

41. Have long had (1 time)

> Artists have long had an interest in observing landscapes.

42. Much, many (1 time)

> The piano is somewhat similar to the harpsichord, a much older instrument.
> The harpsichord is many years older than the piano.

43. Since, for (1 time)

> Since people depend on the forests for so much, every effort must be made to preserve them.

44. Each, every, all (1 time)

> All Native American people arrived on the continent before Europeans.

Each Native American claims a unique heritage.
Every Native American in the county is invited to the celebration.

45. Big, great (1 time)

Laurence Olivier is known as a great actor.
The director is looking for a big actor to play the giant in his new film.

46. Instead of (1 time)

Daylight savings time now begins at the beginning of April instead of the end of April.

EXERCISES WITH THE TWELVE MOST COMMON STRUCTURES

Parallel Construction

Words or phrases that are connected by a conjunction or a connecting word (and, but, or, nor, either . . . or, neither . . . nor, as well as, not only . . . but also) must have the same grammatical function in the sentence. They must all be nouns, adjectives, adverbs, infinitives, or gerunds.

EXAMPLES:

Nouns: *Computer science* and *math* are the biggest departments at this school.
Infinitives: My friends and I like to *hike, swim,* and *play* tennis.

(Note: The word "to" is omitted before "swim" and "play.")

Gerunds: My friends and I like *hiking, swimmimg,* and *playing* tennis.

N O T E

Look for the function of the word or phrase in each sentence, not only its ending.

EXAMPLE: That old dog is *wrinkled* and *graying.*
("Graying" is an adjective and is therefore parallel to "wrinkled" even though one ends in "ing" and the other ends in "ed.")

EXERCISE 10

Parallel Construction

DIRECTIONS: All the sentences below have words or phrases that should be parallel. Some of them are correct, and some are incorrect. If a sentence is correct, write "OK" in the blank, and underline the parallel words. If the sentence is incorrect, mark an "X" in the blank, correct the parallel words, and then underline them. The answers are on page 167.

_____ 1. In this automobile safety class, you will learn how to drive and passing the test.

_____ 2. I'd like to major in international business, and study international trade, bank, and commerce.

_____ 3. I learned a lot in class by writing essays and how to study for exams.

_____ 4. For the American history exam, we had to be able to discuss major holidays, as well as naming famous heroes.

_____ 5. There is a growing problem in the U.S. with people taking drugs like heroin and cocaine.

_____ 6. Hemingway was a gifted journalist, novelist, and wrote short stories.

_____ 7. Fresh pineapple, drinking coffee, and sugar cane are three of Hawaii's main exports.

_____ 8. Macadamia nuts grow well in moist, rich, tropical soil.

_____ 9. Surprisingly, Hawaii has wet forests, desert-like areas, and even snow-covered mountains.

_____ 10. A bicycle not only gives you exercise, but also you can see the countryside as you ride.

Noun, Adjective, Verb, Adverb

Any of these word forms might be written incorrectly on the TOEFL test.

EXAMPLE I

> *Incorrect:* Long exposed to air will cause rust to form on iron.
> The word "exposed" is incorrect. "Exposed" can be a verb or an adjective, but in this sentence a noun is needed. The noun form is 'exposure.'"

Correct: Long exposure to air will cause rust to form on iron. (noun
subject: exposure . . . verb: will cause)

Long exposed to air, the iron turned to rust. (adjective: exposed . . . subject: iron . . . verb: turned)

EXAMPLE 2

Incorrect: Walking every daily is one of the best exercises for overall
health.

"Daily" can be an adjective or an adverb, but it is incorrect
here because a noun must follow "every."

Correct: Walking every day is one of the best exercises.

Walking daily is one of the best exercises.

"Daily" as an adverb: I walk daily.

"Daily" as an adjective: I take a daily walk.

EXAMPLE 3

Incorrect: Changes in daily, seasonally, and yearly temperature affect
the growth cycle in plants.

"Seasonally" is an adverb; "seasonal" is an adjective. In the
sentence above, the adjective "seasonal" describes the noun
"temperature."

Correct: Changes in daily, seasonal, and yearly temperature affect
the growth cycle in plants.

This sentence is confusing since "daily" and "yearly" end in
"ly" even though they are adjectives.

CONFUSING WORDS

marry

1. Verb: *to marry*—must be followed by a name

   EXAMPLE 1: Jill married John. (John is Jill's husband.) This form
   cannot be made passive.

   EXAMPLE 2: The minister married John. (The minister performed
   the marriage ceremony.) This form can be made passive. (John
   was married by the minister.)

2. Adjective: *married*—must follow "to get" or "to be"; can be
   followed by "to"

   EXAMPLES: Jill got married.
   Jill got married to John.

> Jill got married last year.
> Jill is married.

The following sentence has two possible meanings.

> Jill was married last year. (Now she is divorced. She was
> married for five years.)
> Jill was married last year. (Jill and John got married last year.
> They have been married for one year.)

interesting, interested

Both words are adjectives.

> He is an *interesting* person.
> He is an *interested* person.
> He is an interesting person = He does things that interest me. He is
> unusual. I like him.
> He is interested = He is paying attention. He is showing an interest
> in something.

It is unusual to say: "I am very interesting." If you say this, you are talking about yourself and how good you are. You might say, however: "I gave a very interesting speech. The audience loved it." (The audience was interested in my speech.)

A person or an animal can be either interested or interesting. A place or an object cannot be interested.

> The dog is interesting. (He is unusual.)
> The bone is interesting. (It is unusual.)
> The dog is interested. (He probably wants something.)
> The dog is interested in the bone.
> The bone is interested. (impossible)

"To interest" is a verb.

> I interest him. = He likes me.
> The book interests me. = I like the book.

Below is a sample list of words that follow the pattern of "interesting" and prepositions that can follow them:

amazing, amazed (at)
amusing, amused (at)
astonishing, astonished (at)
boring, bored (with)
confusing, confused (about)
embarrassing, embarrassed (about)

exciting, excited (about)
fascinating, fascinated (with)
frightening, frightened (about)
pleasing, pleased (with)
satisfying, satisfied (with)
surprising, surprised (at, about)

EXERCISE 11

Noun, Adjective, Verb, Adverb

DIRECTIONS: Correct the incorrect noun, adjective, verb, or adverb. The answers are on page 167.

1. Many children are now getting the opportune to take a computer programming course in school.

2. A blood clot that comes loose in the body can obstruction the blood vessels in the brain and cause a stroke.

3. Many communities are studying long-range development plans in order to lessen the impacted of population growth on their environment.

4. Anthropologists who study early hominid development look for three features of the brain: the size, the overall shape, and the intricacy of nervous fibers.

5. The ancient philosopher, Confucious, was against writing criminal law, an idea that is precise opposed to Western tradition.

6. The beach is an interested place to walk on a stormy day.

7. After Helen Keller passed the examine, she attended Radcliffe College.

8. Anyone who is in the field of business or mass communicate must have an understanding of statistics.

9. Congress has passed laws require that industries stop discharging pollutants into rivers.

10. Good actors and capably speakers can communicate emotions with regularity.

SINGULAR OR PLURAL NOUN

Some of the questions on the TOEFL exam test your knowledge of irregular plurals:

EXAMPLES

man — men	woman — women
foot — feet	tooth — teeth
child — children	

and uncountable (mass) nouns:

EXAMPLES

furniture   equipment
luggage   traffic
advice   homework

Some names of countries end in "s" even though they are singular:

EXAMPLES

the United States . . . is . . . .
the Netherlands . . . is . . . .
the Philippines . . . is . . . .

On the TOEFL exam the questions will sometimes incorrectly add an "s" where none is needed:

> *Incorrect:* Sixty percents of all the profit goes to the club.
> *Incorrect:* Your economic report is due on the tenth months.

Sometimes the "s" is omitted:

> *Incorrect:* More students enrolled in occupational course this year.
> *Incorrect:* Sometimes a bear can have two cub at the same time.

Here are a few singular/plural clues:

1. When a noun modifies another noun, the first noun does not end in "s."

    EXAMPLES

    a car door   a cat box
    a house boat   a computer disk
    a lamp shade   a milk carton

2. In a phrase that begins with "One of the ...(noun)...," the noun must be plural:

    EXAMPLE: One of the features of the new resort is its shuttle bus.

3. In a phrase modifying a noun, either both nouns will be singular or both will be plural.

    EXAMPLES

    A *freeway, a road* with no stop signs, *is* a major highway.
    Freeways, roads with no stop signs, *are* major highways.

4. A singular countable noun must be preceded by "a," "an," or "the." "A" is used before a consonant sound (a pear). "An" is used before a vowel sound (an apple). "The" is used to refer to a specific noun. A plural noun has no article.

EXAMPLES

Students taking *occupational courses* are learning job skills.
Students taking *an occupational course* learn job skills.

EXERCISE 12

Singular or Plural Nouns

DIRECTIONS: Each of the following sentences has one or more incorrect nouns. Cross out the incorrect words and write in the correct answers. The answers are on page 167.

1. Metropolitan area have increased in the southern part of the country.

2. Only a few wild condor are left in the mountain of California.

3. The population of Chicago is about three millions.

4. All womans over forty should come in for a checkup.

5. New street and highway cover thousand of miles of central farmland.

6. Citizen of a democracy have the rights to vote for government official.

7. Scientists have long known that the additions of calcium to the diet increases bone strength.

8. Silicon chip manufacturer work with precise micro measurements.

9. The fundamental problems of any government is to balance expenses and income.

10. Biofeedback studies give information to peoples about how to monitor their own bodily functions.

NOUN CLAUSE

A noun clause is a group of words with a subject and verb. It can begin with the words: what, where, when, who, why, which, whose, how, that, *or* whether.

The noun clause can be the subject of a sentence:

<u>Where she is going</u> is nobody's business.
        subject

It can also be the object of a sentence:

I didn't know <u>that he was a member of this committee.</u>
                                 object

The subject comes before the verb in a noun clause. Sometimes the questions on the TOEFL test will change the order.

Incorrect: I don't know where is he going.
 Correct: I don't know *where he is* going.

REMEMBER

The main verb of the sentence is not in the noun clause.

<u>Where she is going</u>   is   nobody's business.
    noun clause   main verb

I didn't <u>know</u> <u>that he was coming.</u>
     main verb   noun clause

EXERCISE 13

Noun Clauses

DIRECTIONS: Some of the following sentences are correct and some are incorrect. Underline the noun clause. Write "S" over the main subject of the sentence, and "V" over the main verb. Check to see if the subjects and verbs are correct. Write "OK" in the blank if the sentence is correct. Mark "X" if the sentence is not correct, and then correct it. The answers are on page 168.

1. _X_ That she ~~were~~ *was* crying last night was obvious to everyone.

2. _____ I think that she is a good actress, don't you?

3. _____ I don't know whether he like me.

4. _____ I wonder where does he buy this?

5. _____ What she said surprised me.

6. _____ Police officers say that computer crime is hard to detect.

7. _____ Exactly what an IQ test measures is not agreed upon by all researchers.

8. _____ How to cure the common cold is still a mystery to science.

9. _____ Whether the government, private industry, or individuals themselves are responsible for diseases like cancer is a debatable question.

10. _____ Each political party must consider who is the best candidate for the coming years.

PREPOSITIONS FOLLOWING A VERB OR ADJECTIVE

Below is a list of some of the common prepositions following verbs and adjectives:

capable of	able to	result from
careful of	accustomed to	amazed at
careless of	adjust to	angry at
conscious of	comparable to	shocked at
consists of	essential to	surprised at
critical of	equal to	eager for
inconsiderate of	harmful to	made for
independent of	leading to	prepared for
made of	married to	used for
proud of	parallel to	made by
scared of	relate to	prepared by
tired of	resistant to	symbolized by
similar to	similar to	interested in
careless with	tend to	result in
dissatisfied with	enthusiastic about	used in
pleased with	serious about	placed under

EXERCISE 14

Prepositions After an Adjective

DIRECTIONS: Fill in the correct preposition. Try to answer without looking at the list above. The answers are on page 168.

When I first came to the United States, I was surprised _____

how casually people relate _____ each other. I was also

shocked _____ the informal way that people dress. I felt

that sometimes people were being inconsiderate _____ each other. Now that I have been in the U.S. for a while, I have grown accustomed _____ American life. Even though I am still very conscious _____ some unusual styles of behavior, I have adjusted _____ many new things. I realize that in the past I was too critical _____ American customs. Now I am satisfied _____ my life. I am interested _____ what I see, and enthusiastic _____ learning even more.

ADJECTIVE OR ADVERB CLAUSE BEGINNING WITH A "WH" WORD

On the TOEFL exam there are many questions about agreement of subject and verb. An adjective clause will often separate a main subject and verb, making it difficult to determine whether or not they agree. Recognizing a clause will help you find the main subject and verb. A clause is a group of words with a subject and verb.

The clause can be a sentence (independent clause):

She is late.

The clause can be part of a sentence (dependent clause):

If she is late to the party . . .

Adjective Clause: An adjective clause describes a noun. It usually begins with the words: who, whom, which, where, when, whose, that.

EXAMPLE: The people *who were late* are waiting outside. (What people? . . . the ones who were late . . . .)

Restrictive Clause: A restrictive clause is necessary to the meaning of a sentence. It has no commas around it.

EXAMPLE: My friend *who lives in Canada* is coming to visit me. (I have many friends, but only the one from Canada is coming here.)

Non-restrictive Clause: A non-restrictive clause is not necessary to the meaning of the sentence. It gives extra information. It must be separated by commas.

EXAMPLE: My father, *who lives in Canada*, is coming to visit me. (I have only one father. He lives in Canada.)

Pronouns: The pronoun "that" can be substituted for "who" or "which" in a restrictive clause only.

   Correct: The essay *that favored nuclear disarmament* was published in the school newspaper.

   Correct: The essay *which favored nuclear disarmament* was published in the school newspaper.

   Correct: Sue's essay, *which favored nuclear disarmament,* was published in the school newspaper.

  Incorrect: Sue's essay, that favored nuclear disarmament, was published in the school newspaper.

R E M E M B E R

The adjective clause must begin with a pronoun (who, whom, which, where, when, whose, that). You can never have a complete sentence in the middle of another sentence separated by commas.

  Incorrect: The essay, it was about nuclear disarmament, was published in the school newspaper.

Adverb Clause: An adverb clause answers the questions when, how, how long, where, and why. It also has a subject and verb. The adverb clause usually comes before or after the main part of the sentence, rather than between the main subject and verb.

An adverb clause commonly begins with words such as: even though, before, when, although, after, *or* as.

EXAMPLE: When she dyed her hair pink last year, she liked that punk style. (When did she like that punk style? . . . when she dyed her hair pink.)

EXERCISE 15

Adjective or Adverb Clauses

DIRECTIONS: Some of the following sentences are correct, and some are incorrect. Underline each clause. Write the letter "S" over the main subject and the letter "V" over the main verb. Check for the tense and the agreement of singular and plural. If the sentence is correct, write "OK" in the blank. If it is incorrect, mark "x" and correct the sentence. The answers are on page 169.

1. __OK__ The tea <u>that you sent me from China</u> was excellent.

2. _____ The barber who cut your hair does a good job yesterday.

3. _____ Do you recognize the woman who just came into the room?

4. _____ The movies that were playing last weekend was good.

5. _____ When the Soviet premier and the U.S. president left the summit meeting, they shook hands cordially.

6. _____ As soon as a new student registers, he or she can get a parking sticker for the school parking lot.

7. _____ Orange trees grow well in Florida and California, where is there a lot of sun.

8. _____ I didn't like the vegetables they were soaked in oil.

9. _____ John Lennon shot as he was walking into his apartment building.

10. _____ Marriage, that is a legal contract, can also be seen as an economic institution.

ADJECTIVE OR ADVERB PHRASES

Phrases are groups of words without subjects and verbs.

Adjective Phrase: An adjective phrase describes a noun. Sometimes the adjective phrase renames the noun and can be substituted for that noun.

EXAMPLES:

Alaska, *the largest state in the United States*, has a very small population.
The shortest day of the year, *December 21*, was cold and rainy.
Farmers used to use marl, *a kind of clay mixture,* for fertilizer.

Adverb Phrase: An adverb phrase gives information about how, how long, how often, when, or why.

It often begins with a present participle (verb + -ing), past participle (verb + -ed), or an infinitive (to + verb).

If it begins with a preposition, the preposition must be followed by a noun or gerund (verb + -ing).

EXAMPLES:

A fish breathes under water *by using its gills.*
After serving as U.S. President for four years, Jimmy Carter retired to his peanut farm.
Plants *living under the ocean* are sometimes vividly colored.

On the TOEFL test, the mistake might be in the word order, the use of an article, the addition of a subject or verb, the preposition, the use of "ing."

EXERCISE 16

Adjective or Adverb Phrase

DIRECTIONS: Correct the adjective or adverb phrase in each sentence. The answers are on page 169.

1. My English teacher, is Mrs. Jones, canceled class today.

2. The winner of the contest, the good friend of mine, just gave me a big hug.

3. The President of the Philippines, Aquino is, gave an excellent speech.

4. I was worried when Mr. Stevens, he is my school counselor, told me that I would have to get 550 on the TOEFL exam.

5. Before hand calculators were common, math students usually carried a slide rule, it is a type of calculating ruler.

6. To use a calculator, one can easily convert kilos to pounds and Celsius to Fahrenheit.

7. By study fossil remains, paleontologists gain information about previous life forms.

8. The number of people contracting AIDS, a deadly virus diseases, is escalating every year.

PREPOSITIONAL PHRASE AFTER A NOUN OR ADJECTIVE

A prepositional phrase is a preposition plus an object (a noun or a noun phrase).

EXAMPLE:

in a classroom
prep   object

The following errors are often in TOEFL exam sentences.

Sometimes a TOEFL exam question will substitute a verb or an adverb for a noun.

Incorrect: Fur gives a mark *of elegant* to a jacket.
Correct: Fur gives a mark of elegance to a jacket.

Sometimes the mistake is in the preposition:

Incorrect: The leaves *for the tree* turn golden in the fall.
Correct: The leaves of the tree turn golden in the fall.

Sometimes the order of the noun phrase is reversed:

Incorrect: The professor was deep *in thought abstract.*
Correct: The professor was deep in abstract thought.

EXERCISE 17

Prepositional Phrases

DIRECTIONS: Put parentheses ( ) around each prepositional phrase, and correct the errors. Not all the prepositional phrases contain errors, but each sentence has at least one error of some type. The answers are on page 170.

1. The manner of election the president is written in the Constitution.

2. The hub of bank is in New York City.

3. Water will boil quickly under high pressured.

4. Dolphins can leap out of the water from a deep far below the surface.

5. Scientists are working on a system of recycle food and waste products for lengthy space flights.

6. Is the government or private industry financially responsible for the problem of water pollute?

7. The application of statistic methods to business enterprises has brought radical changes to some businesses in recent years.

8. Both hardware and software engineering are important aspects of build computer systems.

VERB TENSE

On each TOEFL test, there will probably be a few questions that test your ability to choose a correct tense, or to recognize an incorrect tense. Any tense can be used incorrectly.

A past continuous might be substituted for a passive voice.

EXAMPLES:

Incorrect: In 1861, when Abraham Lincoln *was electing* president, many Americans owned slaves.

Correct: In 1861, when Abraham Lincoln was elected president, many Americans owned slaves.

A future perfect might be substituted for a past tense verb.

Incorrect: Before 1920 few people *will have had* washing machines.

Correct: Before 1920 few people had washing machines.

EXERCISE 18

Verbs

DIRECTIONS: Correct the incorrect verbs in the following sentences. The answers are on page 170.

1. Tropical areas of the earth lay near the equator.

2. A well-seasoned traveler always have carried small amenities for personal health and safety.

3. In 1937, Amelia Earhart leaves the United States for her ill-fated flight across the Pacific.

4. The artifacts dug up by the archeologist to be sorted, tagged, and stored for further use.

5. Condors can be having a wing span of up to ten feet.

6. A corporation needed capital in order to start up its business.

7. In advertising, a group of consumers who might buy a product to be known as the target market.

8. In some communities, flouride added to the water supply to reduce tooth decay in children.

COMPARATIVES/PROPORTIONAL STATEMENTS

Comparatives: Comparatives are formed by adding "er" to an adjective with one syllable:

high—higher

If a word has more than one syllable, the word "more" or "less" is added:

expensive—more expensive
compact—less compact

There are a few exceptions:

early—earlier

There are a few irregular adjectives:

good—better
bad—worse

Sometimes the TOEFL exam will test your choice of whether to use "er" or "more" or "less."

Incorrect: These bricks are *longer* and *more strong* than those.

Sometimes the TOEFL exam will test your ability to choose an adjective form:

Incorrect: This book is *less complication* than that one.

Proportional Statements: Proportional statements use a comparative adjective. There are two parts of the sentence, and there is always a comma between the two parts. The meaning of one part increases or decreases in proportion to the other.

EXAMPLE: The stronger the magnet, the greater the force.

The TOEFL question might test your use of an article:

Incorrect: The stronger magnet, the greater the force.

It might test the sentence structure:

Incorrect: The longer the book, the more difficult than read.

EXERCISE 19

Comparatives/Proportional Statements

DIRECTIONS: Find the error in each sentence, and correct it. The answers are on page 170.

1. The harder I study, more tired I become.
2. Doing research proves difficulter than I thought.
3. Pottery dishes painted by hand are more beauty than than the ones painted by machine.
4. The ocean off the Continental Shelf is more depth than the waters of the ocean close to the land.
5. The more you practice your skills, the capabler you become.
6. Medicines with a brand name are usually more expensiver than generic medicines.
7. A doctor has had years of study more than a pharmacist.
8. Researchers say that the faster you read, the more better is your comprehension.

SUPERLATIVES

A superlative is used when three or more things are compared. Both adjectives and adverbs can be superlatives. If the word has one syllable, add "est" to the end:

I am the tallest person in my family.
Your house is the nearest of all our houses.

If the word has two or more syllables, add the word "most" or "least."

Of all the children, John sang the most happily.
My uncle is the most unreasonable man I know.

Look for these words:

> the most
> the least
> the _____est
> the _____est of all

Be sure that you don't omit the word "the." Be sure that you don't use both "most" and "-est."

> *Incorrect:* The *most fastest* trains are in Japan and France.

In the exercises below, while you are looking for the superlative, also look for the main subject and verb. The main subject ("S") and verb ("V") can be at the beginning or the end of the sentence, or they can be separated by a prepositional phrase.

EXAMPLES:

The GRE is the most difficult test I've ever taken.

Of all the tests I've taken, the GRE is the most difficult.

One of the most difficult tests I've taken is the GRE.

Some of the most . . . are . . . .

REMEMBER

The main subject and verb are never in the prepositional phrase. Be sure that the verb agrees with the main subject of the sentence, not necessarily the noun just before the verb.

EXERCISE 20

Superlatives

DIRECTIONS: Correct the errors in the following sentences. Write "S" over the main subject and "V" over the main verb. The answers are on page 170.

1. Busiest airport in the U.S. is in Chicago.

2. The giraffe is one of the least mammals that can't swim.

3. Of all the immigrants that come to live in the U.S., Asians and Hispanics are biggest group.

4. Of the great differences between a St. Bernard and a Chihuahua is the size of the dog.

5. The most usually distinction between a living room and a family room lies in the formality of its use.

6. Of all the world's major mountain chains, the Himalayas have the high peaks.

7. Highest possible score for the TOEFL is 677.

8. The answer sheets with fewest errors have best scores.

WORD ORDER, SUBJECT/VERB

Sometimes the TOEFL test questions will test your ability to choose a correct subject and verb from a variety of clauses and phrases. Sometimes the word order in the choices is mixed up so that the sentence does not make sense.

EXAMPLE: For hundreds of years, _____ feather pens instead of ball point pens.

(A) there were used
(B) people used
(C) that people used
(D) using

The correct answer is (B).

EXERCISE 21

Subject/Verb Order

DIRECTIONS: Choose the correct answer for each sentence. The answers are on page 171.

1. On a cold day, _____ a delicate appearance.

(A) a fresh snowflake has
(B) a snowflake that has fresh
(C) has a fresh snowflake
(D) which snowflake is fresh

2. _____ as a material for women's coats.

   (A) Values mink
   (B) That mink has value
   (C) Mink is valued
   (D) Which mink values

3. The chancellor of the university _____ to all family and friends to attend graduation ceremonies.

   (A) which invites
   (B) invitation extends
   (C) who is inviting
   (D) extends an invitation

4. The _____ has risen in the last five years, but not as fast as the number of miles passengers have flown.

   (A) number of air traffic controllers
   (B) air traffic number controllers
   (C) controller of number air traffic
   (D) air traffic controller number

5. When applying for government grants and loans, _____ an incredible number of forms.

   (A) which one can fill out
   (B) there are to fill out
   (C) they are filling out
   (D) one must fill out

FINDING THE MAIN SUBJECT AND VERB

Many of the problems in the Structure section of the TOEFL depend on your knowing the subject and verb of the main clause of the sentence and being sure that they agree. In a long, complex sentence, it might be hard to find the main clause quickly. To practice finding the main clause, do the following in order:

STEP 1: Look for the prepositional phrases. These are quick and easy to find because they begin with the "little" words (in, on, at, for, etc.). Put parentheses around these prepositional phrases. *The main subject and verb will not be in the prepositional phrases.*

STEP 2: Look for the dependent clauses. Identify them by the transitional words (if, because, when, since, although, etc.) *The main subject and verb will not be in the dependent clause.*

STEP 3: Now look at the words that are left. Find the subject and verb.

STEP 4: Check the subject and verb to see if they are both plural or both singular. Make sure the verb is in the right tense.

STEP 5: Check the sentence for parallel construction in all verbs, adjectives, nouns, and pronouns.

The following sentence is taken from a university application booklet.

If you want to be sure to be considered for admission to the university you want to attend, and to the major or program of study you want to pursue, file your completed application before the deadline.

STEP 1: Put parentheses around the prepositional phrases.

If you want to be sure to be considered (for admission) (to the university) you want to attend, and (to the major or program of study) you want to pursue, file your completed application (before the deadline).

If you take the prepositional phrases out of your sentence, it will look like this:

If you want to be sure to be considered xxx xxxxxxxxx xx xxx xxxxx xxxx you want to attend, and xx xxx xxxxx xx xxxxxxx xx xxxxx you want to pursue, file your completed application xxxxxx xxx xx xxxxxx.

STEP 2: Identify the dependent clause, if any. Look for a transitional word to help you find the beginning of a dependent clause, and a comma to help you find the end.

If you want to be sure to be considered xxx xxxxxxxxx xx xxx xxxxx
transitional word   dependent clause
xxxxxx you want to attend, and xx xxx xxxxx xx xxxxxxx xx xxxxx

you want to pursue, file your completed application xxxxxx xxx
           comma
xxxxxxxx.

Now take out the dependent clause and your sentence will look like this:

> xx xxx xxxx xx xx xxxx xx xx xxxxxxxxx xxx xxxxxxxxx xx xxx
> xxxxxxxxxx xxx xxxx xx xxxxxx, and xx xxx xxxxx xx xxxxxxx xx
> xxxxx xxx xxxx xx xxxxxx, file your completed application xxxxxx
> xxx xxxxxxxx.

STEP 3: Find the subject and verb in the words that are left.

. . . . . . file your completed application . . .
Subject: you (not written)
Verb: file

EXERCISE 22

Finding the Main Subject and Verb

DIRECTIONS: In the following sentences taken from college application forms, put parentheses around the prepositional phrases, mark the dependent clauses, and find the subject and verb of the main clause. The answers are on page 171.

1. After the deadline, some campuses will accept applications if they still have openings for new students.

2. If, after submitting your application, you wish to add more new information to your record, you may mail it in a separate envelope to the admissions office.

3. Most fall term applicants are notified of their admission to the university by late spring.

4. If you are applying as a foreign student, arrange to take the Test of English as a Foreign Language (TOEFL), and if you are applying as a graduate student, you must also take the Graduate Record Examination (GRE).

5. At the time you take these tests, you must ask the testing service to send your scores directly to the admissions office at each of the campuses to which you are applying.

GENERAL ADVICE

Personal Rule Summary

If you have been following the advice of this book, you will have already begun your personal rule summary. (See page 6.) By keeping a personalized rule summary, you will review structures that you have studied in past years, and discover what particular structures you need to study more.

Study Actively

When you study grammar, it is important to be active.

Don't just read the structure rule or the example sentence and say to yourself, "I know that."

Do write your own examples in your own words. Write true sentences that mean something to you.

Do check your sentences using a book or a native speaker. Correct your errors, and copy the sentences again correctly.

Use Your Knowledge of Frequent Structures: When you are taking the TOEFL test, use your knowledge of frequent structures to help you in the Structure section of the exam. Look at the two methods below. Method 1 is the way most people do the Structure exam. They read the sentence and look for the error or the correct answer. But there is another way. You can look for specific types of errors as you read each sentence.

Method 1	Method 2
1. Read the sentence.	1. Read the sentence.
2. Look for the correct answer choice or the sentence error.	2. Look for particular categories of errors based on the Frequency List in this book.

Method 2 is especially helpful if you are running out of time, or if the sentence is very difficult. Even if you don't understand all the sentence, you can check to see if the subject and verb agree, if the verbs or adjectives are parallel, or if the prepositions seem correct. You can sometimes save time by looking quickly for the most common errors before examining each underlined word or phrase separately.

VOCABULARY AND READING COMPREHENSION

The Vocabulary and Reading Comprehension section of the TOEFL measures your reading comprehension skills. You will have forty-five minutes to complete this section.

There are two types of questions. The first thirty questions are vocabulary questions. You will see a sentence with one word underlined. There will be four answer choices. You choose the word that keeps the best meaning of the sentence. The next thirty questions are reading comprehension questions. You will read four or five short paragraphs, each followed by several questions with four answer choices. You choose the best answer.

This workbook section contains exercises to help you practice reading comprehension and vocabulary skills. It is divided into three parts: Prefixes, Suffixes, and Roots; Using Context Clues; and Reading Paragraphs.

PREFIXES, SUFFIXES, AND ROOTS

If you don't know the meaning of a word, you can often guess at the meaning by using the prefixes, suffixes, and roots. A prefix is a word or syllable placed in front of a word. A suffix comes at the end of a word, and a root is the main part of a word. The following exercises will help you learn the meanings of these common parts of words.

EXERCISE 23

Number Prefixes

DIRECTIONS: Study this list of prefixes. Add an example of your own for each prefix. Some examples are listed in the answer key, page 172.

Prefix	Meaning	Example	Your Example
1. mono, uni	one	uniform	_____
2. du, bi	two	binoculars	_____
3. tri	three	tricycle	_____

4. quad	four	quadrangle	_____
5. penta, quint	five	quintuplets	_____
6. deca	ten	decade	_____
7. cent	hundred	centennial	_____
8. poly, multi	many	multilingual	_____

EXERCISE 24

Negative Prefixes

DIRECTIONS: Each of the prefixes below means "no" or "not." Write each negative prefix and the meaning of each example word. Do not use your dictionary. The answers are on page 172.

Example	Prefix	Meaning of Example
1. illegal	_____	_____
2. immature	_____	_____
3. incorrect	_____	_____
4. irregular	_____	_____
5. unattached	_____	_____
6. antiwar	_____	_____
7. disobey	_____	_____
8. misspell	_____	_____

EXERCISE 25

Relationship Prefixes

DIRECTIONS: Study the meanings of the prefixes below, and write a definition for the example word. Do not use your dictionary. If you don't know the word, guess at the meaning. The answers are on page 172.

Prefix	Meaning	Example	Meaning of Example
1. pre	before	to prepay	_____
2. post	after	a postscript	_____
3. inter	between	intermittent rain	_____
4. sur	over	a surtax	_____
5. sub	under	a subgroup	_____
6. peri	around	a perimeter	_____
7. sym, syn	together	to synchronize	_____
8. co, com	together	a coworker	_____

EXERCISE 26

Noun Suffixes

DIRECTIONS: The following suffixes are all used with nouns. Change each verb or adjective into a noun by adding the correct suffix. The answers are on page 173.

Noun Suffixes: -ion, -tion, -sion, -ment, -ness, -ity, -ence, -ance.

Verb or Adjective   Noun

1. intelligent   _____

2. inform   _____

3. shy   _____

4. vain   _____

5. able   _____

6. kind   _____

7. regulate   _____

8. impress   _____

EXERCISE 27

Adjective Suffixes

DIRECTIONS: The following suffixes are all used with adjectives. Change each noun into an adjective by adding the correct suffix. The answers are on page 173.

Adjective Suffixes: -ic, -ish, -ive -y, -ous, -al.

Noun	Adjective
1. child	_____
2. athlete	_____
3. dirt	_____
4. nature	_____
5. explosion	_____
6. mystery	_____
7. volcano	_____
8. bump	_____

EXERCISE 28

"Person" Suffixes

DIRECTIONS: For each of the nouns below, write the suffix and then describe what the person does. The answers are on page 173.

Noun	Suffix	Meaning—A person who:
1. purchaser	_____	_____
2. florist	_____	_____
3. cashier	_____	_____
4. beautician	_____	_____
5. supervisor	_____	_____

6. typist   _____   _____

7. programmer   _____   _____

8. mortician   _____   _____

EXERCISE 29

Root Words

DIRECTIONS: Look at each group of words below, and write the roots that are common to each group. Then guess the meanings of the roots. Do not use your dictionary. The answers are on page 173.

Words	Root	Meaning of Root
1. bicycle, tricycle, cyclone	_____	_____
2. dentist, orthodontist, indent	_____	_____
3. psychology, psychiatrist	_____	_____
4. transcript, description	_____	_____
5. independent, suspend, depend	_____	_____
6. telephone, phonetics	_____	_____
7. manuscript, manufacture	_____	_____
8. microscope, telescope	_____	_____

USING CONTEXT CLUES

Even though you have studied a lot of vocabulary words, you may still come to a word that you don't know. What should you do then? Rather than stop and use your dictionary, you should try to figure out the new word by using other words in the sentence. These are called "context clues." The clues can be found in the same sentence, an adjoining sentence, or anywhere in the paragraph. The clues can also be found in your own background knowledge.

If you always stop to look in a dictionary when you come to a new word, you slow down your reading speed, and you don't comprehend the reading as well as you could. When you practice reading comprehension skills, you should not stop reading to look up new words. After all, you can't use a dictionary during the TOEFL exam. You can use your dictionary while you are studying vocabulary, to check up on your knowledge. But don't rely on that dictionary when you are reading. It will slow you down. What you want to learn is how to read faster.

The following exercises will help you find and use context clues.

Direct Clues: A direct clue is a definition or description of the word in the same sentence. There are several things to look for:

COMMAS: Solar energy, energy from the sun, is now commonly used for heating homes in many parts of the world.
CLUE: "solar energy" = "energy from the sun"

WORDS IN A SERIES: The people were unhappy with the government, so they were working to change the statutes, laws, and regulations.
CLUE: "statutes" = "similar to laws and regulations"

VERB: is, are, was, etc. The dimensions of the box are 2″ × 3″ × 6″.
CLUE: "dimensions" = "size"

"AND": She slipped and fell on the ice.
CLUE: "slipped" = "fell"

Indirect Clues: With an indirect clue, the clue words are in an opposing word or an opposing idea. This type of sentence will have words like "although," "but," "in contrast," "even though," or "while." You should look for opposite words.

Although the material was made of synthetic fiber, it felt just like natural material.

Clue Words: the opposite of "natural material"
Definition: "synthetic" = "made by people, not natural"

Inference and Background Knowledge: Often you can use your own life experience to help you guess a meaning.

After eating a delicious banquet, my appetite was satiated, and I felt sleepy.

Clue: How do I feel after I eat a big meal?
Definition: "satiated" = "full"

EXERCISE 30

Guessing New Words

DIRECTIONS: For each underlined word, guess the meaning using the context clue. Write the clues that helped you guess the meaning. Do not use your dictionary. The answers are on page 174.

1. Even though the water had been churned up by the motor on the boats, it was still smooth and clear enough to see the fish.

   Clue Words: _____

   Meaning of "churned": _____

2. Although his story was plausible, I didn't believe what he was saying.

   Clue Words: _____

   Meaning of "plausible": _____

3. Even though the flood inundated the valley with water, the homes on the hillside stayed dry.

   Clue Words: _____

   Meaning of "inundated": _____

4. Altruistic love and concern for others are difficult to attain if you feel threatened and insecure.

   Clue Words: _____

   Meaning of "altruistic love": _____

5. His candor was shown by his openness and his truthful answers.

   Clue Words: _____

   Meaning of "candor": _____

6. The victims of the tax swindle were given all their money back when the truth was found out.

   Clue Words: _____

   Meaning of "swindle": _____

7. Janet's job barely gave her enough money to live on, so she augmented her income by working at night.

   Clue Words: _____

   Meaning of "augmented": _____

8. Every morning at 5:00 AM, we were <u>rousted</u> out of our warm beds, to face the cold air and round up the cows for milking.

Clue Words: _____

Meaning of "rousted": _____

READING PARAGRAPHS

Finding the Main Idea

When you are reading to get the general meaning of a paragraph, you should practice reading as quickly as possible. Don't stop to look up words in your dictionary because that will slow you down. Instead of concentrating on individual words, look at the relationship between the sentences in the paragraph. Look for clues to the author's organization. These clues will help you find the author's main idea.

The main idea is the most important message presented by the author. In a well-written paragraph, all sentences relate in some way to the main idea. The main idea is stated in the topic sentence, and this sentence is usually the first sentence of the paragraph. It may, however, be the last sentence, a middle sentence, or even implied in several sentences.

In TOEFL exams, almost every paragraph has a question about the main topic or the best title. Understanding the organization of the paragraph will help you to recognize the main idea quickly. Look for the word clues. The following list gives some examples of clues to paragraph organization.

Paragraph Organization—Description: The main idea is often the first general statement.

Clue Words: many, some, others, one, another, also, all.

Possible Paragraph Structure:

There are many xxxxxxxxxxxx. Some of them are xxxx xxxxxxxx. Others are xxxxxxxxxxxx.

There are many xxxxxxxxx. One is xxxxxx. Another is xxxxxxxx xxxxxxx. Also, xxxxxxxxxxxx.

Paragraph Organization—Additional Information: The main idea is usually the addition of the new information.

Clue Words: not only, but also, as well, additionally, moreover, in addition, further, furthermore, what is more.

Possible Paragraph Structure:

> xxxxxxxxxxxxxxx not only xxxxxxxxxxxxxx but also xxxxxxx
> xxxxx.
> xxxxxxxxxxxxxx is not only xxxxx, but xxxxxx as well.

Paragraph Organization—Contradiction: The main idea usually follows the clue word.

Clue Words: but, however, nevertheless, rather.

Possible Paragraph Structure:

> It is said that xxxxxxxxxxxxxx, but xxxxxxxxxxxxx.
> Xxxxxxxxx is supposed to be xxxxxxxxxxxxxxxxxxx; however, xxxxxxxxxxxxx.

Paragraph Organization—Time Order: The main idea usually includes the topic and its time frame.

Clue Words: from . . . to, first, next, last, since, later

Possible Paragraph Structure:

> Xxxxxxxx can be traced from xxxxxxx to xxxxxxxx.
> At the beginning, xxxxxxxxxxxxx. Later, xxxxxxxx.

Paragraph Organization—Reason/Result: The main idea is usually stated in the reason clause of the sentence or the result clause of the sentence.

Clue Words: reason, because, result, consequently, therefore, in consequence, thus, since, if

Possible Paragraph Structure:

> The reason xxxxxxxxxxxxxxxxxx is xxxxxxxxxxxxxxxx. Because xxxxxxxxxxxxxxxx, xxxxxxxxxxxx is xxxxxxxxxx. Xxxxxxxxxx xxxxxxxxxxxxx. As a result, xxxxxxxxxxxx. Xxxxxxxxxxxxxxx xxxx. Consequently, xxxxxxxxxxxxxxxx.

EXERCISE 31

Topic Sentences

DIRECTIONS: For each of the following paragraphs, underline the organization word clues using the list on page 87 and above. Then write the type of paragraph organization and the topic sentence. The answers are on page 174.

1. A new discovery of a dinosaur fossil in Antarctica has confirmed the idea that dinosaurs lived not only in the Northern Hemisphere but in the Southern Hemisphere as well. Up until this discovery, paleontologists had found dinosaur remains on every continent except Antarctica. This new discovery now confirms the idea that dinosaurs were distributed worldwide. If the dinosaur fossil is shown to be related to other dinosaurs of the same period in South America, it will also add evidence to the idea that South America and Antarctica were once linked together.

   Paragraph Organization _____

   Topic Sentence _____

2. A very strong wind of over 75 miles per hour (139 kilometers per hour) is known in different areas of the world by different names. If the wind storm occurs over the North Atlantic Ocean, it is called a hurricane. Another name is used if the storm is centered in the West Pacific area. Here it is called a typhoon. And if the identical phenomenon is over the Indian Ocean, it has a third name: a tropical cyclone. Though hurricanes, typhoons, and cyclones all occur during different times of the year and in different areas, they are all identical. A mature wind storm is almost a complete circle, and its influence often extends over an area of 500 miles (927 km) in diameter. The circumference of the circle is the area of the greatest wind speed, while the center, the eye, is almost calm. The storms move westward at about 10 miles (16 km) per hour, and have a lifespan of from one to thirty days.

   Paragraph Organization _____

   Topic Sentence _____

3. A popular method of treating exposure to very cold weather and frostbite is to slowly rewarm the fingers or toes or to rub them with snow. The best treatment, however, is not slow rewarming but rapid rewarming. Putting the fingers or toes in a warm bath, applying a heating pad, or using a hot water bottle are all good ways to treat frostbite. Hot drinks to warm the body from within are also helpful. One must be careful about burning the skin, however, since the affected parts are anesthetized. The temperature of any heat applied should not be greater than 43° C (110° F).

   Paragraph Organization _____

   Topic Sentence _____

INFERENCES AND RESTATEMENTS

Many of the TOEFL exam questions ask you to infer information from the reading. This means that the questions are not answered directly in the text. You must think of what logical conclusions you can make from the ideas given in the reading. Ask yourself what the author wants you to know that is not directly stated.

What can you infer from the following sentences?

> The village was made up of a few broken-down houses. There was not much for the people to eat.

You can infer that:

The village was poor.
The people were hungry.

What else can you infer? _____

A restatement is a sentence that gives the same information, but says it in a different way. The words might be rearranged, the sentence might be changed from active to passive, or synonyms might be substituted; but the basic information is the same.

A restatement of the above example sentences could be:

> A small number of old, dilapidated houses was all that was in the village. The villagers had very little to eat.

EXERCISE 32

Inferences and Restatements

DIRECTIONS: Each paragraph below is followed by several statements. Mark each statement in one of the following ways;

> R = restatement of ideas in the paragraph
> I = information that can be inferred from the paragraph
> F = false information based on the paragraph
> NG = information not given in the paragraph

> ### N O T E
>
> Do not mark the statements based on common knowledge or your own background knowledge. Use only the information written in the paragraph to mark the answers.

A. Glaciers are ice fields that can be compared to slow-moving rivers of ice. They are formed when the amount of snow that falls during the year is more than the amount that melts. The masses of snow are compressed and slowly turn to ice. As new layers of ice are formed, the layers on the bottom become more and more firmly packed down. Eventually, they begin to move. Glaciers move very slowly, rarely more than twenty-four inches a day. The top and center move more quickly than the sides, and this uneven movement can cause the ice to crack open and form large crevasses. Icebergs are formed when a slow-moving glacier reaches the ocean, and large pieces then break off into the water.

1. _____ In forming a glacier, snow is packed into ice.

2. _____ Glaciers move evenly down a mountain.

3. _____ Glacier crevasses are dangerous for winter hikers.

4. _____ There must be a lot of snow and cold weather before a glacier can form.

5. _____ Icebergs melt more quickly than glaciers.

6. _____ Glaciers begin to move after the snow is compressed into a hard layer of ice.

B. Balloons have recently been used in a new medical procedure to open up stiffened heart valves in aging adults. The four valves in the heart keep the blood going in the right direction, and if the valves become stiff, the result can be deadly. In this procedure, known as balloon valvuloplasty, a small balloon is inserted into the heart and then inflated with a saline solution for up to forty seconds. The inflated balloon will split the valves apart, allowing them to open and close more freely. This procedure has been done since 1979 in children with valve disease, but it has just recently been done with adults. The procedure is especially good for aging people since it can be done without a general anesthetic. The patient can be given a local pain-killer and can leave the hospital in a few days.

1. _____ Balloon valvuloplasty is better to use with children than adults.

2. _____ Stiffened heart valves can cause death.

3. _____ Balloon valvuloplasty was first done in 1979.

4. _____ The opening and closing of the valves is essential for a healthy heart.

5. _____ Stiffened heart valves are painful.

6. _____ Balloon valvuloplasty is a simpler procedure than a surgical operation.

C. New studies have shown that non-smokers can be affected by being around people who smoke. The studies show an increased incidence of lung problems in children of smokers. There is also an increase in the incidence of lung cancer in non-smokers who live with smokers. The studies show a thirty percent higher lung cancer incidence in non-smoking spouses of smokers than in non-smoking couples.

1. _____ Non-smoking people live longer than smokers.

2. _____ Children of smokers are more likely to have lung problems than children of non-smokers.

3. _____ Smoking causes lung cancer.

4. _____ It is healthier to associate with non-smokers than with smokers.

5. _____ You have a thirty percent higher chance of getting lung cancer if you don't smoke but are married to a smoker than if you are married to a non-smoker.

6. _____ It is good not to smoke around children.

GENERAL ADVICE FOR VOCABULARY AND READING COMPREHENSION

Vocabulary Questions

Many people feel that the vocabulary questions are easier than the reading comprehension questions. If you feel like this, be sure not to speed through the vocabulary and make foolish mistakes. Do the questions carefully. You can gain many points in this section if it is easy for you.

Reading Speed

It's true that you need to read and answer the questions quickly. When you first look at a paragraph, however, read the first sentence slowly and carefully. While reading this sentence concentrate on comprehension, not speed. Usually the main idea is in the first sentence. It's important that you understand the main idea.

After you read the first sentence slowly, read the rest of the paragraph as fast as you can. You can skim over it paying particular attention to key words: nouns, numbers, first words of sentences, last words of sentences, capital words, and abbreviations.

Read the last sentence more slowly. It often sums up a major idea.

Answer Choices

After skimming over the paragraph, look at the questions. Answer as many as you can without re-reading the paragraph. Make light marks in front of the questions you are guessing about. Then go back to the paragraph and look for particular answers. Scan the paragraph, looking for word clues to help you get the answer.

Finishing All Paragraphs

Read through all the paragraphs and questions quickly. Answer as many questions as you can without spending a lot of extra time on a hard paragraph or a hard question. If you don't know the answer, make a mark beside that question, and go on to the next paragraph. Work through to the end of the section, and then go back to the difficult ones. Sometimes an easy paragraph follows a difficult paragraph. You want to be sure to have time to read through all the paragraphs. Sometimes when you go back to a hard question, it will seem easier the second time you read it.

Checking

When you have finished all the questions, be sure to go back and check them. Read through everything again. Don't just sit and wait for the time to be up.

WRITING THE TOEFL ESSAY

The Test of Written English (TWE) is a required part of the TOEFL exams given three or four times a year. It is given first, before you open your test booklet. You have thirty minutes to read the question, organize your thoughts, and write your essay. Space will be given for you to make notes, and lined paper is provided for writing the essay. A good length for your essay is about 200 or 300 words, but you should concentrate more on organization than length.

The questions will be on a general topic, one that will allow you to make a statement and defend or support that statement. The questions are of two types: (1) comparing and contrasting two opposing points of view, and defending one of them; and (2) describing and interpreting a chart or graph. You are being tested on your ability to organize your ideas, support them with evidence, and write them down clearly in standard written English.

The essays will be scored on a scale of from 1 to 6, with 6 being the highest. Below is a general description of each level:

6: The writer clearly demonstrates competence on all levels, even though there may be occasional errors.

The essay:

- is well organized and well developed
- clearly answers the question
- supports the main statement and gives examples
- is unified around the main idea
- is consistently able to demonstrate good use of English
- shows variety in the choice of words

5: The writer demonstrates competence on all levels, though there will be occasional errors.

The essay:

- is generally well organized and well developed, but has fewer details than a "6" paper
- answers the question well, but some parts may be more clearly answered than others
- is unified around the main idea

- shows some variety in the choice of words
- is well written, but has more grammatical errors than a "6" paper

4: The writer demonstrates minimal competence.

The essay:

- is adequately organized
- answers most of the question, but not all
- uses some details to support a statement
- is inconsistent in word usage
- may have some serious errors that make the paper difficult to understand

3: The writer demonstrates some competence.

The essay:

- is inadequate in organization
- does not support statements or give enough details
- has many errors in sentence structure
- has incorrect choices of words

2: The writer shows some incompetence.

The essay:

- is not organized or developed around the topic
- has little or no detail, or has irrelevant detail
- has many serious errors in sentence structure

1: The writer shows incompetence.

The essay:

- cannot be understood
- shows that the writer did not understand the question
- has many serious word and sentence errors

ORGANIZING YOUR THOUGHTS

You have thirty minutes for the Test of Written English. Part of this time is for thinking about the question and organizing your thoughts. As a general guide, you might spend about ten minutes on planning, and about twenty minutes on writing. If you plan clearly, the writing will be easier. Here are three possible methods for you to use in organizing your thoughts. Whatever method you choose, however, the first step is the same.

First: Read the question very carefully. Think about all parts of the question. Look for key words to help you in your organization.

Method A: Brainstorming

STEP 1: After reading the question, write down all the ideas that come to your mind about the topic. Do not stop to think of whether they are good or bad. Write either words or phrases or even abbreviations. Write quickly without stopping to consider each item. Do not try to organize anything yet, just write whatever you think.

STEP 2: Look at your list of words and phrases. Read back over the question and think again about what you are asked to discuss. Begin to organize and classify the words and phrases in a way that relates to your question. Mark them in some way, such as:

> Put a circle around the words that relate to one idea. Put a box around words that relate to another idea. Cross out the words that don't relate directly to the question.

STEP 3: Write a brief outline or list of the ideas in each topic.

STEP 4: Begin your essay, organizing your list into unified paragraphs.

Example of Method A—Brainstorming

EXAMPLE QUESTION: Advertising is common throughout the world as a way of letting the public know about a product. Some people feel that advertising is generally helpful, and others feel that it is generally harmful. Discuss your ideas of the good and bad effects of advertising, and decide whether you think it is generally helpful or harmful. Use specific examples to support your discussion.

STEP 1: Brainstorm ideas.

TV
bad
radio
newspapers—can help
songs and stories
too loud

don't like
funny pictures
learn about product
expensive to make
not true info.
billboards—ruin the landscape
helps me know what's on sale
helps me get good prices on groceries
saves time choosing a store
the purse I bought on sale
the stuff I bought I didn't need

Add your own brainstorming ideas on this topic.

STEP 2: Categorize ideas.

   ⬭ = places to advertise   ✖ = examples
   [ ] = harmful   — = doesn't fit
   ⬜ = helpful

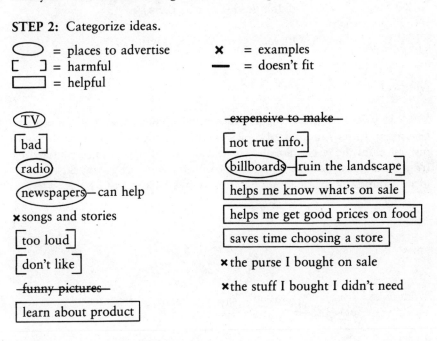

STEP 3: Make a brief outline of categories.

   Places to Advertise:
      TV—effects on watchers
      radio—effects on listeners
      newspapers—effects on readers
      billboards
   (Add your own)

   Harmful Effects:
      too loud on TV

don't like to be disturbed
not true info. sometimes
(Add your own)

Helpful Effects:
learn about product
know what's on sale
know where to get good prices
saves time
(Add your own)

EXAMPLES:
the purse I bought on sale
the things I bought I didn't need (describe them)

STEP 4: Use the list. Organize your essay and write it.

Method B: Clustering

STEP 1: Write the major topic in the center of your paper, and draw a circle around it. As you think of topics to write about, write them on lines going out from the circle. Smaller topics can be written on lines coming out from other lines. You are doing a little bit of organizing as you cluster your ideas around the major topic. Figure 7 shows a cluster of ideas.

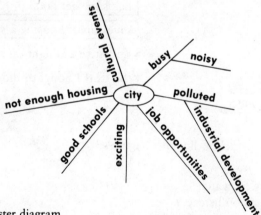

Figure 7. Cluster diagram

STEP 2: Look over your completed cluster of topics. See which ones relate best to your overall topic. Choose one or more to write about.

STEP 3: Begin your essay, keeping your ideas focused on the topic.

Example of Method B—Clustering

EXAMPLE QUESTION: In most of the world now, the cities are growing larger, while the rural towns and villages are declining in population. There are both advantages and disadvantages to living in the city. Discuss some the differences between living in the city and living in the country. Which one would you choose? Why?

STEP 1: Cluster your ideas.

STEP 2: Look at your cluster. Choose the "arms" that are most important for you to write about.

STEP 3: Organize the information; write a brief outline.

STEP 4: Write your essay.

Method C: Outlining

STEP 1: Write an outline, organizing your topic and subtopics in a list.

STEP 2: Write your essay, using your outline to keep the paragraph focused on your main idea.

Example of Method C—Outlining

EXAMPLE QUESTION: People have different preferences for spending leisure time. Some people are very active physically, and will spend free time running, exercising, or participating in a sport like football, soccer, baseball, or tennis. Other people would rather spend their leisure time in more quiet ways, like reading or listening to music. Compare these two ways of spending leisure time. Which type of activity are you more likely to choose. Why?

STEP 1: Write an outline. (Below is a partial outline. You can add to it to make it complete.)

    I. Active activities
      A. Healthy for body
        1. Good for heart
        2. Makes you strong
      B. Number of people

       1. Groups or teams
         a. You make friends
         b. You learn to work together
       2. Individual
         a. You choose your own time
         b. You work at your own pace

  II. Quiet Activities
    A. Healthy for the mind
       1. You can be calm
       2. You can relax
    B. Number of people
       1. Individual
         a. You can choose your own time
         b. You can choose your own thing to do
       2. Group activities
         a. Listening to music with friends is fun
         b. Going to movies, concerts, plays is stimulating

 III. My preferred type of activity
       1. Reasons
       2. Examples

STEP 2: Write your essay on a separate sheet of paper.

READING AND DESCRIBING CHARTS AND GRAPHS

Some of the writing questions on the Test of Written English will ask you to describe the information in a chart or graph. Look for key words in the question to help you in planning your essay. The key words might be:

  describe: present details, present a sequence
  discuss: talk about all aspects
  state: say something briefly
  explain: bring out the details, make clear, interpret
  analyze: interpret and make clear
  interpret: make the information clear, show relationships

  For this type of writing, your paragraphs are usually organized by time order, generalizations and specifics, or classification.

  On the following page there are some words to use for each type of writing:

Time Order	Generalization	Specifics	Classification
always	in general	for example	group
sometimes	on the whole	for instance	type
rarely	in most cases	as an example	kind
never	as a rule		main
now	all		major
when	every		some of
before	usually		most of
after	frequently		all of
once	rarely		include
during			section
since			

Study the following graphs and charts and then write a sample essay. Take no more than thirty minutes to read the question, study the graph, and plan and write your essay. Use brainstorming, clustering, or outlining to organize your thoughts. Decide on which of the above organizations you should use for your essay. Refer to the above list of words to help structure your writing. Save a few minutes near the end of your thirty minutes to go back and check your grammar, punctuation, and spelling.

Circle Graph

The circle graph in Figure 8 shows the income of Valley City for 1986. Discuss this graph, describing the different sources of money the city receives and the relative importance of each source.

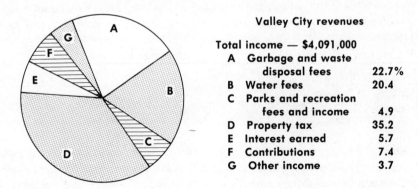

Valley City revenues

Total income — $4,091,000

A	Garbage and waste disposal fees	22.7%
B	Water fees	20.4
C	Parks and recreation fees and income	4.9
D	Property tax	35.2
E	Interest earned	5.7
F	Contributions	7.4
G	Other income	3.7

Figure 8. Circle graph

Bar Graph

Figure 9 is a bar graph. The graph shows that the relationship between the number of businesses and the number of industries has changed in Mountain Town during the last twenty-two years. Describe this change on a separate sheet of paper and give your projection for the next few years.

Line Graph

Figure 10 is a line graph. The graph shows that the ethnic population mix of Western City has changed dramatically since 1940. Discuss the overall changes that have occurred. What are the major changes in different ethnic groups of people that are living in Western City now as compared to those living here in 1940?

COMPARING AND CONTRASTING

Some of the questions in the Test of Written English will be questions of comparison and contrast. Two contrasting ideas may be given, or two aspects of one idea. You will be asked to discuss them both, giving examples or facts to support your statements. You then need to take a stand on one of the ideas and defend that position.

"Comparison" means thinking about the similarities of the two ideas. In your essay you will use words like:

> both, together, more, most, similar to, as...as, also, as well as, too, likewise, is equal to, are alike, in the same way, to compare, just as.

"Contrast" means thinking about the differences between the two ideas. In your essay you will use words like:

> but, however, although, in contrast, on the other hand, is different from, while, whereas, nevertheless, less than, more than, not as...as.

There are two easy ways to organize a comparision/contrast essay. These two examples have four or five paragraphs. Let's assume that you are asked to compare two countries and choose one of them to live in for one year.

Organization Method 1: Your first paragraph will introduce the two countries and mention the particular aspects of each that you will discuss (Your topic sentence). The second paragraph will discuss the aspects for country

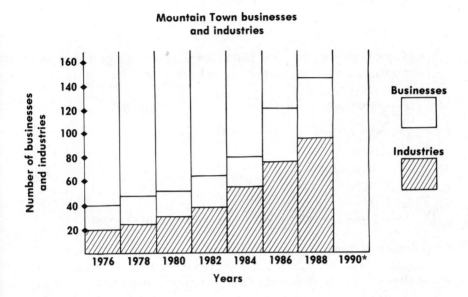

*Make your own projection for 1990.

Figure 9. Bar graph

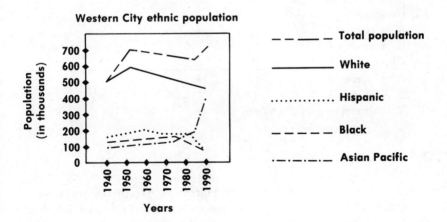

Figure 10. Line graph

A. The third paragraph will discuss the aspects for country B. In the fourth paragraph, you will state your preference for living in one country.

OUTLINE FOR METHOD 1

    I. Topic Sentence (name the two countries and the aspects you will discuss: government, geography, and climate.)
    II. Country A
        A. Government
        B. Geography
        C. Climate
    III. Country B
        A. Government
        B. Geography
        C. Climate
    IV. Your preference (give examples to support your decision.)

Organization Method 2: Your first paragraph is the same—you name the two countries and the aspects you will discuss for each. The number of paragraphs you will have depends on the number of items you are discussing. You will have one paragraph for each aspect. In the final paragraph, you state which country you choose, giving examples to support your decision.

OUTLINE FOR METHOD 2

    I. Topic Sentence (Name the two countries and the aspects of each that you will discuss: government, geography, and climate.)
    II. Government
        A. Country A
        B. Country B
    III. Geography
        A. Country A
        B. Country B
    IV. Climate
        A. Country A
        B. Country B
    V. Your preference and why

TOPIC SENTENCES

In an essay where you are comparing or contrasting two things, you should mention both of them in your topic sentence. You also need to tell whether you will be emphasizing the similarities or the differences. In either your first or last paragraph, you must state which aspect of the question you are supporting or agreeing with, and why you feel that way. Always support your statements with examples.

Look back on page 96 at the example question for brainstorming. Below are some possible topic sentences for this question.

> Though advertising is often thought of as harmful, I feel that overall it has very positive results.

> or

> Advertising has both good and bad effects; however, I believe that the bad effects are more important than the good.

> or

> Advertising is necessary in this modern world, even though it does have a few harmful aspects.

> or

> In a country where people have little money to spend, advertising, though necessary in some respects, is mainly harmful.

PRACTICE: Write practice essays for the questions on pages 96, 99, 101 and 102. Organize your thoughts by brainstorming, clustering, or outlining. You should spend less than thirty minutes in planning and writing these essays, since you have already thought about the topics.

Below is a sample essay using the question on page 96, the brainstorming ideas from page 97, and the outline from page 97.

Sample Essay

Introduction {

In most countries in the world, advertising is common. You can see billboards on the highways, posters in subways, signs in buses, pictures in magazines, and commercials on television. Though these signs of advertising are often thought of as harmful, I feel that, overall, advertising has very positive results.

} **Topic Sentence Clear Point of View**

The harmful effects of advertising are obvious. When driving on a peaceful highway, a large billboard can block your view and disrupt your thoughts. When you are listening to good music on the radio, a commercial is disturbing when it interrupts your program and changes your mood. Television commercials are the worst of all. Your program is stopped, and you are forced to watch an advertisement unless you actively change the channel or leave the room. I feel that there should be laws that limit the advertisers right to put up billboards, interrupt television and radio programs, and in other ways fill our lives with advertisements.

> Description of Harmful Effects; Specific Examples

In general, however, I feel that the positive results of advertisements are beneficial to society and to individuals. When I am making a purchase, I can use advertisements in newspapers and magazines to compare prices, features, and the quality of the product I want. I can use advertisements wisely to inform myself about the item. By being more informed and educated, I can buy something that will benefit me in the long run.

> Description of Helpful Effects; Specific Examples Benefits to Individuals

If individual shoppers are more educated, they are more able to choose between good and bad products. Because of that, the producers of the product will be more careful about what they are making in order to sell more of their products. This will benefit society in general.

> Benefits to Society

All in all, for a wise and educated shopper, the helpful effects of advertising outweigh the harmful effects.

> Conclusion Restatement of Point of View

ESSAY CHECKLIST

1. Did you read the question carefully? Did you look for the key words to guide your organization (i.e. compare, contrast, describe, interpret, support, defend, etc.)?
2. Did you answer the question completely, and answer only the question (no irrelevant material)?

3. Does your first paragraph give the reader enough signals to understand the direction and purpose of the essay? Is your topic sentence clearly written?
4. Did you use examples and facts to support and defend your statements?
5. Does your final paragraph summarize your main points? Did you clearly state your opinion and defend it?
6. Does each paragraph discuss only one idea or topic? Do all the sentences in that paragraph relate to that idea?
7. Did you leave a margin and indent the first word of each paragraph?

> Xxxx xxxxxxx xxxxxx xxx xxxxx xxxxxxxxx. Xxxx xxxx xxxxxx xxxx xxx xx. Xx xx xxxx xxxx xxxxx. Xxx xxx xxxxxxxxx xxxxxx xxxxx xxx xxxx xxxxxx.

8. Did you quickly check your writing for grammar, spelling, and punctuation errors?

OVERALL HINTS AND STRATEGIES FOR TAKING THE TOEFL

LISTENING COMPREHENSION: PART A

One of the difficult parts about this section is that it is the first thing you do on the test. You may be anxious about beginning the test. And, as you know, when the tape is turned on, it continues at a steady pace. Get prepared for this rhythm by practicing for it during the practice tests.

LISTENING COMPRREHENSION: PART B

While you listen to the instructions for Part B, you have a little break. If you feel tense, rub the back of your neck and shoulders. Take a deep breath. Also, since you know the instructions for the test, use this time to read ahead to the answer choices.

Many people feel a little more relaxed about Part B, partly because they have already begun the test (the "inverted V" principle). Part B may also seem a little easier because:

1. You hear the speakers for a longer time.
2. There is a little more background in the conversation and that helps your comprehension.

However, don't relax too much. You don't want to lose this good opportunity. Pay close attention to the speakers on the tape in order to gain all the points that you can.

LISTENING COMPREHENSION: PART C

Before Part C, you have another short break while the tape repeats the instructions. During this time, you can again try to relax by taking a deep breath and rubbing the back of your neck and shoulders.

While the directions are being read, you have a chance again to glance ahead at the questions to get a general idea of what to listen for. You don't have much time to summarize the questions, but even a general idea of the topic can help your listening comprehension. It also can help your listening comprehension just to look at the main words that you might hear on the tape. Reading the words will help you to prepare for the topic you will hear.

In Part C, the mini-talk will cover several questions. First, listen carefully to which questions relate to each mini-talk, and notice where the questions end. There are three main techniques for listening to Part C. The way that helps you most will depend on both your listening ability and your knowledge of the topic. You might even use different methods for different paragraphs on the same test. These are the three methods:

1. Concentrate completely on the tape while you listen to it. Try to figure out the main idea and remember the facts. It might help you to concentrate if you close your eyes while listening. Even though you might not remember all the details, you should get the main points, and you can guess at the details.
2. Before the speakers come on the tape, (probably during the reading of the directions), look at the answer choices. Note the questions that ask for specific details like dates, numbers, or names. Later, as you listen to the tape, listen specifically for these details. Follow along in your answer book just enough to hear these details. For the rest of the time, just concentrate on the speaker, as in (1) above.
3. Follow the answer choices in your answer book all the time that the speaker is on the tape. Since the questions are asked in the order that they are spoken, you can usually guess the question while the tape is on. This method is the most difficult method because it involves listening, reading, and guessing all at the same time. You must continually guess which question the speaker might ask about, while also listening to the details that he or she is talking about. The difficult part is that by concentrating on choosing the answers, you might miss the main points the speaker is saying. If you try this and feel lost, then go back to (1) above and concentrate completely on the speaker.

STRUCTURE AND WRITTEN EXPRESSION

Now that the tape is off, you are on your own time for the next sections. If any question is very difficult, make a very light mark beside that question, and go on to the next. Then at the end, go back to the questions you marked. (You are not allowed to write in the test book, but it is all right to make a very light mark, like a dot, beside a question. Don't, however, do any actual writing in the test book.)

As you go through the questions, keep in mind the common testing points. Look for parallel structure; singular and plural nouns; and nouns, adjectives, or adverbs used incorrectly. One way to begin is to check the main subject and verb to see if they agree. Be sure that you are checking agreement of the *main* verb with the *main* subject, and not mixing up a verb from a dependent clause or a noun from a prepositional phrase.

VOCABULARY

The standard form Vocabulary section has thirty questions which give you thirty points. This is the same number of points as in the Reading Comprehension section, but obviously this part is quicker to read. You have a good chance to gain points in this section, compared to the Reading Comprehension section. Be sure to read each sentence carefully and look for the meaning in the context of the sentence. Remember that words have different meanings depending on their context. Don't just look at the word and choose a meaning without reading the whole sentence.

READING COMPREHENSION

The difficulty of this section is partly determined by your knowledge of the topic. The way that you read the paragraph also depends on how easy or difficult it is for you. Here are three ways to read this section:

1. Read the first sentence slowly; skim quickly through the rest of the paragraph; and then read the last sentence slowly. Then read the questions, answer the ones you can, and read back in the paragraph for the other answers.
2. Quickly look at the questions before reading the paragraph. Get a general focus on what to read for, and then read the paragraph, concentrating on looking for answers.

3. Read the whole paragraph carefully, paying particular attention to names, dates, and the main focus. Then read and answer the questions. If any paragraph is very difficult for you, then skip it and go on to an easier paragraph. You can go back to the difficult one later. Remember that your goal is to gain all the points you can in the whole section, rather than to understand each paragraph completely.

PRACTICE TEST 1

SECTION 1

LISTENING COMPREHENSION

This section of the test is for demontrating your ability to understand spoken English. There are three different parts in this section. Each section has separate directions.

N O T E

You will need the tape to do Section 1. If you do not have the tape, the tapescript for this practice test is on pages 239 to 243. Answer sheets to this test are found on pages 249 and 251. Explanatory answers begin on page 177.

Part A

DIRECTIONS: For each question in Part A, you will hear a short sentence which will be spoken only one time. None of the sentences will be written out for you, so you must listen carefully to understand what the speaker says.

After you hear a sentence, read the four choices in your test book, marked (A), (B), (C), and (D), and decide which one is closest in meaning to the sentence you heard on tape. Then, look on your answer sheet for the number of the question and fill in the space that corresponds to the letter of the answer you have chosen. Fill in the space carefully, dark enough so that the letter inside the oval cannot be seen.

EXAMPLE I   Sample Answer

You will hear: Would you mind opening   (A) ● (C) (D)
                the door for me?

You will read: (A) The door to my office
                   is open.
               (B) Could you please open
                   the door for me?
               (C) Please remind me to
                   open the door.
               (D) I don't mind the door
                   opening.

The speaker said, "Would you mind opening the door for me?"
Sentence (B), "Could you please open the door for me," is closest in
meaning to the sentence you heard. Therefore, you should choose
answer (B).

EXAMPLE 2   Sample Answer

You will hear: There is so much fog that I   (A) (B) ● (D)
                can barely see the cars on
                the road.

You will read: (A) There are a lot of cars
                   on the road.
               (B) I saw a dog on the
                   road.
               (C) It is hard to see
                   anything on the road.
               (D) I was surprised to see
                   bears on the road.

The speaker said, "There is so much fog that I can barely see the cars
on the road." Sentence (C), "It is hard to see anything on the road," is
closest in meaning to the sentence you heard. Therefore, you should
choose answer (C).

1. (A) I want to go early.   2. (A) I want to go less than
   (B) I like to be late.   you.
   (C) I hope you won't be   (B) I'll go if you can't go.
       early.   (C) I won't go even if you go.
   (D) I prefer to be late.   (D) I'll go if you go.

GO ON TO THE NEXT PAGE

3. (A) It's raining.
   (B) It's likely to rain.
   (C) It looks wet.
   (D) It likes rain.

4. (A) I had an argument with my old friend yesterday.
   (B) I passed my friend in town.
   (C) I met my friend in town by accident.
   (D) My friend and I had an accident yesterday.

5. (A) Ann is skeptical about new things.
   (B) Both Ann and her brother are interested in new things.
   (C) Ann likes to try new things, but her brother does not.
   (D) Neither Ann nor her brother are skeptical.

6. (A) I'd like to go running with you after class.
   (B) Please run down to the class for me.
   (C) Let's meet after class.
   (D) Let me tell you about the class.

7. (A) She missed one class this semester.
   (B) She hasn't missed any classes this semester.
   (C) She's missed only a few classes this semester.
   (D) She's missed many classes this semester.

8. (A) Bill forgot to pay the bill, and the phone is not working.
   (B) Bill paid the bill on time, but the phone is still not working.
   (C) Bill forgot the phone was not working when he paid the bill.
   (D) Bill forgot to connect the phone before he paid the bill.

9. (A) She's keeping a secret.
   (B) She doesn't want to tell anyone about the accident to her nose.
   (C) She doesn't know anything.
   (D) She doesn't like to talk about her ideas.

10. (A) It takes a long time to run.
    (B) It's worth it to run a long time in training.
    (C) Your work will be worth the time eventually.
    (D) An old well gets worse in time.

11. (A) The information is old.
    (B) The tape is sold out.
    (C) The quality is poor.
    (D) There is no date on the tape.

12. (A) It seems cheap to buy a car.
    (B) Cheap cars do not run well.
    (C) It's convenient to have a car.
    (D) It's expensive to have a car.

GO ON TO THE NEXT PAGE ➡

13. (A) He isn't growing anymore.
    (B) He seems younger than eighteen.
    (C) He is short for his age.
    (D) He is almost eighteen.

14. (A) Randy thinks pizza is better than tacos.
    (B) Randy likes tacos more than pizza.
    (C) Randy would like a piece of taco.
    (D) Randy likes to talk about pizza.

15. (A) Jim is used to smoking.
    (B) Jim likes to smoke when it's hot.
    (C) Jim does not smoke anymore.
    (D) Jim smoked more before.

16. (A) Exercising can reduce depression.
    (B) Exercise can cause depression.
    (C) Depression helps you exercise better.
    (D) Depression can remind you to exercise.

17. (A) They are different books, but they look alike.
    (B) The covers are different.
    (C) They cover different material.
    (D) Some of the books have soft covers.

18. (A) Mary asked the salesman to be present.
    (B) Mary presented the wrapping.
    (C) The salesman dropped the present.
    (D) The salesman put paper around the present.

19. (A) I am really hungry!
    (B) I have never been hungry!
    (C) I am very angry!
    (D) I'm never angry!

20. (A) Jenny is younger than Jane.
    (B) Jane is smaller than Jenny.
    (C) Jane is older than Jenny.
    (D) Jane is bigger than Jenny.

Part B

DIRECTIONS: In Part B you will hear several short conversations between two speakers. At the end of each conversation, a third person will ask a question about what was said. You will hear each conversation and question only once. Therefore, you must listen carefully to understand what each speaker says. After you hear a conversation and the question about it, read the four possible answers in your test book and decide which one is the best answer to the question. On your answer sheet, find the number of the question and fill in the letter of the answer you have chosen.

EXAMPLE   Sample Answer

You will hear: Ⓐ Ⓑ Ⓒ ●

You will read: (A) Pick up the mail.
               (B) Go home.
               (C) Go to work.
               (D) Buy some milk.

From the conversation, you know that the man is going to stop and pick up some milk. The best answer is (D), "Buy some milk." Therefore, you should choose answer (D).

21. (A) She has to do
        some work.
    (B) She went last week.
    (C) The daylight hours
        are long.
    (D) She is tired.

22. (A) He wishes the professor
        would talk more.
    (B) He doesn't always under-
        stand the professor.
    (C) He thinks the professor
        has an accent.
    (D) He thinks the professor
        talks too quietly.

23. (A) She wants to pay the bill.
    (B) She wants Bill to pay for
        the meal.
    (C) She wants to pay for her
        meal.
    (D) She wants the man
        to pay.

24. (A) He has sour fruit.
    (B) He doesn't feel good.
    (C) He sold some thread.
    (D) He hates Vitamin C.

25. (A) She has had a nice day.
    (B) She is sick.
    (C) She wants to catch some
        fish.
    (D) She works at the beach.

26. (A) Mail a check for her
    (B) Pick up her mail
    (C) Put a check in his
        mailbox
    (D) Take a check from her
        mailbox.

27. (A) She'll take it because she
        likes it.
    (B) She'll take it even though
        she doesn't like it.
    (C) She won't take it because
        she doesn't like it.
    (D) She won't take it even
        though she likes it.

28. (A) She does not like it.
    (B) She is going to dive.
    (C) She is afraid to diet.
    (D) She wants to lose weight.

29. (A) In a dressing room
    (B) In a bedroom
    (C) In a department store
    (D) In a restaurant

GO ON TO THE NEXT PAGE ➡

30. (A) Having a computer
        registered
    (B) Deciding on a computer
        course
    (C) Buying a computer
        tomorrow
    (D) Registering for classes
        tomorrow
31. (A) He will pay for a call
        from Lisa.
    (B) He will make a call to
        Lisa.
    (C) He is collecting money
        for Lisa.
    (D) He is correcting a call
        from Lisa.
32. (A) Life insurance
    (B) Health insurance
    (C) Car insurance
    (D) Theft insurance

33. (A) Take a class for credit
    (B) Add a class
    (C) Drop a class
    (D) Attend a class for no
        credit
34. (A) She misplaced her
        contact lenses.
    (B) She finds her old
        glasses better.
    (C) She couldn't contact her
        optometrist.
    (D) Her contact lenses are
        better.
35. (A) One should write down
        anything important.
    (B) One should do the right
        thing and do it well.
    (C) Doing the right thing is
        the most important.
    (D) The man and the
        woman have different
        opinions.

Part C

DIRECTIONS: In this part of the test, you will hear short talks or conversations. After each of them, you will be asked several questions. The questions, as well as the talks and conversations will be spoken only once. They will not be written out for you. Therefore, you must listen carefully to understand what each speaker says.

After you hear a question, read the four possible answers in your test book and decide which one is the best answer to the question. On your answer sheet fill in the letter of the answer you have chosen.

Listen to this sample talk.

EXAMPLE I   Sample Answer

You will hear: ● Ⓑ Ⓒ Ⓓ

You will read: (A) Students at the
                   university
               (B) Spanish folk singers
               (C) The Scottish country
                   dance group
               (D) The University Interna-
                   tional Dancers

The best answer to the question, "Who is the announcement given to?"
is (A), "Students at the university." Therefore, you should choose
answer (A).

EXAMPLE 2   Sample Answer

You will hear: Ⓐ Ⓑ Ⓒ ●

You will read: (A) learn Scottish dancing
               (B) buy costumes
               (C) eat dinner
               (D) dance to music

The best answer to the question, "What will many people at the
festival be able to do?" is (D), "Dance to music." Therefore, you
should choose answer (D).

---

36. (A) In a doctor's office
    (B) In an exercise class
    (C) In a dentist's office
    (D) In a biology class
37. (A) How to stretch new ideas.
    (B) How to change ideas
    (C) How to pull a tooth
    (D) How to exhale
38. (A) Gaining new concepts
    (B) Releasing stress
    (C) Stretching
    (D) Pulling teeth

39. (A) It is difficult to learn
        something new.
    (B) It always hurts to
        exercise.
    (C) It hurts more to have a
        tooth pulled than it does
        to exercise.
    (D) If you don't feel the pain
        of stretching, you need to
        stretch more.

GO ON TO THE NEXT PAGE ➡

40. (A) The man will learn a new saying.
    (B) The man will go home.
    (C) The man will try a new way to exercise.
    (D) The woman will discuss difficulties of learning

41. (A) A form
    (B) An official notice
    (C) An identification
    (D) A license

42. (A) The newcomer
    (B) The officer
    (C) The bus driver
    (D) The people in line

43. (A) He had no social security number.
    (B) The vocabulary was too specific.
    (C) He couldn't read.
    (D) It was the wrong form.

44. (A) Because the officer laughed at him.
    (B) Because he didn't know what form to get.
    (C) Because he filled out the wrong form.
    (D) Because he didn't realize the form was in Spanish.

45. (A) Yes, he got one in two weeks.
    (B) Yes, he got one right away.
    (C) No, he was too embarrassed to apply for one.
    (D) No, he was told to wait until he could speak English better.

46. (A) Scientists at a research center
    (B) Chemists at a convention
    (C) Students at a university
    (D) Workers at an air-conditioning factory

47. (A) Ultraviolet light
    (B) The use of spray cans
    (C) Air-conditioning systems
    (D) Fluorocarbons and the ozone layer

48. (A) Providing fluorocarbons
    (B) Shielding the sun
    (C) Protecting the earth
    (D) Destroying chemicals

49. (A) Fluorocarbons
    (B) Oxygen
    (C) Shields
    (D) Ultraviolet light

50. (A) How to Make Air-Conditioners with Fluorocarbons
    (B) Harmful Effects of Ultraviolet Light
    (C) The Make-up of the Ozone Layer
    (D) The Sun as a Cause of Ozone Layer Depletion

THIS IS THE END OF SECTION 1.

The next part of the test is Section 2. Turn to the directions for section 2 in your test book, read them, and begin work. Do not read or work on any other section of the test.

STOP   STOP   STOP   STOP   STOP   STOP

SECTION 2

STRUCTURE AND WRITTEN EXPRESSION

Time — 25 minutes

This section measures your ability to recognize standard written English. There are two types of questions in this section. Each of the sections has different directions.

DIRECTIONS: Questions 1–15 are not complete sentences. One or more words are left out of each sentence. Under the sentences you will see four words or phrases, marked (A), (B), (C), and (D). Choose the one word or phrase that completes the sentence correctly. Then, on your answer sheet, find the number of the question and fill in the correct space dark enough so that the letter inside the oval cannot be seen.

EXAMPLE 1   Sample Answer

Many people came to the museum to look   ● Ⓑ Ⓒ Ⓓ
_____ the exhibit of Van Gogh's paintings.

  (A) at
  (B) up
  (C) on
  (D) in

The sentence should read, "Many people came to the museum to look at the exhibit of Van Gogh's paintings." Therefore, you should choose answer (A).

EXAMPLE 2   Sample Answer

_____ not enough food for all the people who   Ⓐ Ⓑ Ⓒ ●
are suffering from the recent famine.

  (A) There are
  (B) Is
  (C) All is
  (D) There is

The sentence should read, "There is not enough food for all the people who are suffering from the recent famine." Therefore, you should choose answer (D).

After you read the directions, begin work on the questions.

1. The population of cities in the Eastern and Northern areas of the United States is declining, while _____ Southern cities is growing.
   (A) that in
   (B) that of
   (C) those of
   (D) those in

2. Some people find it surprising _____ his career as an actor in California.
   (A) when Ronald Reagan began
   (B) Ronald Reagan began
   (C) that Ronald Reagan began
   (D) to know Ronald Reagan

3. The travels of Marco Polo in the twelfth century would not have been so well known _____ for the book he wrote while in jail.
   (A) it not have been
   (B) is not been
   (C) had it not been
   (D) has not been

4. The Caspian Sea, a salt lake, is _____ any other lake in the world.
   (A) largest
   (B) the largest
   (C) larger than
   (D) the larger than

5. 3,810 meters above sea level in Bolivia stands Lake Titicaca, _____ in the world.
   (A) the highest large lake
   (B) highest large lake
   (C) highest largest lake
   (D) the high largest lake

6. _____ in an electric typewriter is the ability to correct spelling errors.
   (A) There are many new features
   (B) New features
   (C) The new features
   (D) One of the new features

7. Ballet dancers, _____ actors, must spend many hours a day practicing before a performance.
   (A) like
   (B) the like
   (C) the same
   (D) same as

8. It is a sign _____ fall when the leaves on the trees begin to change color.
   (A) for
   (B) at
   (C) to
   (D) of

9. Bees have compound eyes _____ almost 6000 tiny lenses.
   (A) made of
   (B) made in
   (C) made on
   (D) made up

GO ON TO THE NEXT PAGE ➡

10. _____ the reactions of people
with amnesia, scientists are
learning more about the pro-
cess of memory in the brain.
(A) By studying
(B) To study
(C) They study
(D) They're studying

11. The White House is where the
president lives, while the Capi-
tol Building is where _____.
(A) laws made
(B) the laws are making
(C) the laws are made
(D) are making the laws

12. High levels of hazardous
waste _____ in soil near many
nuclear defense facilites.
(A) have been measured
(B) has been measured
(C) is measuring
(D) are measuring

13. Bigamy is a situation where a
man _____ two women at the
same time.
(A) marries to
(B) is marry to
(C) married
(D) is married to

14. _____ the rainfall was ade-
quate this year, the apricot
trees still did not produce a
high yield.
(A) Since
(B) However
(C) Although
(D) Due to

15. Ludwig van Beethoven is con-
sidered one of the greatest
composers _____.
(A) who ever lived
(B) he lived
(C) when living
(D) while he lived

DIRECTIONS: In questions 16–40 you will see sentences with four under-lined words or phrases. The four underlined parts of the sentence are marked (A), (B), (C), and (D). Find the one word or phrase that must be changed in order to make a correct sentence. On your answer sheet, find the number of the answer you have chosen, and fill in the space completely.

EXAMPLE 1   Sample Answer

Large forest fires can produce a significant   Ⓐ Ⓑ ● Ⓓ
<u>A</u>   <u>B</u>

amounts of air pollution.
      <u>C</u>   <u>D</u>

The sentence should read, "Large forest fires can produce a significant amount of air pollution." Therefore, you should choose answer (C).

EXAMPLE 2   Sample Answer

Vegetables such a tomatoes, cucumbers, and   ● Ⓑ Ⓒ Ⓓ
          <u>A</u>

celery are usually eaten raw.
  <u>B</u>   <u>C</u>   <u>D</u>

The sentence should read, "Vegetables such as tomatoes, cucumbers, and celery are usually eaten raw." Therefore, you should choose answer (A).

After you read the directions, begin work on the questions.

16. The research works of paleontologists comes to life with paintings
     <u>A</u>   <u>B</u>   <u>C</u>

    and sculptures of dinosaurs.
        <u>D</u>

17. According to a *Newsweek* magazine poll taken in 1986, seventy-seven
        <u>A</u>   <u>B</u>

    percent of Americans want the U.S. and the Soviet Union to sign an

    arms agreement limits nuclear weapons.
         <u>C</u>   <u>D</u>

18. In 1963, the Beatles, with their haircuts, clothes, and joking, drew
                 A   B   C

    crowds of shrieking teenagers.
              D

19. Conditions which are necessary for a sucessful business includes
       A   B   C

    consumer demand and adequate supply.
                   D

20. On New Year's Day, most Americans watch football on TV, visiting
          A   B   C

    friends, and relax around the house.
                   D

21. Scientists have been studying the effects of aspirin on lower the
                      A   B   C

    instances of heart attacks in people.
       D

22. The more you pull on a square knot, the tightest it gets.
            A   B   C   D

23. The koto, a Japanese string instrument, consists in a long wooden
                                    A   B   C

    body and seven to thirteen strings.
                          D

24. Much of the beautifully spring color in the mountain meadows comes
       A   B   C

    from the flower of the wild lupine plant.
       D

25. The earliest suspension bridges in the United States were built by
               A   B   C

    American building James Finley.
            D

26. Caterpillars have three pairs of legs, two row of eyes, and strong jaws.
                      A   B   C   D

27. Cro-Magnon man, a human being that lived about 35,000 years ago,
                                A

    was about six feet tall, stood straight, and with a large brain and a
      B   C   D

    high forehead.

GO ON TO THE NEXT PAGE ➡

28. The boll weevil, a cotton-eating insect, was a major reason for the
                    A   B
    change from a one-crop ecomony to diversified agricultural in the U.S.
                        C   D

29. Scientists predict that there would be an earthquake of great magnitude
                            A   B
    in California within the next few years.
                  C   D

30. The number of wild condors, an endangered species of bird, have been
                                  A   B
    steadily increasing this year because of the work of scientists and
      C   D
    environmentalists.

31. Since the last explore voyage into space, we have increased our knowl-
      A   B   C
    edge about the planet Jupiter.
      D

32. Mahogany wood, what is used for making furniture, is resistant to ter-
                 A   B   C
    mites, and is a beautiful color.
           D

33. Muscular dystrophy is a disease of the muscles, which commonly afflicting
                          A   B   C
    boys more than girls.
      D

34. Yellowstone National Park is well known for its beautiful canyon, its
                                   A   B
    amazed geysers, and its wild life.
      C   D

35. Having red leaves in the fall, the poison oaks plant is easy to see.
      A   B   C D

36. A planetarium, with his domed ceiling and many projectors, is capable of
     A   B   C
    showing the position of the stars in any season.
          D

37. Both scientists and treasure seekers are interesting in uncovering the
     A   B   C   D
    mysteries of the sunken ship, the Titanic.

38. Harvard University, that is the oldest American college, was founded
                 A   B   C   D

    in 1636.

39. Showing great talent as a child, Franz Schubert, the famous Austrian
         A

    composer, was first taught to play the violin and piano from his father.
          B   C   D

40. A few of the works in art of the French painter Cezanne are part of
      A   B   C

    the permanent collection of the Museum of Modern Art in New York
                  D

    City.

THIS IS THE END OF SECTION 2.

If you finish before time is called, check your work on Section 2 only. Do not read or work on any other section of the test. The supervisor will tell you when to begin work on Section 3.

STOP   STOP   STOP   STOP   STOP   STOP

SECTION 3

VOCABULARY AND READING COMPREHENSION

Time — 45 minutes

This section measures your comprehension of standard written English. There are two types of questions in this section. Each section has different directions.

DIRECTIONS: In questions 1–30, you will see sentences with one word or phrase underlined. Below each sentence are four other words or phrases, marked (A), (B), (C), and (D). You are to choose the one word or phrase that is the most similar to the word in the original sentence. On your answer sheet, find the number of the question and fill in the space with the letter of the answer you have chosen. Fill in the space completely so that the letter inside the oval cannot be seen.

EXAMPLE　　　　　　　　　　　　　　　　　Sample Answer

Leif Ericsson made his famous <u>journey</u> across the Atlantic Ocean in the year 1000.　　　Ⓐ Ⓑ ● Ⓓ

   (A)　activity
   (B)　ride
   (C)　trip
   (D)　fight

The best answer is (C) because "Leif Ericsson made his famous trip across the Atlantic Ocean in the year 1000" is closest in meaning to the original sentence. Therefore, you should choose answer (C).

After you read the directions, begin work on the questions.

1. Vincent Van Gogh is <u>renowned</u> for his post-impressionist painting.
   (A)　regarded
   (B)　applauded
   (C)　accomplished
   (D)　famous

2. Extreme sunburn can cause small <u>blisters</u> on the skin.
   (A)　spots
   (B)　swellings
   (C)　wounds
   (D)　bites

3. Natural occurrences such as hurricanes, earthquakes, and tornadoes can have <u>catastrophic</u> effects on people.
   (A)　disastrous
   (B)　killing
   (C)　categorical
   (D)　unimaginable

4. Jane Goodall has written a new, <u>comprehensive</u> book on her study of the chimpanzees in Africa.
   (A)　complete
   (B)　factual
   (C)　festive
   (D)　illustrated

5. The earthworm is a <u>segmented</u> worm found in almost all parts of the world.
   (A)　plated
   (B)　round
   (C)　long
   (D)　pieced

6. Ammonia is a chemical with a penetrating <u>odor</u>.
   (A)　smell
   (B)　flavor
   (C)　sting
   (D)　burn

GO ON TO THE NEXT PAGE ➡

7. After the American Civil War, the Southern armies were granted amnesty.
   (A) punished
   (B) frightened
   (C) pardoned
   (D) separated

8. Amphibians like frogs and toads have moist skin.
   (A) wet
   (B) slimy
   (C) sticky
   (D) tough

9. The Bay of Pigs invasion in 1961 resulted in severe criticism of President Kennedy by the American people.
   (A) deep
   (B) special
   (C) tight
   (D) harsh

10. Coral is made by a small, sedentary animal that lives in the ocean.
    (A) secluded
    (B) hard-working
    (C) immobile
    (D) lively

11. Charles Darwin formulated his famous theory of evolution during his five-year cruise on the "Beagle."
    (A) expanded
    (B) developed
    (C) critiqued
    (D) finished

12. By the end of the Crimean War, the name of Florence Nightingale was legendary.
    (A) imaginary
    (B) novel
    (C) gratifying
    (D) famous

13. The most devastating earthquake in North America occurred in Alaska in 1964.
    (A) damaging
    (B) divisive
    (C) crushing
    (D) shocking

14. In many coastal areas of the U.S. there is a deficiency of sand, causing an erosion problem.
    (A) quality
    (B) propagation
    (C) movement
    (D) lack

15. The increase in world population was negligible until around 1900.
    (A) unimportant
    (B) needless
    (C) average
    (D) misleading

16. A credit card allows the user to receive credit at the time of a purchase.
    (A) donate
    (B) arbitrate
    (C) reject
    (D) obtain

GO ON TO THE NEXT PAGE ➡

17. Credit card holders can
    <u>postpone</u> payment on their
    purchases by accepting a
    monthly interest charge.
    (A) provide
    (B) decrease
    (C) mail
    (D) defer

18. William Faulkner, a <u>brilliant</u>
    American novelist, was award-
    ed the 1949 Nobel Prize in
    literature.
    (A) intelligent
    (B) starry
    (C) captive
    (D) well-known

19. When frost appears on a win-
    dow, it often has a delicate
    and <u>curious</u> pattern.
    (A) special
    (B) strange
    (C) fine
    (D) cute

20. The American Dental Associa-
    tion cautions people not to
    <u>neglect</u> their teeth during their
    growing years.
    (A) abuse
    (B) damage
    (C) disrupt
    (D) disregard

21. When the earth turns, the
    moon <u>appears</u> to rise in the
    east and set in the west.
    (A) refers
    (B) seems
    (C) is likely
    (D) is supposed

22. One goal of a physical fitness
    program is to <u>maximize</u> a per-
    son's strength and endurance.
    (A) split
    (B) distinguish
    (C) increase
    (D) combine

23. Among the dangers of drilling
    for oil in the ocean is the pro-
    blem of <u>potential</u> leaks.
    (A) serious
    (B) dangerous
    (C) imminent
    (D) possible

24. Kangaroos give birth to
    babies that develop within
    their mothers' <u>pouches</u>.
    (A) sacks
    (B) bodies
    (C) eggs
    (D) nests

25. Unicorns, dragons, and cen-
    taurs are all <u>imaginary</u>
    animals.
    (A) magic
    (B) unimportant
    (C) pictorial
    (D) unreal

26. The Milky Way <u>consists</u> of
    about a hundred billion stars.
    (A) is consious of
    (B) surrounds
    (C) contains
    (D) makes

GO ON TO THE NEXT PAGE

27. Blizzards in the high moun-
    tains can be dangerous for
    hikers and skiers.
    (A) Snow storms
    (B) High winds
    (C) Avalanches
    (D) Slippery ice

28. To make raisins, the ripened
    grapes are usually picked
    by hand, placed on trays, and
    set in the sun for several days.
    (A) dried
    (B) cleaned
    (C) crushed
    (D) mature

29. Of the Olympic ski events, ski
    jumping is the most spectacular.
    (A) striking
    (B) dangerous
    (C) appealing
    (D) difficult

30. The central states in the U.S.
    are noted for their production
    of wheat and corn.
    (A) applauded for
    (B) informed of
    (C) known for
    (D) described by

DIRECTIONS: In this final part of the section, you will read several short
passages. Each one is followed by several questions. You are to choose the
answer, (A), (B), (C), or (D), which is the best answer to the question. On
the answer sheet, find the number of the question and fill in the answer you
have chosen.

All of the answers you choose should be answered on the basis of what is
either stated or implied in that passage.

Read the following passage:

Honeybees communicate by dancing. When a honeybee finds
flowers, it flies back to its hive to communicate the location to other
bees. At the beehive, the bee will wiggle its body and buzz loudly. The
speed and the direction of the bee's dance tell the other bees where the
flowers are. If the flowers are near, the bee dances very fast in a circle.
If the flowers are far away, it dances slowly in a strange figure eight.

EXAMPLE 1   Sample Answer

How does a honeybee communicate?

   (A) by flying
   (B) by smelling and tasting
   (C) by wiggling and buzzing
   (D) by singing a song

According to the passage, the bee will wiggle its body and buzz loudly. Therefore, you choose answer (C).

EXAMPLE 2   Sample Answer

Other bees can tell the direction of the   ● Ⓑ Ⓒ Ⓓ
flowers by

   (A) the speed and direction of the dance
   (B) the length of the dance
   (C) the time of day
   (D) the size and color of the bee

The passage states, "The speed and the direction of the bee's dance tell the other bees where the flowers are." Therefore, you should choose answer (A).

After you read the directions, begin work on the questions.

Questions 31–34

     The American architect and engineer, Buckminster Fuller, was born in 1895 in Massachusetts. He devoted his life to the invention of revolutionary technological designs to solve problems of modern living. He is best known for his development of the geodesic dome, which is an extremely light and yet enormously strong spherical structure composed of triangular pieces. The geodesic dome is an application of his principle of deriving maximum output from a minimum input of material and energy. In the 1950s many of these domes were built for military and industrial uses. A considerable number of homes have also been built using geodesic dome structures. Fuller was also a controversial writer. Among his many books are *Nine Chains to the Moon* (1938), *Ideas and Integrities* (1963 — an autobiography), *Utopia or Oblivion* (1970), and *Earth, Inc.* (1973).

31. Which of the following would be the most appropriate title for this passage?
    (A) The Geodesic Dome
    (B) An American Architect
    (C) American Architecture
    (D) Revolutionery Designs

32. Which statement best describes the dome?
    (A) It uses a lot of material, but takes less energy to construct than traditional structures.
    (B) It puts out maximum energy for its size.
    (C) It uses very little material even though it is spacious.
    (D) It takes less material and energy than traditional structures of the same size.

33. A geodesic dome is closest in shape to
    (A) a length of tube
    (B) the end of a box
    (C) a half of a ball
    (D) the tip of a triangle

34. Fuller wrote about his life in his book
    (A) *Ideas and Integrities*
    (B) *Utopia or Oblivion*
    (C) *Nine Chains to the Moon*
    (D) *Earth, Inc.*

Questions 35–40

Water on the earth is being continuously recycled in a process known as the hydrologic cycle. The first step of the cycle is the evaporation of water in the oceans. Evaporation is the process of water turning into vapor, which then forms clouds in the sky. The second step is the water returning to the earth in the form of precipitation, either rain, snow, or ice. When the water reaches the earth's surface, it runs off into the rivers, lakes, and the ocean, where the cycle begins again.

Not all water, however, stays on the surface of the earth in the hydrologic cycle. Some of it seeps into the ground through infiltration and collects under the earth's surface as groundwater. This groundwater is extremely important to life on earth since 95% of the earth's water is in the oceans, and is too salty for humans or plants. Of the 5% on land, only .05% is above ground in rivers or lakes. The rest is underground water. This groundwater is plentiful and dependable, as it doesn't depend on seasonal rain or snow. It is the major source of water for many cities. But as the population increases and the need for water also increases, the groundwater in some areas is getting dangerously low. Added to this problem is an increasing amount of pollution that seeps into the groundwater. In the future, with an increasing population and more toxic waste, the hydrologic cycle we depend on could become dangerously imbalanced.

35. Clouds are formed from
    (A) water vapor
    (B) evaporation
    (C) the hydrologic cycle
    (D) groundwater
36. Water returns to the earth by
    (A) infiltration
    (B) pollution
    (C) precipitation
    (D) evaporation
37. Groundwater
    (A) depends on seasonal rain
    (B) comes from toxic waste
    (C) is .05% of all water
    (D) collects under the earth
38. The amount of groundwater is
    (A) about 95% of all water
    (B) less than 5% of all water
    (C) .05% of above ground water
    (D) 95% of above ground water

39. The supply of groundwater is getting low because of
    (A) conservation
    (B) toxic waste
    (C) pollution
    (D) population increase
40. The best title for this passage is
    (A) Water Conservation
    (B) The Hydrologic Cycle
    (C) Underground Water
    (D) Polluted Groundwater

Questions 41–47

The Library of Congress in Washington, D.C., which houses the largest collection of books in the world, is fighting a battle against paper deterioration. The pages of old books, often yellowed and torn, sometimes crumble when they are touched. The main culprit in the battle is the acidic paper which has been used for making books since the nineteenth century.

Air pollution and moisture have added to the problem. Strangely, the books that are most in danger of destruction are not the oldest books. The paper in books made before the last century was made from cotton and linen rags, which are naturally low in acid. And the Gutenberg Bible, printed five centuries ago, was made of thin calfskin, and is in remarkably good shape. But in the nineteenth century, with widespread literacy bringing a demand for a cheaper and more plentiful supply of paper, the industry began using chemically treated wood pulp for making paper. It is the chemical in this paper that is causing today's problem.

This problem of paper deterioration is one of global concern. France, Canada, and Austria are all doing research into new methods of deacidification. A new technology has recently been developed, in fact, that allows for mass deacidification of thousands of books at the same time. It costs less than microfilming and still preserves books in their original form. It is hoped there will soon be treatment facilities all over the world to preserve and deacidify library book collections.

41. The Library of Congress
    (A) is headed for destruction
    (B) is fighting a battle
    (C) is causing paper deterioration
    (D) is implementing new techniques

42. According to this passage, libraries are trying to stop
    (A) the tearing of books
    (B) the yellowing of pages
    (C) the problem of air pollution
    (D) the deterioration of paper

43. Before the nineteenth century,
    (A) most books crumbled
    (B) the industry used wood pulp
    (C) paper had less acid
    (D) thousands of books were deacidified

44. We can assume from this passage that
    (A) cotton and linen rags are not good for making paper
    (B) calfskin is low in acid
    (C) wood pulp is expensive
    (D) microfilming is an inexpensive way to preserve old books

45. Many countries in the world are
    (A) deacidifying their book collections
    (B) producing books from cotton and linen rags
    (C) doing research into methods of mass preservation
    (D) building treatment facilities

46. A new technique in deacidification
    (A) uses microfilm to save books
    (B) will save the Gutenberg Bible
    (C) uses chemically treated wood pulp
    (D) can treat thousands of books at a time

47. The best title for this passage is
    (A) Paper Deterioration
    (B) Techniques of Deacidification
    (C) Microfilming vs. Deacidification
    (D) Types of Paper Used in Bookmaking

Questions 48–53

Impressionism, in painting, developed in the late nineteenth century in France. It began with a loosely structured group of painters who got together mainly to exhibit their paintings. Their art was characterized by the attempt to depict light and movement by using pure broken color. The movement began with four friends who met in a cafe: Monet, Renoir, Sisley, and Bazille. They were reacting against the academic standards of their time and the romantic emphasis on emotion as a subject matter. They rejected the role of imagination in art. Instead, they observed nature closely, painting with a scientific interest in visual phenomena. Their subject matter was as diverse as their personalities. Monet and Sisley painted landscapes with changing effects of light, while Renoir painted idealized women and children. The works of impressionists were received with hostility until the 1920s. By the 1930s impressionism had a large cult following, and by the 1950s even the least important works by people associated with the movement commanded enormous prices.

48. Impressionism began with a small group of artists who wanted to
    (A) use light colors
    (B) fight the government
    (C) become scientists
    (D) show their paintings

49. The first impressionists
    (A) supported the academic standards
    (B) began a new academy
    (C) did not like the academic standards
    (D) developed new official standards

50. The early impressionist artists painted
    (A) with imagination
    (B) different subject matter
    (C) landscapes
    (D) diverse personalities

51. What subject matter did Monet and Sisley usually paint?
    (A) country scenes
    (B) portraits
    (C) skyscrapers
    (D) animals in nature

52. Which of the following typifies the early impressionists?
    (A) They had a romantic emphasis.
    (B) They tried to see nature unemotionally.
    (C) They worked toward a unified goal.
    (D) They idealized life.

53. Most people did not like impressionistic painting
    (A) before 1920
    (B) between 1920 and 1930
    (C) between 1930 and 1950
    (D) after 1950

Questions 54–60

Tissue transplants and organ transplants are both used in the treatment of disease. Tissue transplants include the transplanting of skin, bones, and the cornea of the eye; whereas organ transplanting includes replacing the kidney, heart, lung, and liver. Skin and cornea transplants are very common and successful, and have been performed for hundreds of years. In fact, there is evidence that skin transplants were done as early as 600 B.C. in India. Organ transplants, on the other hand, are quite recent. They are also more difficult to perform. Moreover, it is not always easy to find a suitable donor. Even if a healthy organ is found, the receiver's body may reject it. This is the major reason for problems with organ transplants.

The first heart transplant was performed by Dr. Christiaan Barnard in 1967 in South Africa. Many successful heart transplant operations have been performed since then. In 1982, Dr. Barney Clark was the first to receive an artificial heart. Research into organ transplants continues all the time. Doctors are continuing to find new ways to combat the problems, and make transplants safer and more available to needy people.

54. Which of the following is a tissue transplant?
    (A) liver
    (B) lung
    (C) bone
    (D) kidney

55. In 600 B.C., there were
    (A) organ transplants
    (B) skin transplants
    (C) cornea replacements
    (D) artificial hearts

56. A cornea is located in the
    (A) heart
    (B) skin
    (C) bone
    (D) eye

57. The most common problem with organ transplants is
    (A) rejection of the tissue
    (B) finding a donor
    (C) finding a healthy organ
    (D) replacing the organ

58. Successful heart transplants have been performed since
    (A) 600 B.C.
    (B) 1967
    (C) 1982
    (D) 600 A.D.

59. The first heart transplant was
    (A) received by Dr. Christiaan Barnard
    (B) performed by Dr. Barney Clark
    (C) performed in South Africa
    (D) with an artificial heart

60. The best title for this passage is
    (A) The Treatment of Disease
    (B) The First Heart Transplants
    (C) Successful Organ Transplants
    (D) Transplants: Past and Present

THIS IS THE END OF SECTION 3.

If you finish before time is called, check your work on Section 3 only. Do not read or work on any other section of the test.

STOP   STOP   STOP   STOP   STOP   STOP

PRACTICE TEST 2

SECTION 1

LISTENING COMPREHENSION

This section of the test is for demonstrating your ability to understand spoken English. There are three different parts in this section. Each section has separate directions.

N O T E

You will need the tape to do Section 1. If you do not have the tape, the tapescript for Section 1 is on pages 243 to 248. Answer sheets to this tape are found on pages 250 and 252.

Part A

DIRECTIONS: For each question in Part A, you will hear a short sentence which will be spoken only one time. None of the sentences will be written out for you, so you must listen carefully to understand what the speaker says.

After you hear a sentence, read the four choices in your test book, marked (A), (B), (C), and (D), and decide which one is closest in meaning to the sentence you heard on tape. Then, look on your answer sheet for the number of the question and fill in the space that corresponds to the letter of the answer you have chosen. Fill in the space carefully, dark enough so that the letter inside the oval cannot be seen.

EXAMPLE 1   Sample Answer

You will hear: Would you mind opening
the door for me?

You will read: (A) The door to my office
is open.
(B) Could you please open
the door for me?
(C) Please remind me to
open the door.
(D) I don't mind the door
opening.

The speaker said, "Would you mind opening the door for me?"
Sentence (B), "Could you please open the door for me," is closest in
meaning to the sentence you heard. Therefore, you should choose
answer (B).

EXAMPLE 2   Sample Answer

You will hear: There is so much fog that I
can barely see the cars on
the road.

You will read: (A) There are a lot of cars
on the road.
(B) I saw a dog on the
road.
(C) It is hard to see
anything on the road.
(D) I was surprised to see
bears on the road.

The speaker said, "There is so much fog that I can barely see the cars
on the road." Sentence (C), "It is hard to see anything on the road," is
closest in meaning to the sentence you heard. Therefore, you should
choose answer (C).

1. (A) The train is early.   (B) Grandma should walk
   (B) You missed the train.   slowly so she doesn't fall.
   (C) You must hurry.   (C) Since Grandma's fall, she
   (D) You hurry too much.   should do less work.
                                         (D) Since Grandma did so
2. (A) Grandma had an easy   much work in the fall,
       fall, but she's all right.   she should rest this winter.

3. (A) John has already left for the party.
   (B) The director will get to the party before John.
   (C) John will leave before the director comes.
   (D) The director has already gone to the party.

4. (A) Sandra didn't have enough time to finish the work.
   (B) There was no clock in the room Sandra finished the work in.
   (C) It took more time than she thought to finish.
   (D) Sandra worked quickly and finished the work.

5. (A) The front door is for the handicapped only.
   (B) You can use the back door if the front door is locked.
   (C) The disabled can use the back door if necessary.
   (D) I left your cap on the red door.

6. (A) Representing the whole group, the student gave a talk.
   (B) The group discussed whether or not the project should be presented.
   (C) The student was supported by the entire group.
   (D) The group discussed the student's project.

7. (A) In the past, Jenny wanted to be a world-class gymnast.
   (B) Jenny almost won the gold medal in gymnastics.
   (C) Jenny used to be a very good gymnast.
   (D) Jenny took part in the gymnastics event in the Olympics.

8. (A) You have to move to the left.
   (B) Watch out! The track is on your right.
   (C) If you continue on the right side, you'll get there.
   (D) You are doing all right so far.

9. (A) Mr. Wilson retired when he got rich.
   (B) Mr. Wilson could stop working because he has enough money.
   (C) Rich people don't have to work anymore.
   (D) Health is more important than wealth.

10. (A) The black clothes fit you better than the white clothes.
    (B) The white clothes fit you better than the black ones, now that it is summertime.
    (C) It's better to wear white clothes than black clothes in the summertime.
    (D) Your black clothes have gotten too tight to wear in the summer.

GO ON TO THE NEXT PAGE ➡

11. (A) They resigned their jobs when there was too much work.
    (B) They had a lot more work to do after finishing the design.
    (C) They fulfilled their plans when they began to work.
    (D) They were beginning to work on designing.

12. (A) They were small planets.
    (B) They were large planets.
    (C) They were too small to be called planets.
    (D) They were too large for small planets.

13. (A) You should do more because I have to rest.
    (B) I will cook the rice if you cook everything else.
    (C) I will do everything that you don't do.
    (D) Since you have to rest, I will prepare everything.

14. (A) His determination was the most important reason that he succeeded.
    (B) It seemed impossible for him to be so determined.
    (C) It was impossible for him to be successful.
    (D) The key to success was impossible, it seemed.

15. (A) The computer room is very crowded.
    (B) Computer science has been applied to many fields.
    (C) Too many people are studying computer science today.
    (D) Computer science is developing very quickly.

16. (A) I want to know what it costs.
    (B) I want to buy a coat that fits me.
    (C) I want it, but it's too expensive.
    (D) I'll buy it for any price.

17. (A) My uncle is a famous speaker.
    (B) My uncle speaks well when he lectures.
    (C) My uncle's lecture was excellent.
    (D) I knew my uncle would lecture me on speech.

18. (A) George stopped going to class because he didn't like it.
    (B) George couldn't take the class because he had another class at the same time.
    (C) The class was about conflicts of schedule.
    (D) George needed another class in his busy schedule.

19. (A) We should have gone to the beach on a warmer day.
    (B) Today was not a good day for me to go to the beach.
    (C) The weather is just right for the beach today.
    (D) This beach is not good enough to go to.

20. (A) I can't work any faster.
    (B) I will work faster.
    (C) I am not able to work.
    (D) It's bad to work too fast.

Part B

DIRECTIONS: In Part B you will hear several short conversations between two speakers. At the end of each conversation, a third person will ask a question about what was said. You will hear each conversation and question only once. Therefore, you must listen carefully to understand what each speaker says. After you hear a conversation and the question about it, read the four possible answers in your test book and decide which one is the best answer to the question. On your answer sheet, find the number of the question and fill in the letter of the answer you have chosen.

EXAMPLE: Sample Answer

You will hear: Ⓐ Ⓑ Ⓒ ●

You will read: (A) Pick up the mail
               (B) Go home
               (C) Go to work
               (D) Buy some milk

From the conversation, you know that the man is going to stop and pick up some milk. The best answer is (D) "Buy some milk." Therefore, you should choose answer (D).

---

21. (A) She will not say what the boss will do.
    (B) The boss will not do anything.
    (C) Don't tell the boss the bad news.
    (D) She doesn't know what he will do.

22. (A) She wants him to stay longer.
    (B) She wishes he had left sooner.
    (C) She knows he must go soon.
    (D) She wants him to go now.

23. (A) In a post office
    (B) In a department store
    (C) At a party
    (D) In a grocery store

24. (A) 3 hours if working by hand
    (B) A minimum of 3 hours
    (C) 3 hours at the maximum
    (D) 3 hours, more or less

GO ON TO THE NEXT PAGE

25. (A) He wants to wait until the class is full.
    (B) He will wait for the list.
    (C) He hopes someone will drop the class.
    (D) He is late and there are no more chairs.
26. (A) In a library
    (B) In a hotel
    (C) In a restaurant
    (D) In a bank
27. (A) He should go first and she will catch up to him later.
    (B) She will go have coffee and then do her work.
    (C) She will do her work instead of having coffee.
    (D) She will do her work at the coffee house.
28. (A) A room with a balcony
    (B) A room with two beds
    (C) A room and transportation
    (D) A room and meals
29. (A) In a clothes store
    (B) In a shoe store
    (C) In a gymnasium
    (D) At a swimming pool
30. (A) Go to the gym and work out
    (B) Be calm and patient
    (C) Listen carefully to John
    (D) Do the easiest thing

31. (A) In a delicatessen
    (B) In a grocery store
    (C) In a candy store
    (D) In an ice cream store
32. (A) She lost her job.
    (B) She mislaid her money.
    (C) She got divorced.
    (D) She's in the hospital.
33. (A) He will call Pete before he goes home.
    (B) He will call Pete after he gets home.
    (C) He called Pete at home.
    (D) He will call Pete tomorrow.
34. (A) She doesn't want pumpkin or apple.
    (B) She can't decide. She likes them both the same.
    (C) She doesn't know the difference between pumpkin and apple pie.
    (D) She likes pumpkin pie better than apple pie.
35. (A) Bill had to pay $54.
    (B) It was a little more than $54.
    (C) It was a little less than $54.
    (D) The whole bill was $54.

Part C

DIRECTIONS: In this part of the test, you will hear short talks or conversations. After each of them, you will be asked several questions. The questions, as well as the talks and conversations will be spoken only once. They will not be written out for you. Therefore, you must listen carefully to understand what each speaker says.

After you hear a question, read the four possible answers in your test book and decide which one is the best answer to the question. On your answer sheet fill in the letter of the answer you have chosen.

Listen to this sample talk.

EXAMPLE 1   Sample Answer

You will hear: ● Ⓑ Ⓒ Ⓓ

You will read: (A) Students at a university
          (B) Spanish folk singers
          (C) The Scottish country
               dance group
          (D) The University Interna-
               tional Dancers

The best answer to the questions, "Who is the announcement given to?" is (A) "Students at a university." Therefore, you should choose answer (A).

EXAMPLE 2   Sample Answer

You will hear: Ⓐ Ⓑ Ⓒ ●

You will read: (A) learn Scottish dancing
          (B) buy costumes
          (C) eat dinner
          (D) dance to music

The best answer to the questions, "What will many people at the festival be able to do?" is (D) "Dance to music." Therefore, you should choose answer (D).

---

36. (A) A nurse
    (B) A dentist
    (C) A patient
    (D) An assistant

37. (A) Just before pulling a
        tooth
    (B) Just after pulling a tooth
    (C) At a consultation about
        pulling a tooth
    (D) While another person is
        pulling a tooth

38. (A) For a half hour
    (B) For a few hours
    (C) Until tomorrow
    (D) Until the swelling goes
        down

39. (A) Rinse your mouth
    (B) Take aspirin
    (C) Sleep
    (D) Keep ice on it

GO ON TO THE NEXT PAGE ➡

40. (A) Every 20 minutes tomorrow
    (B) In a half hour
    (C) Every 3 hours tomorrow
    (D) In 4 or 5 hours

41. (A) Keep the mouth clean
    (B) Prevent pain
    (C) Stop bleeding
    (D) Prevent swelling

42. (A) It is normal.
    (B) It should stop in a half hour.
    (C) It is not bleeding.
    (D) There will be a lot of bleeding.

43. (A) Angry
    (B) Worried
    (C) Helpful
    (D) Excited

44. (A) New students
    (B) Old students
    (C) Faculty
    (D) Staff

45. (A) Desks
    (B) Suites
    (C) Kitchens
    (D) Closets

46. (A) Children
    (B) Cooking
    (C) Spouses
    (D) Single students

47. (A) Foreign only
    (B) Resident only
    (C) Either foreign or resident
    (D) Only Spanish-speaking

48. (A) Spanish nationals
    (B) Spanish majors
    (C) Spanish speaking
    (D) Spanish cooking

49. (A) Co-ed dorms
    (B) Married student apartments
    (C) International Houses
    (D) Spanish House

50. (A) Visit the housing they like
    (B) Move into the housing
    (C) Fill out forms
    (D) Buy a meal ticket

THIS IS THE END OF SECTION 1.

The next part of the test is Section 2. Turn to the directions for Section 2 in your test book, read them, and begin work. Do not read or work on any other section of the test.

STOP   STOP   STOP   STOP   STOP   STOP

SECTION 2

STRUCTURE AND WRITTEN EXPRESSION

Time — 25 Minutes

This section measures your ability to recognize standard written English. There are two types of questions in this section. Each of the sections has different directions.

DIRECTIONS: Questions 1–15 are not complete sentences. One or more words are left out of each sentence. Under the sentences you will see four words or phrases, marked, (A), (B), (C), and (D). Choose the one word or phrase that completes the sentence correctly. Then, on your answer sheet, find the number of the question and fill in the correct space so that the letter inside the oval cannot be seen.

EXAMPLE 1   Sample Answer

Many people came to the museum to look   ● Ⓑ Ⓒ Ⓓ
_____ the exhibit of Van Gogh's paintings.

  (A) at
  (B) up
  (C) on
  (D) in

The sentence should read, "Many people came to the museum to look at the exhibit of Van Gogh's paintings." Therefore, you should choose answer (A).

EXAMPLE 2   Sample Answer

_____ not enough food for all the people   Ⓐ Ⓑ Ⓒ ●
who are suffering from the recent famine.

  (A) There are
  (B) Is
  (C) All is
  (D) There is

The sentence should read, "There is not enough food for all the people who are suffering from the recent famine." Therefore, you should choose answer (D).

After you read the directions, begin work on the questions.

1. Even though woodpeckers _____ as a nuisance to many people, they are actually helpful since they feed on harmful insects.
   (A) are seen
   (B) which are seen
   (C) being seen
   (D) to be seen

2. The first clock, made nearly a thousand years ago, had neither a face nor hands, _____ that rang each hour.
   (A) it had bells
   (B) rather than bells
   (C) though bells
   (D) but had bells

3. _____ on the floor of the ocean is a big farming industry.
   (A) Oysters raising
   (B) Oysters are raised
   (C) The raising of oysters
   (D) The oysters raised

4. A barbershop _____ a red and white striped pole.
   (A) what symbolizes
   (B) is symbolized by
   (C) is symbolized to
   (D) was symbolized

5. Llamas are used as _____ by the Indians in the Andes Mountains.
   (A) beasts in burden
   (B) beasts of burden
   (C) burden beasts
   (D) beasts' burden

6. The moon, _____ no air around it, grows extremely hot in the daytime and extremely cold at night.
   (A) which has
   (B) has
   (C) having had
   (D) what has

7. Even though they are not liquid, cottage cheese, sour cream, and yogurt, are sold _____ liquid measurements.
   (A) to
   (B) for
   (C) through
   (D) by

8. To plant rice, farmers, _____, set young plants in the mud.
   (A) they wade with bare feet in the water
   (B) water wading in their bare feet
   (C) wading in the water in their bare feet
   (D) whose bare feet wading in the water

9. _____, farmers cut holes in the bark of maple trees.
   (A) Maple syrup is collected
   (B) To collect maple syrup
   (C) The collection of maple syrup
   (D) When collect maple syrup

GO ON TO THE NEXT PAGE

10. The boll weevil, an insect
_____ cotton plants, is native
to Central America.
(A) destroys
(B) to destroy
(C) has destroyed
(D) that destroys

11. _____ humans, toads have
tongues fastened at the front
of their mouths which allow
them to catch insects.
(A) Not the same
(B) Unlike
(C) Except for
(D) Dislike

12. _____ on a hot fire is a
delicacy in many parts of the
world.
(A) Lamb roasted
(B) Lamb roasts
(C) Lambs roast
(D) Lambs roasting

13. _____ determines a good meal
varies from country to country.
(A) Which
(B) Why
(C) What
(D) How

14. _____, the pecan is the second
most popular nut in the
United States.
(A) The rich food
(B) Food is rich
(C) To be rich
(D) A rich food

15. More ivory is obtained from
elephants in Africa _____
elephants in Asia.
(A) rather than
(B) more than
(C) than from
(D) as well as

DIRECTIONS: In questions 16–40 you will see sentences with four underlined words or phrases. The four underlined parts of the sentence are marked (A), (B), (C), and (D). Find the one word or phrase which must be changed in order to make a correct sentence. On your answer sheet, find the number of the answer you have chosen, and fill in the space completely.

EXAMPLE 1   Sample Answer

Large forest fires can produce a significant   Ⓐ Ⓑ ● Ⓓ
   A   B

amounts of air pollution.
     C   D

The sentence should read, "Large forest fires can produce a significant amount of air pollution." Therefore, you should choose answer (C).

EXAMPLE 2   Sample Answer

Vegetables such a tomatoes, cucumbers,   ● Ⓑ Ⓒ Ⓓ
        A

and celery are usually eaten raw.
   B   C   D

The sentence should read, "Vegetables such as tomatoes, cucumbers, and celery are usually eaten raw." Therefore, you should choose answer (A).

After you read the directions, begin work on the questions.

16. One of the most important discovery of the nineteenth century was a
                            A   B

    method of using natural gas for cooking and heating.
           C   D

17. The Netherlands, a country with much of the land lying lower than
                               A   B

    sea level, have a system of dikes and canals for controlling water.
          C   D

18. Davy Crockett, a famed American pioneer, was known for his
                              A   B

    hunting, trapping, tell stories, and quick wit.
                         C   D

19. The movement of ocean waves can be compared to the waves caused by
            A   B   C

    the wind in a field or grass.
                    D

20. Milk, often considered a nearly perfect food, contains fat, sweet, and
                                   A   B   C   D

    protein.

21. Only after they themselves become parents, do people realize the dif-
                        A   B   C

    ficulties of raised children.
                 D

22. Aviators, fish, and sailors are among those who rely on weather
         A   B   C   D

    predictions.

23. Mohandas K. Gandhi, who was called Mahatma, lived a noble life of

    fasting and poverty in order to work for peaceful and independence.
         A   B   C   D

24. Soybean, which sometimes grow seven feet tall, have thick, woody
         A   B   C   D

    stems.

25. When settling the old west in pioneer times, American families build
            A   B   C

    their homes from split logs.
                       D

26. Venus's Flytrap are small plants which have leaves that snap together
              A   B   C

    like traps.
       D

GO ON TO THE NEXT PAGE ➡

27. *The Last of the Mohicans* are a famous book about frontier life by the
                   A B   C   D
    American author James Fenimore Cooper.

28. The Treaty of Ghent, signed in 1814, ends the last war between
                          A   B C D
    England and the United States.

29. In the year 500, ancient Greece was reaching its highest level of
                              A   B
    civilization, with great achievements in the fields of art, architecture,
                                          C
    politic, and philosophy.
       D

30. A fever, the elevations of body temperature above 98.6° F, is
                A
    considered to be a symptom of a disorder rather than a disease in
       B   C
    itself.
      D

31. Lacrosse is a ball game played on a field outdoors similar soccer.
                          A   B   C   D

32. The manufactural of ice cream in the United States on a
          A   B
    commercial scale began in 1851.
       C   D

33. People with two family members which suffer heart attacks before age
                          A   B
    fifty-five are likely to have early heart attacks themselves.
            C   D

34. Children's games, which are amusements involve more than one in-
                                     A
    dividual, appear to be a cultural universal.
            B   C   D

35. During times of war, political groups will sometimes kidnap foreign
    diplomats and hold them as hostage until the government meets certain
                A   B   C
    demands.
      D

36. The first year of a child's life is characterized in rapid physical growth.
                  A   B   C   D

37. A trial by juries is guaranteed by the American Constitution.
         A   B   C   D

38. Since ancient times, water from rivers and smaller streams are used for
               A   B   C   D

    irrigation.

39. Khaki is a cloth made in linen or cotton and dyed a dust color.
            A   B   C   D

40. The symptom of leukemia include weakness, general ill feelings, and
          A   B   C   D

    fever.

THIS IS THE END OF SECTION 2

If you finish before time is called, check your work on Section 2 only. Do not read or work on any other section of the test. The supervisor will tell you when to begin work on Section 3.

STOP   STOP   STOP   STOP   STOP   STOP

SECTION 3

VOCABULARY AND READING COMPREHENSION

Time—45 minutes

This section measures your comprehension of standard written English. There are two types of questions in this section. Each section has different directions.

DIRECTIONS: In questions 1–30 you will see sentences with one word or phrase underlined. Below each sentence are four other words or phrases, marked (A), (B), (C), and (D). You are to choose the one word or phrase that is the most similar to the word in the original sentence. On your answer sheet, find the number of the question and fill in the space completely so that the letter inside the oval cannot be seen.

EXAMPLE: Sample Answer

Leif Ericsson made his famous <u>journey</u>   Ⓐ Ⓑ ● Ⓓ
across the Atlantic Ocean in the year
1000.

    (A) activity
    (B) ride
    (C) trip
    (D) fight

The best answer is (C) because "Leif Ericsson made his famous trip across the Atlantic Ocean in the year 1000" is closest in meaning to the original sentence. Therefore, you should choose answer (C).

After you read the directions, begin work on the questions.

1. Produce is commonly shipped across the United States in large <u>crates.</u>
    (A) wooden boxes
    (B) box cars
    (C) trucks
    (D) quantities

2. Because of the baby boom of 1980s, preschools in the US have <u>proliferated.</u>
    (A) changed in philosophy
    (B) increased in numbers
    (C) become more crowded
    (D) become more expensive

3. Even though he was <u>obese,</u> Oliver Hardy gained fame as a comedian.
    (A) dying
    (B) crazy
    (C) unhappy
    (D) fat

4. Crimes against property have risen in the USA and other <u>urbanized</u> countries.
    (A) rich
    (B) large
    (C) multicultural
    (D) metropolitan

5. Racoons and dormice are examples of animals that <u>hibernate</u> several months of the year.
    (A) sleep
    (B) fast
    (C) lose hair
    (D) store food

GO ON TO THE NEXT PAGE

6. The California condor has become scarce during this century.
   (A) easily frightened
   (B) prone to disease
   (C) fewer in numbers
   (D) difficult to catch

7. Charles Darwin and A.R. Wallace published their ideas on evolution simultaneously in 1858.
   (A) in the same book
   (B) for the same people
   (C) on the same topic
   (D) at the same time

8. In coastal areas where there is an abundance of fish, the fishing industry prospers.
   (A) more than sufficient quantity
   (B) a wide variety
   (C) a unique type
   (D) a common diet

9. There is a common superstition that a ring around the moon means that rain will come soon.
   (A) attitude
   (B) speculation
   (C) belief
   (D) approach

10. Political refugees often find sanctuary in churches.
    (A) happiness
    (B) protection
    (C) peace
    (D) charity

11. Many pesticides are available for insects like termites and cockroaches.
    (A) poisons
    (B) deterrents
    (C) sprays
    (D) medicines

12. Two animals that thrive at high altitudes are llamas and alpacas.
    (A) survive
    (B) settle down
    (C) flourish
    (D) die out

13. If you are going to be in a swamp area, you should take a mosquito repellent.
    (A) marsh
    (B) jungle
    (C) savanna
    (D) tropical

14. Ralph Nader is an advocate of consumer rights.
    (A) an opponent of
    (B) a believer in
    (C) a politician for
    (D) a supporter of

15. A backyard swimming pool can be a hazard for small children.
    (A) pleasure
    (B) disaster
    (C) danger
    (D) thrill

16. When the New York Giants lost the football game, the citizens of New York were abject.
    (A) surprised
    (B) disgusted
    (C) relieved
    (D) depressed

17. Canada is a vast country in terms of its area.
    (A) concerning
    (B) in regard to
    (C) in spite of
    (D) because of

GO ON TO THE NEXT PAGE ➡

18. Tenzing Norkay and Sir Edmund Hillary were the first people to <u>scale</u> Mount Everest.
    (A) climb
    (B) camp on
    (C) discover
    (D) survive on

19. At a high temperature, <u>evaporation</u> is more rapid than at a lower temperature.
    (A) absorption of a liquid
    (B) decreased energy of molecules
    (C) change of a solid into a liquid
    (D) change of liquid into vapor

20. A huge mountain chain in Europe is formed by <u>linking</u> the Alps, the Pyrenees, the Balkans, the Caucasus, and the Carpathians.
    (A) dividing
    (B) surpassing
    (C) surrounding
    (D) joining

21. John Foster Dulles <u>achieved</u> recognition in the USA as an international lawyer in the 1930s.
    (A) fought for
    (B) gained
    (C) wrote about
    (D) chose

22. In 1936, Edward VIII <u>renounced</u> his title to the British throne to marry Wallis Warfield Simpson.
    (A) gave up
    (B) threw away
    (C) let down
    (D) put in

23. Many children looked <u>emaciated</u> during the drought.
    (A) sick
    (B) unhappy
    (C) thin
    (D) lonely

24. An increasing number of women in the 1980s have delayed marriage and childbirth in order to <u>launch</u> their careers.
    (A) postpone
    (B) expand
    (C) begin
    (D) participate in

25. According to Carl Sagan the Earth is a tiny and fragile world that needs to be <u>cherished.</u>
    (A) explored
    (B) valued
    (C) unified
    (D) developed

26. In certain areas of many cities, it is against the law to <u>loiter.</u>
    (A) throw paper
    (B) stand around
    (C) join a mob
    (D) carry a weapon

27. During the 1980s women have entered the work force <u>in droves.</u>
    (A) seriously
    (B) fervently
    (C) in large numbers
    (D) in management positions

GO ON TO THE NEXT PAGE

28. Taking some kinds of medicine will cause your body to <u>retain</u> fluids.
    (A) sustain
    (B) inject
    (C) lose
    (D) keep

29. <u>Down</u> pillows are becoming very popular.
    (A) Floor
    (B) Beanbag
    (C) Feather
    (D) Polyester

30. In most public buildings, <u>ramps</u> are installed for handicapped people.
    (A) sloped walkways
    (B) safe handrails
    (C) low telephones
    (D) wide doorways

DIRECTIONS: In the final part of the section you will read several short passages. Each one is followed by several questions. You are to choose the answer, (A), (B), (C), or (D), which is the best answer to each question. On your answer sheet, find the number of the question and fill in the answer you have chosen.

All of the answers you choose should be answered on the basis of what is stated or implied in that passage.

Read the following passage:

Honeybees communicate by dancing. When a honeybee finds flowers, it flies back to its hive to communicate the location to other bees. At the beehive, the bee will wiggle its body and buzz loudly. The speed and the direction of the bee's dance tell the other bees where the flowers are. If the flowers are near, the bee dances very fast in a circle. If the flowers are far away, it dances slowly in a strange figure eight.

EXAMPLE I   Sample Answer

How does a honeybee communicate?

  (A) by flying
  (B) by smelling and tasting
  (C) by wiggling and buzzing
  (D) by singing a song

According to the passage, the bee will wiggle its body and buzz loudly.
Therefore, you choose answer (C).

EXAMPLE 2   Sample Answer

Other bees can tell the direction of the   ● Ⓑ Ⓒ Ⓓ
flowers by

  (A) the speed and direction of the dance
  (B) the length of the dance
  (C) the time of day
  (D) the size and color of the bee

The passage states that "the speed and the direction of the bee's dance
tell the other bees where the flowers are." Therefore, you should
choose answer (A).

After you read the directions, begin work on the questions.

Questions 31–34

Halley's comet has become the best observed comet in history, but the information that has been gathered is only the beginning of what is needed to
understand this comet, one of the most primitive bodies in the solar system.
During the recent appearance of Halley's comet, a research corps of over
1000 professional astronomers gathered data around the world. The data
revealed intriguing new information. For the first time ever, European and
Soviet spacecraft have photographed the comet's nucleus. The photographs
now show the mass of dirty ice and gas that makes up the comet's center.

In spite of close-up photos revealing one of the oddest-looking objects in
the solar system, comet scientists still can't decide how fast Halley's nucleus
spins. Some experts believe it spins once every 2.2 days, some determine the
spin to be once in 7.4 days, and other scientists suggest that the comet ex-
hibits both motions superimposed together.

Astronomers monitor Halley each time it comes close enough to the earth, so that we can see the bright cloud of vaporized dust and gas that forms its tail. It is easiest to get a clear look at the comet when it is far away from the sun so that its activity dies down.

31. The word "primitive" in Line 3 means
    (A) mysterious
    (B) singular
    (C) original
    (D) simple

32. According to the article scientists are puzzled about
    (A) why we see a cloud of dust and gas
    (B) how quickly Halley's comet turns
    (C) what the tail consists of
    (D) when Halley will return

33. The passage implies that many scientists think that Halley's comet is
    (A) strange-looking
    (B) misunderstood
    (C) dirty
    (D) dying

34. It is easiest to see Halley when
    (A) it is dead
    (B) it has less activity
    (C) it is closer to the sun
    (D) it is active

Questions 35–40

Compact discs (CDs) have revolutionized the music industry with their surprisingly realistic sound. The six-inch discs look like thin, plastic sandwiches with aluminum in the center. They have digitally recorded material that is read by laser beams, so the sound has none of the crackling of vinyl records. CDs are also virtually indestructible, lighter, and smaller than conventional records (LPs). CDs are becoming more widely available than LPs: they're sold in electronics and video stores that haven't formerly carried records or cassettes. Many record stores are now cutting their prices on LPs to make room for the new CDs.

There has been a phenomenal growth in the sale of CDs. Sales were up almost 150 percent in the first half of 1986 as compared to the first half of 1985. While fewer than 6 million CDs were sold in the US in 1984, there were approximately 50 million sold in 1986. The sales would likely be even higher were it not for the price: CDs cost nearly twice as much as LPs. In the near future, however, prices should lower as more production facilities open.

35. The main appeal of CDs is their
    (A) price
    (B) size
    (C) sound
    (D) availability

36. The author refers to CDs as "sandwiches" because they
    (A) are light
    (B) are small
    (C) are layered
    (D) don't crackle

GO ON TO THE NEXT PAGE ➡

37. This passage states that it is
    difficult to
    (A) play a CD
    (B) produce a CD
    (C) record a CD
    (D) destroy a CD
38. Many record stores are
    currently
    (A) lowering CD prices
    (B) raising LP prices
    (C) lowering LP prices
    (D) raising CD prices

39. According to this passage,
    which one of the following is
    true?
    (A) Different kinds of stores
        are selling CDs.
    (B) More CDs are available
        than LPs.
    (C) Stores are selling more
        CDs than LPs.
    (D) Stores are losing money
        on their LPs.
40. The author's main purpose
    is to
    (A) tell how CDs are made
    (B) discuss the growth of CDs
    (C) compare CDs and LPs
    (D) describe the technology
        that produces CDs

Questions 41–46

A national political struggle is continuing over the issue of protection for the remnants of vast ancient forests that once covered the northwestern areas of the United States. These old forests, called "old growth," contain trees from 200 to 1200 years old. There are now about 6 million acres of virgin forest in Washington and Oregon, only about one-tenth of what existed before the 1800s. This old growth contains some of the most valuable timber in the nation, but its economic worth is also contained in its water, wildlife, scenery, and recreational facilities.

Conservationists want the majority of existing old growth protected from harvesting. They emphasize the vital relationship between old growth and the health of the forest's ecosystem. They cite studies which show that both downed and standing old trees store and release nutrients necessary to younger trees.

On the other hand, much of the Northwest's economy is developed around the logging industry. Trees are cut down to make wood products, and many mills are geared for old-growth industry. In recent years 500 acres of old growth have been logged, including trees up to 500 years old and eight feet in diameter. While the U.S. Forest Service wrestles with the problem of how much of the forest to save, the harvesting of timber continues. The district office refuses to remove any of the old growth from timber production. The struggle is continuing at the national level with strong proponents on both sides.

41. The best title for this passage is
    (A) Ancient Forests of the Northwest
    (B) The US Forest Service
    (C) The Harvesting of Old-Growth Timber
    (D) The Wood-Based Economy of the Northwest

42. According to this passage, conservationists would agree that
    (A) old-growth trees are not necessary for the health of the forest
    (B) fallen trees should not be taken away
    (C) most of the old-growth trees do not need protection
    (D) young trees should not be logged

43. The struggle is between
    (A) Oregon and Washington
    (B) Oregon and the U.S. Forest Service
    (C) Conservationists and the logging industry
    (D) Conservationists and Oregon state

44. Before the 1800s
    (A) there were six million trees
    (B) old-growth was not cut down
    (C) the trees had more economic value
    (D) there were more virgin forests

45. Studies show that young trees gain nutrients from
    (A) wildlife
    (B) virgins
    (C) old trees
    (D) wood products

46. This passage implies that the economy of the Northwest is dependent on
    (A) the U.S. Forest Service
    (B) harvesting trees
    (C) ancient forests
    (D) the forest ecosystem

Questions 47–53

Like other Inuit artists in Canada, Saila Kipanek is now benefiting from a resurgence of interest in Indian and Inuit art. During the 1970s, there was such a rise in the sale of soapstone carvings and prints that the quality deteriorated. Then, in the 1980s, there was an economic slump in the industrial world. These two factors resulted in slow sales in the early 1980s. Now, however, there is a new enthusiasm for both Inuit and Indian art. There are more and more retail stores opening all the time. In the West Coast province of British Columbia there are some 2000 Indians making their living by producing arts and crafts. Both Indians and Inuit have far more artists per capita than does the non-native Canadian population. One reason for this is that both cultures had no written language before the arrival of white people. They expressed their culture and beliefs through carvings, drawings, and baskets. Art was a way of life. A second reason is economic. Indians have been selling their arts and crafts for hundreds of years, as early as the 17th century. Thirdly, art was an interesting occupation for the Inuit when the weather was too cold to leave the shelters. In the last years, the quality of Kipanek's work has improved dramatically. "It could go in any museum in the world," says an art dealer in Montréal.

47. In the early 1980s
    (A) more retail stores opened
    (B) there was renewed interest in Indian and Inuit art
    (C) the desire for Indian art decreased
    (D) the quality of art deteriorated

48. We can infer from this passage that
    (A) all Indians are artistic
    (B) Indians and Inuit have the same culture
    (C) Inuit live where it is cold
    (D) British Columbia has more Indian arts and crafts than other provinces

49. We can assume that the quality of Kipanek's art has improved because of
    (A) the rise in the sale of soapstone carvings
    (B) the resurgence of interest in art
    (C) the slow sales of the early 1980s
    (D) the economic slump

50. According to this author, "Inuit" refers to
    (A) a native Canadian
    (B) an Indian
    (C) a soapstone artist
    (D) a non-native Canadian

51. This passage implies that
    (A) white people came to Canada before the 17th century
    (B) Indians and Inuit came to Canada at the same time
    (C) Indians and Inuit lived in Canada before white people
    (D) white men taught Inuit and Indians how to speak

52. Both Inuit and Indians
    (A) have no written language
    (B) live in the snow
    (C) are non-native Canadians
    (D) have a history based on art

53. The best title for this passage is
    (A) New Interest in Indian and Inuit Art
    (B) The Rise and Fall of Inuit Art
    (C) Saila Kipanek's Art
    (D) Indian *vs.* Inuit Art

Questions 54–60

The excellence of ancient Chinese bronze casting has never been equaled. Though the earliest bronzes predated the Shang dynasty (1523 B.C.–1028 B.C.), general use in state worship rituals by the ruling elite became common early in that period. Towards the end of the Shang dynasty, bronze vessels were also used in private rituals. After that, and up to 220 A.D., bronze vessels were widely used as utensils for daily life.

The Chinese made bronzes by methods that differed greatly from those used in ancient Mesopotamia and Greece. Instead of cold-working the alloy to make the shapes and designs, they used a direct-casting process. In this process, clay molds were assembled around a clay core. The mold sections contained a negative image of the design which had been carved directly into the clay. To make the vessel, the hot molten alloy (a combination of tin and copper) was poured into the mold assembly and left to cool. The finished vessel required no more carving.

The decoration of the vessels developed through the years. Early designs had a narrow band of geometric designs, while later designs had complex patterns covering the entire vessel. Often the design included stylized dragons, birds, or snakes. Inscriptions of ancient script were also cast into vessels, with inlaid gold and silver adding contrasting color to the designs.

54. This passage mainly discusses the
    (A) excellence of Chinese bronze vessels
    (B) techniques of producing bronze
    (C) types of decorations on bronze vessels
    (D) time period of the use of bronze vessels

55. It can be inferred from this passage that
    (A) commoners shared in worship services with the elite
    (B) Chinese script was understood by most people
    (C) dragons, birds, and snakes were feared
    (D) the direct-casting process is superior to cold-working the alloy

56. The earliest bronzes were made
    (A) before 1523 B.C.
    (B) between 1523 B.C. and 1028 B.C.
    (C) just after 1028 B.C.
    (D) around 220 A.D.

57. Around 1500 B.C., bronze vessels were probably most commonly used
    (A) in private family rituals
    (B) for drinking wine
    (C) in official ceremonies
    (D) as common eating bowls

58. Which of the following was not used in design?
    (A) writing
    (B) landscapes
    (C) animals
    (D) precious metals

GO ON TO THE NEXT PAGE ➡

59. What must happen to all vessels before they are complete?
    (A) The gold and silver must be inlaid.
    (B) The negative image must be carved.
    (C) The alloy in the mold must have cooled.
    (D) The ancient inscriptures must be cast.

60. What does "band" mean in line 16?
    (A) a musical group
    (B) a picture of ancient instruments
    (C) a complete covering
    (D) a strip around the edge

THIS IS THE END OF SECTION 3.

If you finish before time is called, check your work on Section 3 only. Do not read or work on any other section of the test.

STOP   STOP   STOP   STOP   STOP   STOP

ANSWERS TO WORKBOOK EXERCISES

Exercise 1: Sample Testing Points, p. 11

1. Conditional
2. Negative
3. Superlative
4. Reference
5. Parallel Construction

Exercise 2: Discrimination between Similar-Sounding Words, p. 34

EXAMPLE: The speaker is talking about a day. (Thursday, not thirsty)
1. He left his job. (resigned, not signed)
2. The people working on the ship were nice. (crew, not cruise)
3. He didn't like the wet air. (fog, not frog)
4. The company gave money to the school. (funded, not founded)
5. They ate beef. (steak, not mistake)
6. It's not a good award. (prize, not price)
7. The speaker is talking about several people. (they, not he)
8. Where is the woman? (Sue, not zoo)
9. He answered fifty. (fifty, not fifteen)
10. Are you getting something clean? (washing, not watching)

Exercise 3: Synonyms, p. 36

These are sample answers. Other sentences are possible.

EXAMPLE: I don't like it.
1. I would prefer to stay home.
2. Tell me when you are ready.
3. You don't have to hurry.
4. The last day of school is next week.
5. I wouldn't do that without thinking carefully.
6. The children walked together in pairs.
7. The professor figured out an answer to our problem.
8. I know this town very well.
9. Don't exercise too much.
10. I can do this by myself.
11. The teacher emphasized that we must arrive early.
12. My mother doesn't smoke anymore.

13. We almost ran out of water, but we had just enough to do the washing.
14. You should see this show. You would appreciate it.
15. I would like to work now.

Exercise 4: Determining Testing Points, p. 38

A. 1. up-to-date = newest
   2. "due date" and "to date" "late" and "date"
   3. (A) This book has the newest information.

B. 1. "glanced" = "looked"
   2. "danced" sounds like "glanced" "threw" sounds like "through"
   3. (D) She looked at him.

C. 1. "overcook" = "cook too long"
   2. "put it" and "pudding"
   3. (C) Don't cook the pudding too long.

D. 1. "high rent" = "expensive"
   2. "I'd rather" and "is rather" "don't think" and "don't you think"
   3. The speaker thinks that the listener will agree that the high rent is too expensive for them to afford.

E. 1. a) "a record" = "a round disk used for playing music"
      b) "a record" = "the highest or farthest score or mark ever made"
      c) "broke the record" = "destroyed or cracked the sound disk"
      d) "broke the record" = "made a higher mark than has ever been done before"
   2. (A) He jumped higher than anyone else.

F. 1. "don't take" and "not to take" "more than" and "too much"
   2. "can't eat" sounds like "can eat"
   3. (D) Don't take too much.

G. 1. The thing that Jim did for me was so important to me that I will never forget it.

H. 1. (A) No one was home when the man knocked.
   2. It is implied that the delivery man knocked on the door, and that, since no one answered the door, no one was home.

Exercise 5: Word Groups, p. 42

1. at a bank
2. at a university graduation
3. at a dentist's office
4. at a concert or performance

5. at a wedding
6. at a pharmacy
7. at a laundry or dry cleaner's
8. at a beauty parlor
9. at a university
10. at a restaurant

Exercise 6: Word Categories, p. 42

at a bank: checking account, overdrawn, (credits), (quarter)
at a graduation: degree, cap and gown
at a wedding: honeymoon, toast
at a dentist's office: cavity
at a performance: curtain, clap
at a beauty parlor: curl, wave
at a drugstore: prescription
at a laundromat: spin dry
at a university: credits, lab, quarter, (degree)
at a restaurant: roquefort, (toast)

Exercise 7: Place and Speaker, p. 43

Other answers may also be correct.

	Place	Speaker
1.	college or university	student
2.	grocery store	shopper
3.	bank	customer
4.	college or university	person-in-charge or student
5.	restaurant	waitress
6.	business, school, or company	director, supervisor, worker, secretary
7.	airport, bus, or train terminal	person-in-charge, worker, friend
8.	doctor's office, university	secretary, friend
9.	courthouse	judge or other person in courthouse
10.	elementary school	teacher, office worker, principal

Exercise 8: Guess the Question, p. 44

1. The best choices are "The Poems of Walt Whitman" and "The Poems of Emily Dickinson." The other two answers are not good guesses because they are both plural, whereas the topic is singular: "an American poet."

2. The lecture must be about a female poet because of the pronoun, "she." "Emily" is a woman's name, while "Walt" is a man's name, so the answer must be "A" in question 1.

3. Any question for number 2 must ask why something happened. A possible question is, "What characterized Emily Dickinson's life during (some period)?" Many other questions are possible, as long as they can be answered by the answer choices in question 2.

4. Any question for number 4 must ask about when something happened. A possible question is, "When did Emily Dickinson (do something)?" Other questions are possible.

5. A likely question for number 5 is, "What will we do in the next class?" Other questions are possible.

Exercise 9: Guess the Answer, p. 46

1.   Question: Who is speaking?

Most likely choices: (A) Professor Smith
                      (B) A teaching assistant
        Answer: (B) A teaching assistant

2.   Question: At what point in the term is the speaker giving this talk?

Most likely choices: (A) At the beginning
        Answer: (A) At the beginning

3.   Question: What is the most important information given by the speaker?

Most likely choices: (A) To explain the grading procedures
                      (D) To teach important safety precautions
        Answer: (D) To teach important safety precautions

4.   Question: Which one of the following can be worn in the lab?

Most likely choices: (A) Loose scarves
                      (B) Open sandals
                      (C) Long necklaces
        Answer: (D) eyeglasses
(For the above question, it is difficult to guess the answer.)

5.   Question: What must the students do before the next class?

Most likely choices: (A) Wash their lab equipment
                      (C) Buy a notebook
                      (D) Put waste in the proper container
        Answer: (C) Buy a notebook

Exercise 10: Parallel Construction, p. 58

1. X. how to drive and how to pass the test
2. X. trade, banking, and commerce
3. X. writing essays and studying for exams
4. X. discuss major holidays as well as name famous heroes
5. OK. heroin and cocaine
6. X. journalist, novelist, and short story writer (writer of short stories)
7. X. fresh pineapple, coffee, and sugar cane
8. OK. moist, rich, tropical soil
9. OK. wet forests, desert-like areas, and even snow-covered mountains
10. X. not only gives you exercise, but also allows you to see the country-side as you ride (gives you the opportunity to see the country-side . . .) Other answers are possible if the verbs are both present.

Exercise 11: Nouns, Adjectives, Verbs, Adverbs, p. 61

1. the opportunity
2. can obstruct
3. the impact
4. nerve fibers
5. precisely opposed
6. an interesting place
7. the examination (the exam)
8. mass communications
9. requiring that
10. capable speakers

Exercise 12: Singular or Plural Nouns, p. 63

1. areas
2. condors, mountains
3. million
4. women
5. streets, highways, thousands
6. citizens, the right, officials
7. addition
8. manufacturers
9. problem
10. people

Exercise 13: Noun Clauses, p. 64

1. X. That she was crying last night was obvious to everyone. Subject and noun clause: that she was crying last night; verb: was
2. OK. Subject: I; verb: think; noun clause: that she is a good actress
3. X. I don't know whether he likes me. Subject: I; verb: do(n't) know; noun clause: whether he likes me.
4. X. I wonder where he buys this? Subject: I; verb: wonder; noun clause: where he buys this.
5. OK. Subject and noun clause: what she said; verb: surprised.
6. OK. Subject: officers; verb: say; noun clause: that computer crime is hard to detect.
7. OK. Subject and noun clause: exactly what an IQ test measures; verb: is.
8. OK. Subject and noun clause: how to cure the common cold; verb: is.
9. OK. Subject and noun clause: whether the government, private industry, or individuals themselves are responsible for diseases like cancer; verb: is.
10. X. Each political party must consider who the best candidate is for the coming years. Subject: party; verb: must consider; noun clause: who the best candidate is for the coming years.

Exercise 14: Preposition after an Adjective, p. 65

When I first came to the United States, I was surprised at how casually people relate to each other. I was also shocked at (or by) the informal way that people dress. I felt that sometimes people were being inconsiderate of each other.

Now that I have been in the U.S. for a while, I have grown accustomed to American life. Even though I am still very conscious of some unusual styles of behavior, I have adjusted to many new things. I realize that in the past I was too critical of American customs. Now I am satisfied with my life. I am interested in what I see, and enthusiastic about learning even more.

Exercise 15: Adjective or Adverb Clause, p. 67

1. OK. Subject: tea; verb: was; adjective clause: that you sent me from China.
2. X. The barber who cut your hair did a good job yesterday. Subject: barber; verb: did; adjective clause: who cut your hair.
3. OK. Subject: you; verb: recognize; adjective clause: who just came into the room.
4. X. The movies that played last weekend were good. Subject: movies; verb: were; adjective clause: that were playing last weekend.
5. OK. Subject: they; verb: shook; adverb clause: when the Soviet premier and the U.S. president left the summit meeting.
6. OK. Subject: he or she; verb: can get; adverb clause: as soon as a new student registers.
7. X. Orange trees grow well in Florida and California, where there is a lot of sun. Subject: trees; verb: grow; adjective clause: where there is a lot of sun.
8. X. I didn't like the vegetables that were soaked in oil. Subject: I; verb: did(n't) like; adjective clause: that were soaked in oil.
9. X. John Lennon was shot as he was walking into his apartment building. Subject: John Lennon; verb: was shot (passive); adverb clause: as he was walking into his apartment building.
10. X. Marriage, which is a legal contract, can also be seen as an economic institution. Subject: marriage; verb: can be seen (passive); adjective clause: which is a legal contract.

Exercise 16: Adjective or Adverb Phrases, p. 69

1. My English teacher, Mrs. Jones, canceled class today.
2. The winner of the contest, a good friend of mine, just gave me a big hug.
3. The President of the Philippines, Aquino, gave an excellent speech.
4. I was worried when Mr. Stevens, my school counselor, told me that I would have to get 550 on the TOEFL exam.
5. Before hand calculators were common, math students usually carried a slide rule, a type of calculating ruler.
6. By using a calculator, one can easily convert kilos to pounds and Celsius to Fahrenheit.
7. By studying fossil remains, paleontologists gain information about previous life forms.
8. The number of people contracting AIDS, a deadly virus disease, is escalating every year.

Exercise 17: Prepositional Phrase, p. 70

1. (of *electing*) (in the Constitution)
2. (of *banking*) (in New York City)
3. (under high *pressure*)
4. (of the water) (from a *depth*) (below the surface)
5. (on a system) (of *recycling* food and waste products) (for lengthy space flights)
6. (for the problem) (of water *pollution*)
7. (of *statistical* methods) (to business enterprises) (to some businesses) (in recent years)
8. (of *building* computer systems)

Exercise 18: Verbs, p. 71

1. lie, not "lay"
2. carries, not "have carried"
3. left, not "leaves"
4. were or are, not "to be"
5. can have, not "can be having"
6. needs, not "needed"
7. is, not "to be"
8. is added, not "added"

Exercise 19: Comparatives/Proportional Statements, p. 73

1. The harder I study, *the more tired* I become.
2. Doing research proves *more difficult* than I thought.
3. Pottery dishes painted by hand are *more beautiful* than the ones painted by machine.
4. The ocean off the Continental Shelf is *deeper* than the waters of the ocean close to the land.
5. The more you practice your skills, *the more capable* you become.
6. Medicines with a brand name are usually *more expensive* than generic medicines.
7. A doctor has had *more years of study* than a pharmacist.
8. Researchers say that the faster you read, *the better your comprehension.*

Exercise 20: Superlatives, p. 74

1. *The* busiest airport.
   Subject: airport; verb: is.
2. one of the *few* mammals
   Subject: giraffe; verb: is.
3. *the* biggest group
   Subject: Asians and Hispanics; verb: are.

4. *One* of the great differences
   Subject: One; verb: is.
5. most *usual* distinction
   Subject: distinction; verb: lies.
6. the *highest* peaks
   Subject: Himalayas; verb: have.
7. *The* highest possible score
   Subject: score; verb: is.
8. with *the* fewest errors
   Subject: answer sheets; verb: have.

Exercise 21: Word Order/Subject/Verb, p. 75

1. (A) a fresh snowflake has
2. (C) Mink is valued
3. (D) extends an invitation
4. (A) number of air traffic controllers
5. (D) one must fill out

Exercise 22: Finding the Main Subject and Verb, p. 78

1. (After the deadline), some campuses will accept applications if they
   ——————— DEPENDENT CLAUSE ———————
   still have openings (for new students).

2. If, (after submitting) your application, you wish to add more new in-
   —————————————— DEPENDENT CLAUSE ——————————————
   formation (to your record), you may mail it (in a separate envelope)
   (to the admissions office).

3. Most fall term applicants are notified (of their admission) (to the
   university) (by late spring).

4. If you are applying (as a foreign student), (you) arrange to take the Test
   ——————— DEPENDENT CLAUSE ———————
   (of English) [as a Foreign Language (TOEFL)], and if you are applying
   —————— DEPENDENT CLAUSE ——————
   (as a graduate student), you must also take the Graduate Record Examination (GRE).

```
        ┌────────── DEPENDENT CLAUSE ──────────┐   s        v
```
5. (At the time) you take these tests, you must ask the testing service to

send your scores directly (to the admissions office) (at each) (of the

campuses) (to which you are applying).

Exercise 23: Number Prefixes, p. 80

These are possible answers. There are many others.

1. unify
2. bicycle
3. triangle
4. quarter
5. Pentagon
6. decimal
7. century
8. polygon

Exercise 24: Negative Prefixes, p. 81

Prefix	Meaning
1. *il*	not legal; against the law
2. *im*	not mature; acting young
3. *in*	not correct; wrong
4. *ir*	not regular; not the same
5. *un*	not attached; loose
6. *anti*	against war
7. *dis*	not obey
8. *mis*	spell wrong

Exercise 25: Relationship Prefixes, p. 81

1. to prepay—to pay before you buy; to pay early
2. a postscript—something written after the main message
3. intermittent rain—rain off and on, in between sun or clouds
4. a surtax—an extra tax on something already taxed
5. a subgroup—a group of a smaller classification
6. a perimeter—the distance around something
7. to synchronize—to happen at the same time
8. a coworker—a working partner

Exercise 26: Noun Suffixes, p. 82

1. intelligence
2. information
3. shyness
4. vanity
5. ablity
6. kindness
7. regulation
8. impression

Exercise 27: Adjective Suffixes, p. 83

1. childish
2. athletic
3. dirty
4. natural
5. explosive
6. mysterious
7. volcanic
8. bumpy

Exercise 28: "Person" Suffixes, p. 83

	Suffix	A person who:
1.	er	purchases
2.	ist	sells flowers
3.	ier	takes in money or gives change in a store
4.	cian	fixes hair
5.	or	supervises
6.	ist	types
7.	er	prepares computer programs
8.	cian	supervises and directs funeral procedures

Exercise 29: Root Words, p. 84

	Root	Meaning of Root
1.	cycle	circle, wheel
2.	dent, dont	tooth
3.	psych	mind
4.	script	write
5.	pend	hanging down or closely connected
6.	phon	hear
7.	manu	hand
8.	scope	instrument for seeing

Exercise 30: Guessing New Words, p. 86

Clue Words	Meaning
1. even though . . . smooth and clear	shaken or stirred, foamy
2. although . . . didn't believe	probably true
3. even though . . . stayed dry	flooded
4. concern for others	unselfish love
5. openness and truthful	truth, sincerity
6. victims . . . given money back	take money falsely, cheat
7. barely enough income	increase
8. out of our warm beds	made to get out

Exercise 31: Topic Sentences, p. 88

1.   Word Clues: not only . . . but . . . as well; also
    Organization: Additional Information
    Topic Sentence: A new discovery of a dinosaur fossil in Antarctica has confirmed the idea that dinosaurs lived not only in the Northern Hemisphere but in the Southern Hemisphere as well.
2.   Word Clues: another; all
    Organization: Description
    Topic Sentence: Though hurricanes, typhoons, and cyclones all occur during different times of the year and in different areas, they are all identical.
3.   Word Clues: however, is not . . . but
    Organization: Contradiction
    Topic Sentence: The best treatment, however, is not slow rewarming but rapid rewarming.

Exercise 32: Inferences and Restatements, p. 90

A.		B.		C.	
1.	R	1.	F	1.	NG
2.	F	2.	R	2.	R
3.	NG	3.	R	3.	I
4.	I	4.	I	4.	I
5.	NG	5.	NG	5.	R
6.	R	6.	I	6.	I

PRACTICE TEST 1—ANSWER KEY

Listening Comprehension, Part A

1. A	5. C	9. A	13. B	17. B
2. D	6. D	10. C	14. A	18. D
3. B	7. B	11. A	15. D	19. C
4. C	8. A	12. D	16. A	20. D

Listening Comprehension, Part B

21. A	24. B	27. A	30. D	33. D
22. B	25. D	28. D	31. A	34. A
23. C	26. B	29. D	32. C	35. C

Listening Comprehension, Part C

36. B	39. A	42. B	45. A	48. C
37. A	40. C	43. D	46. C	49. B
38. C	41. C	44. D	47. D	50. D

Structure and Written Expression

1. B	9. A	17. D	25. D	33. C
2. C	10. A	18. B	26. B	34. C
3. C	11. C	19. C	27. D	35. B
4. C	12. A	20. C	28. D	36. B
5. A	13. D	21. C	29. A	37. C
6. D	14. C	22. C	30. B	38. A
7. A	15. A	23. A	31. B	39. D
8. D	16. B	24. B	32. A	40. B

Vocabulary and Reading Comprehension

1. D	13. A	25. D	37. D	49. C
2. B	14. D	26. C	38. B	50. B
3. A	15. A	27. A	39. D	51. A
4. A	16. D	28. D	40. B	52. B
5. D	17. D	29. A	41. B	53. A
6. A	18. A	30. C	42. D	54. C
7. C	19. B	31. B	43. C	55. B
8. A	20. D	32. D	44. B	56. D
9. D	21. B	33. C	45. C	57. A
10. C	22. C	34. A	46. D	58. B
11. B	23. D	35. A	47. A	59. C
12. D	24. A	36. C	48. D	60. D

PRACTICE TEST 2—ANSWER KEY

Listening Comprehension, Part A

1. C	5. C	9. B	13. C	17. A
2. C	6. D	10. C	14. A	18. B
3. B	7. A	11. B	15. C	19. C
4. D	8. D	12. A	16. D	20. A

Listening Comprehension, Part B

21. D	24. D	27. C	30. B	33. B
22. A	25. C	28. D	31. D	34. B
23. B	26. B	29. A	32. A	35. D

Listening Comprehension, Part C

36. B	39. D	42. A	45. C	48. C
37. B	40. C	43. C	46. D	49. D
38. B	41. C	44. A	47. C	50. C

Structure and Written Expression

1. A	9. B	17. C	25. C	33. B
2. D	10. D	18. C	26. A	34. A
3. C	11. B	19. D	27. A	35. B
4. B	12. A	20. D	28. B	36. C
5. B	13. C	21. D	29. D	37. B
6. A	14. D	22. B	30. A	38. C
7. D	15. C	23. C	31. D	39. B
8. C	16. A	24. A	32. A	40. A

Vocabulary and Reading Comprehension

1. A	13. A	25. B	37. D	49. B
2. B	14. D	26. B	38. C	50. A
3. D	15. C	27. C	39. A	51. C
4. D	16. D	28. D	40. B	52. D
5. A	17. B	29. C	41. C	53. A
6. C	18. A	30. A	42. B	54. A
7. D	19. D	31. D	43. C	55. D
8. A	20. D	32. B	44. D	56. A
9. C	21. B	33. A	45. C	57. C
10. B	22. A	34. B	46. B	58. B
11. A	23. C	35. C	47. C	59. C
12. C	24. C	36. C	48. C	60. D

SECTION 1: LISTENING COMPREHENSION

General Guidelines: The following explanatory answers for the Listening Comprehension section of the TOEFL explain a process of looking at each question as a whole. They do not go through each answer separately. This is because the skills needed for answering questions from a tape recording are different from the skills needed for reading.

When you hear a conversation or a discussion, your brain understands the message as a whole, rather than hearing each individual word. This is good. This is your goal in listening comprehension. You want to learn to summarize the whole message. In fact, the hardest part of the listening test is not usually the vocabulary or the grammar, even though those may be the testing points. The hardest part is comprehending the whole message quickly. TOEFL students who have a study book and a tapescript to read can often figure out the correct answers if they have enough time. The difficulty with the listening tape is that there isn't much time. You hear the tape only once, and you have only a few seconds to choose the correct answer.

Because time is important in the listening test, you must learn to summarize the questions and find the answers quickly. Therefore, you must practice a thinking process that saves you time. The steps on the next few pages may seem long. You may look at them and say to yourself, "I don't have time to do all that." But, in fact, your brain works very quickly. You do have time, and the more you practice this thinking process, the quicker you will get at it. Practice these steps as you might practice the scales on a piano, or the kicking of a soccer ball. As you practice, you will be able to go through the steps more quickly.

This section presents five steps for figuring out the answers to the listening questions on the tape:

FIRST: BEFORE YOU HEAR THE TAPE

STEP 1: Briefly read the answer choices and look for similarities and differences in the words.

STEP 2: Make a guess about the topic and the possible testing points.

NEXT: FOCUS ON LISTENING TO THE TAPE

STEP 3: Summarize the question.

STEP 4: Determine the testing point (usually structure, vocabulary, or listening discrimination).

STEP 5: Choose and mark the answer.

A you practice the steps that are outlined here, you may develop a process that is more meaningful to you. Good! Then you can use your own process. These steps provide you with a guide to follow. If you create a process that is quicker and more reliable for you, then you should follow your own system.

The steps to follow are outlined for each question in the practice tests. Below are the explanations of each step.

STEP 1: *Similar/different*—Briefly look at the answer choices. You don't need to read every word; in fact, you don't have time for that. You are just looking for similar words, opposites, or differences that are quick to see. Let your eyes go across the lines first ⟶ . Then let your eyes go down the answer choices:

STEP 2: *Listening attention*—After you have noted similarities or differences, you can make a guess about what to focus on. You may be able to guess the topic, or you may guess possible questions. Focus your attention on the topic.

STEP 3: *Summarize*—After hearing the statement or conversation, think about what it means to you. What is the main idea?

STEP 4: *Testing point*—What particular structures or vocabulary words are you being asked about?

STEP 5: *Answer*—Choose the best answer and mark your answer sheet.

Part A: Steps to the Answers

> ### N O T E
>
> The answer choices are given before the tapescript in order to help you practice the process of looking at the answer choices first.

Steps to the Answers

1. Before you hear the tape, read: ⟶

STEP 1 — Similar/Different

 Similar: I want
     I like
     I hope
     I prefer
 Different: early
      late

STEP 2 — Listening Attention:

Speaker will probably talk about "early" and "late."

Focus on the tape ⟶

STEP 3 — Summarize:

I want to be early.

STEP 4 — Testing Point:
Structure:
 I'd rather . . . than . . .
 "I'd rather" = "prefer"
 "prefer" = "want"

STEP 5 — Choose answer (A) ⟶ ● Ⓑ Ⓒ Ⓓ

Answers B, C, and D all give the meaning of wanting to be late.

Answer Choices and Tapescript

(A) I want to go early.
(B) I like to be late.
(C) I hope you won't be
  early.
(D) I prefer to be late.

> I'd rather go early than late.

2. Before you hear the tape, read: ⟶ (A) I want to go less than you.

STEP 1 — Similar/Different:

(B) I'll go if you can't go.
(C) I won't go even if you go.
(D) I'll go if you go.

    I . . . go
    I . . . go . . . if
    I . . . not . . . go . . . if
    I . . . go . . . if

STEP 2 — Listening Attention:

    probably about going or not going;
      maybe a conditional idea

Focus on the tape ⟶ | Unless you go to the party, I won't go.

STEP 3 — Summarize:

    If you don't go to the party with me,
      I won't go.

STEP 4 — Testing Point:
Structure:
    "unless" = "if . . . not"

STEP 5 — Choose answer (D) ⟶ Ⓐ Ⓑ Ⓒ ●

    Don't be confused by the similar sounds
      of "less" and "unless."

3. Before you hear the tape, read: ⟶ (A) It's raining.
(B) It's likely to rain.
(C) It looks wet.
(D) It likes rain.

STEP 1 — Similar/Different:

    It's raining
    It's . . . rain
    It . . . wet
    It . . . rain

STEP 2 — Listening Attention:

    topic: rain

Focus on the tape ⟶ | It looks like rain.

STEP 3 — Summarize:

    It's going to rain.

STEP 4 — Testing Point:
Vocabulary:
   "looks like" = "might"
   or "likely to"

STEP 5 — Choose answer (B) ———————▶ Ⓐ ● Ⓒ Ⓓ

   Don't be fooled by the individual
      meanings of "look" and "like."

4. **Before you hear the tape, read:** ——▶ (A) I had an argument
                                              with my old friend
STEP 1 — Similar/Different: yesterday.
                                          (B) I passed my friend in
   I . . . argument   town.
   I passed   (C) I met my friend in
   I met   town by accident.
   I and friend . . . accident   (D) My friend and I had
                                              an accident yesterday.
STEP 2 — Listening Attention:

   "I" or "I and friend" — which verb?

Focus on the tape ————————————▶ | I ran into my old
                                         | friend in town
STEP 3 — Summarize: | yesterday.

   I saw my friend.

STEP 4 — Testing Point:
Vocabulary/idiom:
   "ran into" = "saw" or
   "met by chance"

STEP 5 — Choose answer (C) ——————▶ Ⓐ Ⓑ ● Ⓓ

   "To run into" can also mean "to have
      an accident." You run into an object.
      You run over a person or animal. "By
      accident" = "by chance."

5. **Before you hear the tape, read:** ——▶ (A) Ann is skeptical about
                                              new things.
STEP 1 — Similar/Different: (B) Both Ann and her
                                              brother are interested
   Ann   in new things.
   Both Ann and

Ann
Neither Ann nor

STEP 2 — Listening Attention:

"Ann" or "Ann and"

Focus on the tape ─────────────▶

STEP 3 — Summarize:

Ann is open-minded; her brother is not.

STEP 4 — Testing Point:
Structure:
unlike . . . Ann is . . .
Vocabulary:
"unlike " = "different"
"open-minded" =
"interested in new things"

STEP 5 — Choose answer (C) ─────▶ Ⓐ Ⓑ ● Ⓓ

6. **Before you hear the tape, read:** ─────▶

STEP 1 — Similar/Different:

I'd . . . after class
Let's . . . after class
Let . . . about the class

STEP 2 — Listening Attention:

when? what verb?

Focus on the tape ─────────────▶

STEP 3 — Summarize:

Come in so I can tell you about
the class.

STEP 4 — Testing Point:
Vocabulary/idiom:
"a run-down" =
"give brief information"

(C) Ann likes to try new
things but her brother
does not.
(D) Neither Ann nor her
brother are skeptical.

> Unlike her brother,
> Ann is open-minded.

(A) I'd like to go running
with you after class.
(B) Please run down to
the class for me.
(C) Let's meet after class.
(D) Let me tell you about
the class.

> Come in a minute so
> I can give you a run-
> down on the class.

STEP 5 — Choose answer (D) ———————➤ Ⓐ Ⓑ Ⓒ ●

> Don't be confused by the similar sounds of "run-down" and "running," and the verb "to run."

---

7. Before you hear the tape, read: ———➤

(A) She missed one class this semester.
(B) She hasn't missed any classes this semester.
(C) She's missed only a few classes this semester.
(D) She's missed many classes this semester.

STEP 1 — Similar/Different:

> She . . . missed . . .
> She . . . not . . . missed
> She . . . missed
> She . . . missed

STEP 2 — Listening Attention:

> "missed" or "not missed"

Focus on the tape ————————————➤

> Not once has she missed class this semester!

STEP 3 — Summarize:

> She hasn't missed a class once.

STEP 4 — Testing Point:
Structure:
> not once = never

STEP 5 — Choose answer (B) ———————➤ Ⓐ ● Ⓒ Ⓓ

---

8. Before you hear the tape, read: ———➤

(A) Bill forgot to pay the bill, and the phone is not working.
(B) Bill paid the bill on time, but the phone is still not working.
(C) Bill forgot the phone was not working when he paid the bill.
(D) Bill forgot to connect the phone before he paid the bill.

STEP 1 — Similar/Different:

> Bill . . . forgot
> Bill . . . paid
> Bill . . . forgot
> Bill . . . forgot

STEP 2 — Listening Attention:

> Bill forgot what?
> Bill paid what?

Focus on the tape ——————————►

> The telephone is disconnected; Bill must have forgotten to pay the bill.

STEP 3 — Summarize:

The telephone doesn't work because Bill didn't pay the bill.

STEP 4 — Testing Points:
Vocabulary:
"disconnected" = "not working"
Structure:
must have forgotten

STEP 5 — Choose answer (A) ——————————► ● ⒝ ⒞ ⒟

Don't be confused by "a bill" and "Bill."

9. Before you hear the tape, read: ——————►

(A) She's keeping a secret.
(B) She doesn't want to tell anyone about the accident to her nose.
(C) She doesn't know anything.
(D) She doesn't like to talk about her ideas.

STEP 1 — Similar/Different:

She is keeping
She doesn't want
She doesn't know
She doesn't like

STEP 2 — Listening Attention:

What verb?

Focus on the tape ——————————►

> Whatever she knows, she's not telling anyone.

STEP 3 — Summarize:

If she knows anything, she is not telling.

STEP 4 — Testing Point:
Vocabulary:
"whatever = anything"

STEP 5 — Choose answer (A) ——————————► ● ⒝ ⒞ ⒟

Don't be fooled by "knows" and "nose." "Keeping a secret" means that she doesn't want to tell. The meaning is different from "doesn't like to talk."

10. Before you hear the tape, read: ➡

STEP 1 — Similar/Different:

a long time
a long time
worth the time
in time

STEP 2 — Listening Attention:

What verb?
What noun?

Focus on the tape ➡

STEP 3 — Summarize:

It will take a long time to finish, but it's good for you to do.

STEP 4 — Testing Point:
Vocabulary/idiom:
"in the long run" = "eventually"
"to be worth it" = "you will be pleased"

STEP 5 — Choose answer (C) ➡   Ⓐ Ⓑ ● Ⓓ

Don't be confused by "to run" and "in the long run," or "worth" and "worse."

(A) It takes a long time to run.
(B) It's worth it to run a long time in training.
(C) Your work will be worth the time eventually.
(D) An old well gets worse in time.

It takes a long time, but in the long run, it's well worth it.

11. Before you hear the tape, read: ➡

STEP 1 — Similar/Different:

The . . . is
The . . . is
The . . . is
There is

(A) The information is old.
(B) The tape is sold out.
(C) The quality is poor.
(D) There is no date on the tape.

STEP 2— Listening Attention:

> What noun?
> What adjective?

Focus on the tape ⟶

> This tape is out-of-date.

STEP 3— Summarize:

> The tape is not new (not a new date).

STEP 4— Testing Point:
Vocabulary:
> "out of date" = "old"

STEP 5— Choose answer (A) ⟶ ● Ⓑ Ⓒ Ⓓ

12. Before you hear the tape, read: ⟶

(A) It seems cheap to buy a car.

(B) Cheap cars do not run well.

(C) It's convenient to have a car.

(D) It's expensive to have a car.

STEP 1— Similar/Different:

> It's . . . cheap . . . car
> Cheap car . . .
> It's . . . convenient . . . car
> It's . . . expensive . . . car

STEP 2— Listening Attention:

> Listen for adjective

Focus on the tape ⟶

> Having a car is by no means cheap.

STEP 3— Summarize:

> It's not cheap to have a car.

STEP 4— Testing Point:
Vocabulary:
> "by no means" = "not"

STEP 5— Choose answer (D) ⟶ Ⓐ Ⓑ Ⓒ ●

13. **Before you hear the tape, read:** ➤ (A) He isn't growing anymore.

STEP 1 — Similar/Different:

   He . . . not growing
   He . . . younger
   He . . . short
   He . . . 18

(B) He seems younger than eighteen.
(C) He is short for his age.
(D) He is almost eighteen.

STEP 2 — Listening Attention:

   Listen for adjective

Focus on the tape ━━━━━━━━━➤

> Although he's eighteen, he doesn't act very grown-up.

STEP 3 — Summarize:

   He doesn't act like he is eighteen.

STEP 4 — Testing Points:
Structure: Contrast
   although . . . is not
Vocabulary:
   "grown-up" = "adult"

STEP 5 — Choose answer (B) ━━━━━➤ Ⓐ ● Ⓒ Ⓓ

   Don't be confused by "grown" and
     "growing."

14. **Before you hear the tape, read:** ➤ (A) Randy thinks pizza is better than tacos.

STEP 1 — Similar/Different:

   Randy . . . pizza better
   Randy . . . tacos more than
   Randy . . . piece of taco
   Randy . . . about pizza

(B) Randy likes tacos more than pizza.
(C) Randy would like a piece of taco.
(D) Randy likes to talk about pizza.

STEP 2 — Listening Attention:

   Topic is food —
   pizza vs. tacos

Focus on the tape ━━━━━━━━━➤

> Randy prefers pizza to tacos.

STEP 3 — Summarize:

Randy likes pizza more than tacos.

STEP 4 — Testing Points:
Vocabulary:
   "pizza" and "tacos" = "things to eat"
Structure:
Comparison: prefer X to X
   "prefer" = "to think X is better than Y"

STEP 5 — Choose answer (A) ——————▶ ● Ⓑ Ⓒ Ⓓ

15. Before you hear the tape, read: ——▶ (A) Jim is used to
                                                    smoking.
STEP 1 — Similar/Different: (B) Jim likes to smoke
                                                    when it's hot.
   Jim . . . smoking   (C) Jim does not smoke
   Jim . . . smoke   anymore.
   Jim . . . not smoke   (D) Jim smoked more
   Jim . . . smoked   before.

STEP 2 — Listening Attention:

   Tense: When smoke?

Focus on the tape ————————————————▶ | Jim used to smoke a lot more. |

STEP 3 — Summarize:

   In the past, Jim smoked more than he
   does now.

STEP 4 — Testing Point:
Structure:
   . . . used to . . . .

STEP 5 — Choose answer (D) ——————▶ Ⓐ Ⓑ Ⓒ ●

   Learn the difference between "to be
   used to" + verb + ing and "used to"
   + verb: I am used to smoking. I used
   to smoke.

16. Before you hear the tape, read: ➡️

(A) Exercising can reduce depression.
(B) Exercise can cause depression.
(C) Depression helps you exercise better.
(D) Depression can remind you to exercise.

STEP 1 — Similar/Different:

Exercising . . . depression
Exercise . . . depression
Depression . . . exercise
Depression . . . exercise

STEP 2 — Listening Attention:

What verb?
What causes what?

Focus on the tape ➡️

Exercise is a good remedy for depression.

STEP 3 — Summarize:

Exercise will help cure depression.

STEP 4 — Testing Point:
Vocabulary:
"a remedy" = "a cure"

STEP 5 — Choose answer (A) ➡️ ● Ⓑ Ⓒ Ⓓ

17. Before you hear the tape, read: ➡️

(A) They are different books, but they look alike.
(B) The covers are different.
(C) They cover different material.
(D) Some of the books have soft covers.

STEP 1 — Similar/Different:

They . . . different
The covers . . . different
They cover . . . different
Some . . . covers

STEP 2 — Listening Attention:

What is different?
a cover (noun)
to cover (verb)

Focus on the tape ➡️

They are the same books except for their covers.

STEP 3 — Summarize:

The books are the same, but they have different covers.

STEP 4 — Testing Point:
Structure:
  "covers" used as a noun

STEP 5 — Choose answer (B) ——————▶   Ⓐ ● Ⓒ Ⓓ

18. Before you hear the tape, read: ——▶ (A) Mary asked the
                                                    salesman to be
STEP 1 — Similar/Different: present.
                                                (B) Mary presented the
  Mary . . . the salesman   wrapping.
  Mary   (C) The salesman dropped
  The salesman   the present.
  The salesman   (D) The salesman put
                                                    paper around the
STEP 2 — Listening Attention: present.

  Relationship between Mary and the
    salesman
  Who did what?

Focus on the tape ———————————————▶

> Mary had the
> salesman wrap the
> present.

STEP 3 — Summarize:

  Mary asked the salesman to wrap up
    the present.

STEP 4 — Testing Points:
Vocabulary:
  "to wrap" = "to put paper around"
  "a present" = "a gift"
Structure:
  had . . . do something

STEP 5 — Choose answer (D) ——————▶   Ⓐ Ⓑ Ⓒ ●

Don't be confused by the different
    meanings of:
  "to be present" = "here"
  "to present" = "to give"
  "a present" = "a gift"

19. Before you hear the tape, read: ➝ (A) I am really hungry!
(B) I have never been
hungry!
(C) I am very angry!
(D) I'm never angry!

STEP 1 — Similar/Different:

I . . . hungry
I . . . never . . . hungry
I . . . angry
I . . . never . . . angry

STEP 2 — Listening Attention:

angry or hungry

Focus on the tape ————————➝

> Never have I been so angry!

STEP 3 — Summarize:

I have never been as mad as I am now!

STEP 4 — Testing Points:
Structure:
  "Never have I been . . . " =
  "I have never been . . . "
Structure:
  "so" can be comparison
  "so angry" = "as angry as"
Pronunciation:
  hungry vs. angry

STEP 5 — Choose answer (C) ————————➝ Ⓐ Ⓑ ● Ⓓ

20. Before you hear the tape, read: ➝ (A) Jenny is younger than
Jane.
(B) Jane is smaller than
Jenny.
(C) Jane is older than
Jenny.
(D) Jane is bigger than
Jenny.

STEP 1 — Similar/Different:

Jenny is . . . than Jane
Jane is . . . than Jenny
Jane is . . . than Jenny
Jane is . . . than Jenny

STEP 2 — Listening Attention:

Comparison/Adjective
name

Focus on the tape ————————————▶ | Jenny is smaller than her younger sister, Jane. |

STEP 3 — Summarize:

   Jenny is smaller even though Jane is
      younger.

STEP 4 — Testing Point:
Structure:
Comparison: is . . . -er than

STEP 5 — Choose answer (D) ————————▶ Ⓐ Ⓑ Ⓒ ●

   You must convert to the opposite: if
      Jenny is smaller, then Jane is bigger.

Part B: Steps to the Answers

N O T E

In the following section, the answer choices are written
before the tapescript. This is to help you with the process
of looking at the answers before hearing the tape.

Steps to the Answers

*Answer Choices and
Tapescript*

21. Before you hear the tape, read: ——▶ (A) She has to do some
                                                   work.

STEP 1 — Similar/Different: (B) She went last week.
                                               (C) She wants to catch
   She has   some fish.
   She went   (D) She works at the
   She wants   beach.
   She works

STEP 2 — Listening Attention:

What verb?
Doing what?

Focus on the tape ——————————————————▶

> MAN: Can you go to the beach with me tomorrow?
>
> WOMAN: I wish I could, but I have to catch up on last week's work.
>
> What does the woman mean?

STEP 3 — Summarize:

I can't go to the beach because I have work to do.

STEP 4 — Testing Points:

Structure:
"I wish I could" = "I can't."
Vocabulary:
"to catch up on" = "to do the work you should have done earlier"

STEP 5 — Choose answer (A) ——————————▶ ● Ⓑ Ⓒ Ⓓ

22. Before you hear the tape, read: ——▶

(A) He wishes the professor would talk more.
(B) He doesn't always understand the professor.
(C) He thinks the professor has an accent.
(D) He thinks the professor talks too quietly.

STEP 1 — Similar/Different:

He wishes . . . professor
He doesn't understand . . . professor
He thinks . . . professor
He thinks . . . professor

STEP 2 — Listening Attention:

What verb?

Focus on the tape ——————————————————▶

> WOMAN: How's your class going?
>
> MAN: Terrible! It seems like the more the professor talks, the less I understand.
>
> How does the man feel about the class?

STEP 3 — Summarize:

When the professor talks a lot, I don't understand him.

STEP 4 — Testing Point:

Structure:
"the more . . . the less"

STEP 5 — Choose answer (B) ⟶ Ⓐ ● Ⓒ Ⓓ

23. Before you hear the tape, read:

STEP 1 — Similar/Different:

She . . . pay bill
She . . . Bill pay
She . . . pay meal
She . . . man pay

STEP 2 — Listening Attention:

Who pays?
Pay what?

Focus on the tape ⟶

> MAN: Shall we eat lunch out today?
>
> WOMAN: Only if we split the bill.
>
> What does the woman want to do?

(A) She wants to pay the bill.
(B) She wants Bill to pay for the meal.
(C) She wants to pay for her meal.
(D) She wants the man to pay.

STEP 3 — Summarize:

I want to pay half of the bill.

STEP 4 — Testing Point:
Vocabulary:
"to split the bill" = "to divide the cost"

STEP 5 — Choose answer (C) ⟶ Ⓐ Ⓑ ● Ⓓ

Don't be confused by "Bill" (a name) and "a bill" (money you pay for a service).

24. Before you hear the tape, read:

STEP 1 — Similar/Different:

He

STEP 2 — Listening Attention:

Verb

(A) He has sour fruit.
(B) He doesn't feel good.
(C) He sold some thread.
(D) He hates Vitamin C.

Focus on the tape ———————▶

> MAN: I have a sore throat.
>
> WOMAN: You'd better take some Vitamin C.
>
> What does the man mean?

STEP 3 — Summarize:

You should take some Vitamin C for your sore throat.

STEP 4 — Testing Points:

Structure:
   "you'd better" = "you should"
Vocabulary:
   "sore throat" = "a little sick; to hurt when swallowing"

STEP 5 — Choose answer (B) ————▶ Ⓐ ● Ⓒ Ⓓ

Don't be confused by the sounds of "sore," "sour," and "sold" or "throat" and "thread."

25. Before you hear the tape, read: ——▶

(A) She has had a nice day.
(B) She is sick.
(C) The daylight hours are long.
(D) She is tired.

STEP 1 — Similar/Different:

She
She
. . .
She

STEP 2 — Listening Attention:

Verb

Focus on the tape ———————————▶

> MAN: Hi, Mary. How're you doing?
>
> WOMAN: Oh, it's been a long day!
>
> What does the woman mean?

STEP 3 — Summarize:

Mary feels like the day has been long.

STEP 4— Testing Point:

Vocabulary/idiom:
"It's been a long day" = "I'm tired."

STEP 5— Choose answer (D) ————▶ Ⓐ Ⓑ Ⓒ ●

26. Before you hear the tape, read:

(A) Mail a check for her.
(B) Pick up her mail.
(C) Put a check in his mailbox.
(D) Take a check from her mailbox.

STEP 1— Similar/Different:

mail . . . check
mail
check . . . mailbox
check . . . mailbox

STEP 2— Listening Attention:

Relationship between "check" and "mail"

Focus on the tape ————————▶

> WOMAN: Jack, would you please check my mailbox while I'm gone?
>
> MAN: Sure, no problem.
>
> What does the woman want Jack to do?

STEP 3— Summarize:

Would you look in my mailbox to see if I have any mail?

STEP 4— Testing Point:

Vocabulary:
"to check the mail" = "to see if there are any letters in the mailbox" (Im plied meaning: If there is any mail, please pick it up for me.)

STEP 5— Choose answer (B) ————▶ Ⓐ ● Ⓒ Ⓓ

Don't be confused by the verb "to check" and the noun "a check."

27. Before you hear the tape, read: ———▶

STEP 1 — Similar/Different:

She'll take
She'll take
She won't take
She won't take

STEP 2 — Listening Attention:

Will she or won't she?

Focus on the tape ————————————▶

STEP 3 — Summarize:

I like it, so I want to take it.

STEP 4 — Testing Point:

Structure:
conditional
contradiction

STEP 5 — Choose answer (A) ————————▶ ● Ⓑ Ⓒ Ⓓ

The answer is implied in this conversation. The woman does not say that
she will take it; but the implication is
that because she likes it, she will take
it. It is the opposite of the man's
statement.

(A) She'll take it because
she likes it.
(B) She'll take it even
though she doesn't like
it.
(C) She won't take it
because she doesn't
like it.
(D) She won't take it even
though she likes it.

MAN: If you don't
like it, you don't
have to take it.

WOMAN: Thanks,
but I like it.

What will the woman
do?

---

28. Before you hear the tape, read: ———▶

STEP 1 — Similar/Different:

She

STEP 2 — Listening Attention:

Verb

(A) She does not like it.
(B) She is going to dive.
(C) She is afraid to diet.
(D) She wants to lose
weight.

Focus on the tape ───────────►

STEP 3 — Summarize:

  She doesn't want any cake because she is too fat.

STEP 4 — Testing Point:

Vocabulary:
  "to be on a diet" = "to eat special foods in order to lose weight"

> MAN: Would you like to have a piece of cake?
>
> WOMAN: No, thanks. I'm on a diet.
>
> What does the woman mean?

STEP 5 — Choose answer (D) ──────► Ⓐ Ⓑ Ⓒ ●

---

29. Before you hear the tape, read: ──────►

STEP 1 — Similar/Different:

  In a

STEP 2 — Listening Attention:

  Where?

(A) In a dressing room
(B) In a bedroom
(C) In a department store
(D) In a restaurant

Focus on the tape ───────────►

STEP 3 — Summarize:

  I would like Italian dressing on my salad.

STEP 4 — Testing Point:

Vocabulary:
  "dressing" = "salad dressing"; a sauce put over salads

> WOMAN: What kind of dressing would you like?
>
> MAN: Italian, please.
>
> Where does this conversation probably take place?

STEP 5 — Choose answer (D) ──────► Ⓐ Ⓑ Ⓒ ●

  Don't be confused by the different meanings of "dress":
  "to dress" = "to put clothes on"
  "to dress a salad" = "to put sauce on"
  "a dressing room" = "a place to dress"

30. Before you hear the tape, read: ——▶

STEP 1 — Similar/Different:

computer
computer
computer
classes

STEP 2 — Listening Attention:

Computer or classes?

Focus on the tape ——————————————▶

STEP 3 — Summarize:

I don't know which course to take, and
I must decide by tomorrow.

STEP 4 — Testing Points:

Vocabulary:
"deadline" = "the last day for finishing
something"
Structure:
"but" introduces a contrasting idea

STEP 5 — Choose answer (D) ——————▶ Ⓐ Ⓑ Ⓒ ●

"Computer registration" means
registration by computer, not
registration for computers.

(A) Having a computer
registered
(B) Deciding on a com-
puter course
(C) Buying a computer
tomorrow
(D) Registering for classes
tomorrow.

> WOMAN: The
> deadline for com-
> puter registration is
> tomorrow.
>
> MAN: But I haven't
> decided which course
> to take yet.
>
> What are they talking
> about?

31. Before you hear the tape, read: ——▶

STEP 1 — Similar/Different:

He . . . a call . . . Lisa
He . . . a call . . . Lisa
He . . . Lisa
He . . . a call . . . Lisa

STEP 2 — Listening Attention:

What verb?

(A) He will pay for a call
from Lisa.
(B) He will make a call to
Lisa.
(C) He is collecting money
for Lisa.
(D) He is correcting a call
from Lisa.

Focus on the tape: ━━━━━━━▶

STEP 3 — Summarize:

   I agree to pay for the phone call that
   Lisa is making to me.

STEP 4 — Testing Point:

Vocabulary/cultural:
   "a collect call" = "a phone call for
   which the receiver pays instead of the
   caller"
   "accept a collect call" = "to agree to
   pay for a phone call from someone"

STEP 5 — Choose answer (A) ━━━━━━━▶ ● Ⓑ Ⓒ Ⓓ

   Don't be confused by the similar sounds
   of "collect" and "correct."

WOMAN: Will you accept a collect call from Lisa?
MAN: Yes, I will.
What will the man do?

   32. Before you hear the tape, read: ━━▶ (A) Life insurance
                                               (B) Health insurance
STEP 1 — Similar/Different: (C) Car insurance
                                               (D) Theft insurance
   insurance

STEP 2 — Listening Attention:

   What kind of insurance?

Focus on the tape ━━━━━━━━▶

STEP 3 — Summarize:

   If you have had any accidents or tickets,
   the cost of your car insurance will be
   higher.

STEP 4 — Testing Point:

Vocabulary/cultural:
   "tickets and accidents" refer to driving cars

STEP 5 — Choose answer (C). ━━━━━━━▶ Ⓐ Ⓑ ● Ⓓ

MAN: Hello. I'm interested in the rates for Triple S insurance.
WOMAN: Okay. Have you had any tickets or accidents in the last three years?
What are they talking about?

33. Before you hear the tape, read: ———▶ (A) Take a class for credit.

STEP 1 — Similar/Different:

a class

(B) Add a class.
(C) Drop a class
(D) Attend a class for no credit.

STEP 2 — Listening Attention:

Verb?

Focus on the tape ————————————▶

STEP 3 — Summarize:

Can I come to your class without being a regular student?

STEP 4 — Testing Point:

Vocabulary:
"to audit a class" = "to attend a class without being a regular student" (no grade or credit)

MAN: Dr. Smith, could you let me audit your class?

WOMAN: Sure, officially or unofficially?

What does the man want to do?

STEP 5 — Choose answer (D) ————▶ Ⓐ Ⓑ Ⓒ ●

34. Before you hear the tape, read: ———▶ (A) She misplaced her contact lenses.

STEP 1 — Similar/Different:

She . . . contact lenses
She . . . glasses
She . . . contact
Her . . . contact lenses

(B) She finds her old glasses better.
(C) She couldn't contact her optometrist.
(D) Her contact lenses are better.

STEP 2 — Listening Attention:

What verb?

Focus on the tape ————————————▶

STEP 3 — Summarize:

I'm wearing my glasses because I couldn't find my contact lenses.

MAN: You're wearing your glasses again!

WOMAN: I couldn't find my contact lenses.

What does the woman mean?

STEP 4 — Testing Point:

Vocabulary:
   "could not find" = "misplaced"

STEP 5 — Choose answer (A) ──────▶ ●ⒷⒸⒹ

   This dialogue shows an implied result.
   She is wearing her glasses because
   she can't find her contact lenses.

   35. Before you hear the tape, read: ──▶

STEP 1 — Similar/Different:

   One should . . . write
   One should . . . right
   Doing . . . right

STEP 2 — Listening Attention:

   One should do what?

(A) One should write
     down anything im-
     portant.
(B) One should do the
     right thing and do it
     well.
(C) Doing the right thing
     is the most important.
(D) The man and the
     woman have different
     opinions.

Focus on the tape ──────────────▶

STEP 3 — Summarize:

   It's more important to do the right thing
      than to do something well.

STEP 4 — Testing Point:

Structure/negative:
   It's not important
Structure/negative agreement:
   "No" = "I agree with your negative
      statement."

WOMAN: It's not im-
portant how well you
do something.

MAN: No, it's impor-
tant that you do the
right thing.

What do they mean?

STEP 5 — Choose answer (C) ──────▶ ⒶⒷ●Ⓓ

   Don't be confused by the sounds of
      "write" and "right."

Part C: Steps to the Answers

FIRST MINI-TALK

FIRST — Listen for which questions will relate to the first reading:

36–40

SECOND — Listen to the tape:

Professor: (woman)	Good afternoon. In today's class, I want to discuss and demonstrate one of the principles of relaxation and exercise. This might be different from other ways you've been taught to exercise. What I want you to do is this: stretch your body to the point where you feel a little pull. Then stop stretching, but keep the same posture and exhale deeply. By doing this, you will allow your body to release the stress and reduce the resistance. Then you will be able to stretch further, and relax, and have no pain.	1 2 3 4 5 6 7 8 9 10 11
Student: (man)	But Mrs. Jones, I've done exercises all my life, and I know that it always hurts to stretch. In fact, if you don't feel any pain, it means that you're not stretching enough. You know the old saying, "No pain, no gain!"	12 13 14 15 16
Professor:	Oh yes, I'm well aware of that saying, and, in fact, I agree with it. But let's look at this saying in another way. "No pain, no gain." It can be painful to gain a new concept. Sometimes, it's even more painful to change your ideas than it is to have a tooth pulled. Now let's apply this idea to your exercises for today.	17 18 19 20 21 22 23

THIRD — Briefly summarize the mini-talk:

Main idea: The woman is teaching the students a new form of exercise.

FOURTH — Listen and decide:

> ### NOTE
>
> Refer to page 90 for exercises on inferences and restatements.

36. Where does this conversation probably take place?

(A) In a doctor's office   There is no mention of a doctor.

(B) In an exercise class   *Correct* (inference; Lines 1, 2–3): "In to-day's class . . . demonstrate relaxation and exercise."

(C) In a dentist's office   There is no mention of a dentist.

(D) In a biology class   In biology an instructor might discuss principles of relaxation and exercise, but would not teach the students how to exercise.

37. What does the woman mainly want to explain?

(A) How to stretch   *Correct* (restatement; Lines 4–5): "I want you to . . . stretch . . . ."

(B) How to change ideas   Mentioned, but not the main point.

(C) How to pull a tooth   Used as example only.

(D) How to exhale   Mentioned, but not main point.

38. According to the man, what is painful?

(A) Gaining new concepts   The woman said this.

(B) Releasing stress   No one said this was painful.

(C) Stretching   *Correct* (restatement; Line 13): "It always hurts to stretch . . . ."

(D) Pulling teeth   The woman used this as an example.

39. Which statement would both speakers probably agree to?

(A) It is difficult to learn something new.   *Correct* (inference; Lines 15–16, 19–20): "No pain, no gain . . . it can be painful to gain a new concept."

(B) It always hurts to exercise.   Only the man said this.

(C) It hurts more to have a tooth pulled than it does to exercise.   No one said this.

(D) If you don't feel the pain of stretching, you need to stretch more.   Only the man said this.

40. What will probably happen next?

(A) The man will learn a new saying.	This was not mentioned.
(B) The man will go home.	This was not mentioned.
(C) The man will try a new way to exercise.	*Correct* (inference; Lines 22–23): " . . . let's apply this idea to your exercises today."
(D) The woman will discuss difficulties of learning new ideas.	Used as an example; not a main topic.

SECOND MINI-TALK

FIRST—Listen for which questions will relate to the second reading:

41–45

SECOND—Listen to the tape:

In the United States, social security numbers are used to identify peo-   1
ple for work, for school, and for other official business. You need to   2
know your social security number when you apply for a job, when you   3
fill out tax forms, and when you register for school. Basically, you   4
need a social security number in order to survive in American society.   5
   When I first came to the United States, I was told that I should apply   6
for my social security number. So I took the bus down to the social   7
security office. The office was busy, with several people waiting in   8
line. When it was my turn, the officer gave me a long form and told me   9
to fill it out and return it to him. I took my form, found a seat, and sat   10
down to fill it out.   11
   I read over the form several times, but, to my frustration, I still   12
could not make any sense out of it. I felt terrible, and began to doubt   13
my ability to survive in America. "Oh dear," I thought. "If this is so   14
difficult for me, how will I ever get through school?" After trying   15
again and again to read and understand the form, I finally said to   16
myself, "Even with all the years I've studied English, I haven't learned   17
enough vocabulary to fill out a basic form. But I must apply for a   18
social security number. There is no way around it. I will have to get   19
help." So I reluctantly approached the officer for help. "Excuse me,   20
sir. Could you help me with this form? I'm a newcomer here, and I   21

can't understand it." The officer looked over the form, and said in sur- **22**
prise, "Oh no, I've made a mistake. This form is in Spanish. Here, **23**
take a new form." Was I embarrassed! He gave me the new form, and **24**
I filled it out in a few minutes. Two weeks later, I received notice of **25**
my social security number. **26**

  I have been in the United States for two years now, but I still can't **27**
forget that embarrassing moment during my first visit to the Social **28**
Security office. **29**

THIRD — Briefly summarize the mini-talk:

> Main point: He was embarrassed because he didn't realize that his
>   social security form was written in Spanish.

FOURTH — Listen and decide:

41. What is a social security number?

(A) A form	You need this to get your number.
(B) An official notice	This was not mentioned.
(C) An identification	*Correct* (restatement; Lines 1–2): " . . . used to identify people . . . ."
(D) A license	This was not mentioned.

42. Who said he made a mistake?

(A) The newcomer	He was embarrassed, but he didn't make the main mistake.
(B) The officer	*Correct* (restatement; Line 23): "I've made a mistake."
(C) The bus driver	This was not mentioned.
(D) The people in line	This was not mentioned.

43. Why couldn't the newcomer fill out the form?

(A) He had no social security number	This didn't prevent him from filling out the form.
(B) The vocabulary was too specific.	This was mentioned, but it is not the reason.
(C) He couldn't read.	Too general: "couldn't read" means "He couldn't read any language."
(D) It was the wrong form.	*Correct* (inference; Line 23): "This form is in Spanish."

44. Why was the newcomer embarrassed?

(A) Because the officer laughed at him.	This was not mentioned.
(B) Because he didn't know what form to get.	This was not mentioned.
(C) Because he filled out the wrong form.	He had the wrong form, but he didn't fill it out.
(D) Because he didn't realize the form was in Spanish.	*Correct* (inference; Lines 12–13, 20, 23): "I still could not make any sense out of it . . . reluctantly approached . . . form is in Spanish."

45. Did the newcomer get a social security number?

(A) Yes, he got one in two weeks.	*Correct* (restatement; Line 25): "Two weeks later I received . . . "
(B) Yes, he got one right away.	He got the number in two weeks so he could not have gotten it right away.
(C) No, he was too embarrassed to apply for one.	This was not mentioned. He was embarrassed to talk to the officer, and then he was embarrassed because he didn't realize the form was not in English.
(D) No, he was told to wait until he could speak English better.	This was not mentioned.

THIRD MINI-TALK

FIRST—Listen for which questions will relate to the third mini-talk:

46–50

SECOND—Listen to the tape:

Today I'd like to begin a discussion on the problem of the heating	1
up of the earth. First we'll touch on the relationship between fluoro-	2
carbons and the ozone layer. You probably remember that the ozone	3
layer is the protective shield around the earth. It is important to all life	4
because it filters out harmful ultraviolet light from the sun. Ozone	5
itself, a form of oxygen, is regularly made by the action of the sun in	6

the upper atmosphere. It is also regularly destroyed by natural chemical   **7**
processes. The problem now is that too much of the ozone layer is be-   **8**
ing destroyed. Scientists suspect that certain chemicals, such as   **9**
fluorocarbons, are contributing to this depletion of the ozone layer.   **10**
And how do we use fluorocarbons? Well, the most common uses are   **11**
in spray cans and automobile cooling systems. The chemical pollution   **12**
from these fluorocarbons can account for some of the ozone losses   **13**
that have been reported. There are, however, new studies linking the   **14**
sun itself to the depletion of the ozone layer. We'll go into that new   **15**
study next time.   **16**

THIRD — Briefly summarize the mini-talk:

    Main topic: Too much of the earth's ozone layer is being destroyed, prob-
                  ably by flourocarbons.

FOURTH — Listen and decide:

46. Who is the speaker probably addressing?

(A) Scientists at a research   Topic is too general for for a research
     center   center; would probably not be a continu-
                                ing topic.
(B) Chemists at a convention   Same as (A) above.
(C) Students at a university   *Correct* (inference; Lines 1, 2): "Today
                                I'd like to begin a discussion . . . first
                                we'll touch on . . . ."
(D) Workers at an air-   This was not mentioned.
     conditioning factory

47. What is the speaker's main topic?

(A) Ultraviolet light
                                Too narrow: This tells why ozone is
                                important.
(B) The use of spray cans   Too narrow: This is an example of
                                fluorocarbon use.
(C) Air-conditioning systems   Too narrow: This is an example of
                                  fluorocarbon use.
(D) Fluorocarbons and the   *Correct* (restatement; Lines 2–3):
     ozone layer   " . . . the relationship between fluorocar-
                                bons and the ozone layer."

48. What is the most important purpose of the ozone layer?

(A) Providing fluorocarbons   This was not mentioned.
(B) Shielding the sun   No, it is shielding the earth.
(C) Protecting the earth   *Correct* (restatement; Line 4): " . . . is the protective shield around the earth."

(D) Destroying chemicals   This was not mentioned.

49. What is the ozone layer made of?

(A) Fluorocarbons   A chemical used on earth.
(B) Oxygen   *Correct* (restatement; Lines 5–6): "Ozone . . . a form of oxygen."

(C) Shields   Ozone shields the earth from the sun ("shields" is a verb here).

(D) Ultraviolet light   Harmful rays from the sun.

50. What will the speaker probably discuss next?

(A) How to Make Air-Conditioners with Fluorocarbons.   Idea mentioned as example only.

(B) Harmful Effects of Ultraviolet Light   This was mentioned, but not main topic.

(C) The Make-up of the Ozone Layer   This was mentioned, but not main topic for next time.

(D) The Sun as a Cause of Ozone Layer Depletion   *Correct* (inference; Lines 14–16): " . . . new studies linking the sun . . . to the depletion of the ozone layer. We'll go into that . . . next time."

SECTION 2: STRUCTURE AND WRITTEN EXPRESSION

Steps to the Answers

The main testing point for each question is listed after each sentence. Refer to the Frequency of Structures (pages 51–57) for examples of each testing point.

1. The population of cities in the Eastern and Northern areas of the United States is declining, while _____ Southern cities is growing.

Testing Points: Prepositional Phrase, Pronoun

Refer to Structures 8 and 14, pages 52, 53.

(A) that in	Incorrect preposition.
(B) that of	**Correct**
(C) those of	Must be singular because of "population."
(D) those in	Must be singular; incorrect preposition.

2. **Some people find it surprising _____ his career as an actor in California.**

Testing Point: Noun Clause as Object

Refer to Structure 1, page 51.

(A) when Ronald Reagan began	Adjective or adverb clause; answers question "when."
(B) Ronald Reagan began	New subject and verb; makes two sentences.
(C) that Ronald Reagan began	Correct: Noun clause as object.
(D) to know Ronald Reagan	No verb.

3. **The travels of Marco Polo in the 12th century would not have been so well known _____ for the book he wrote while in jail.**

Testing Point: Conditional "had it not been"

Refer to Structure 28, page 55.

(A) it not have been	Incorrect combination of words.
(B) is not been	Incorrect combination of verb forms.
(C) had it not been	**Correct**
(D) has not been	Not past tense form.

4. **The Caspian Sea, a salt lake, is _____ any other lake in the world.**

Testing Point: Comparison

Refer to Structure 10, page 53.

(A) largest	"Largest" must be preceded by "the." It cannot be followed directly by "any other."
(B) the largest	This would be correct without the words "any other" in the sentence.
(C) larger than	**Correct**
(D) the larger than	This would be correct without the word "the."

5. 3,810 meters above sea level in Bolivia stands Lake Titicaca, _____ in the world.

Testing Point: Superlative

Refer to Structure 11, page 53.

(A) the highest large lake	**Correct**
(B) highest large lake	This answer needs the word "the."
(C) highest largest lake	You can't use two "est" endings together.
(D) the high largest lake	The "est" word must come after "the."

6. _____ in an electric typewriter is the ability to correct spelling errors.

Testing Point: Noun/Verb Agreement

Refer to Structure 3, page 52.

(A) There are many new features	This adds another subject and verb.
(B) New features	This sentence can't have a plural subject because the verb is singular.
(C) The new features	See answer (B).
(D) One of the new features	**Correct:** singular subject ("one").

7. Ballet dancers, _____ actors, must spend many hours a day practicing before a performance.

Testing Point: "like"

Refer to Structure 17, page 54.

(A) like	**Correct**
(B) the like	The word "the" can't be used in front of "like" here.
(C) the same	This would be correct if it said, "the same as."
(D) same as	This would be correct with the word "the."

8. It is a sign _____ fall when the leaves on the trees begin to change color.

Testing Point: Prepositional Phrase after Noun

Refer to Structure 8, page 52.

(A) for	The word "for" introduces a reason.
(B) at	The word "at" introduces a place.

(C) to   The word "to" before "fall" changes
                                       "fall" from a noun to the infinitive form of
                                       the verb "fall." This doesn't make sense
                                       in the sentence.
(D) of   **Correct**

9. **Bees have compound eyes _____ almost 6000 tiny lenses.**

Testing Point: Preposition

Refer to Structure 5, page 52.

(A) made of   Correct: "made of" = "consisting of."
(B) made in   This is followed by a place.
(C) made on   This is followed by a place.
(D) made up   This means "imagined"; it would be cor-
                                       rect if it said, "made up of."

10. **_____ the reactions of people with amnesia, scientists are learning more about the process of memory in the brain.**

Testing Point: Adverb Phrase

Refer to Structure 7, page 52.

(A) By studying   **Correct**
(B) To study   Implies future; "in order to."
(C) They study   Adding a subject and verb makes two
                                       sentences, not one.
(D) They're studying   See answer (C).

11. **The White House is where the President lives, while the Capitol Building is where _____.**

Testing Points: Parallel Construction; Passive Voice

Refer to Structures 1 and 9, pages 51, 53.

(A) laws made   Incorrect passive.
(B) the laws are making   The laws don't "make" anything.
(C) the laws are made   Correct: passive.
(D) are making the laws   No subject, not parallel.

12. **High levels of hazardous waste _____ in soil near many nuclear defense facilities.**

Testing Points: Verb Tense, Passive Voice

Refer to Structures 9 and 24, pages 53 and 54.

(A) have been measured	Correct: plural verb.
(B) has been measured	This is not plural.
(C) is measuring	The verb must be in the passive voice. "Levels" don't measure things.
(D) are measuring	See answer (C).

13. **Polygamy is a situation where a man _____ two women at the same time.**

Testing Point: Verb Tense, Passive Voice

Refer to Structures 9 and 24, pages 53 and 54.

(A) marries to	"To" cannot follow "marry" or "marries."
(B) is marry to	This would be correct if it said, "is married to."
(C) married	Possible only if main verb of the sentence is "was."
(D) is married to	**Correct**

14. **_____ the rainfall was adequate this year, the apricot trees still did not produce a high yield.**

Testing Point: Adverb Clause

Refer to Structure 6, page 52.

(A) Since	This is used for cause and result.
(B) However	This would be correct if it said, "however adequate the rainfall was."
(C) Although	**Correct: shows contrast.**
(D) Due to	Used for cause and result.

15. **Ludwig van Beethoven is considered one of the greatest composers _____.**

Testing Point: Noun Clause

Refer to Structure 6, page 52.

(A) who ever lived	**Correct**
(B) he lived	Subject and verb add new sentence.
(C) when living	This would be correct if the main verb were past tense.
(D) while he lived	See answer (C).

For the following section, only the correct choice will be given and the error explained.

16. (B) *Subject/verb agreement:* Verb is "comes" which is singular; therefore, subject must be singular. Refer to Structure 3.

N O T E

Subject/verb agreement is a common testing point in the TOEFL. To save time, look quickly for subject/verb agreement when you first read the questions.

---

17. (D) *Adjective phrase:* "agreement limiting nuclear weapons." Refer to Structure 7.

18. (B) *Parallel construction:* "joking" should be "jokes." Refer to Structure 1.

19. (C) *Subject/verb agreement:* "include" must be plural to agree with "conditions." "Conditions" cannot be changed because there is no article. Refer to Structure 20.

Check for clauses that come between nouns and verbs.

20. (C) *Parallel construction:* "watch, visit, and relax." Refer to Structure 1.

21. (C) *Adverb phrase:* gerund ("ing") form after preposition—"on lowering the instances." Refer to Structure 7.

22. (C) *Comparative:* "the more . . . the tighter . . . ." Refer to Structure 10.

23. (A) *Preposition after verb:* "consists of." Refer to Structure 5.

24. (B) *Adjective:* "beautiful" and "spring" both modify "color." Refer to Structure 2.

25. (D) *Reference to person:* "American builder." Refer to Structure 27.

26. (B) *Plural noun:* "rows of eyes." Refer to Structure 3.

27. (D) *Parallel construction; verb:* "was . . . stood . . . had . . . ." The word "who" is usually used to describe a person, but "that" is not incorrect. Refer to Structure 1.

28. (D) *Noun* vs. *adjective:* "diversified agriculture." Refer to Structure 2.

29. (A) *Conditional:* "Scientists predict that there will be . . . ." Future conditional uses future tense verb. Refer to Structure 28.

30. (B) *Subject/verb agreement:* "number . . . has been increasing." Refer to Structure 20.

N O T E

Check for prepositional phrases that come between nouns and verbs.

---

31. (B) *Adjective or noun* vs. *verb:* The words "explorer's voyage, exploration voyage, explorative voyage" are all possible. Refer to Structure 2.

32. (A) *Adjective clause:* The word "which" must begin this nonrestrictive clause. Adjective clauses never begin with "what." Refer to Structure 6.

33. (C) *Adjective clause/verb:* Present tense verb—"which commonly afflicts." Refer to Structure 6.

34. (C) *Adjective:* "its amazing geysers" "Amazing" describes one's feelings about the geysers. "Amazed" would describe feelings the geyser would have about itself (impossible). Refer to Structure 2.

35. (B) *Plural noun:* The word "oak" modifies "plant." Refer to Structure 3.

36. (B) *Pronoun:* "with its domed ceiling." A planetarium is not a person; use "it" for things. Refer to Structure 14.

37. (C) *Adjective:* "are interested in." "People are interested in the Titanic" = People want to find out about the Titanic." Refer to Structure 3.

38. (A) *Adjective clause:* A non-restrictive clause cannot begin with "that." Refer to Structure 6.

39. (D) *Preposition after verb:* "was taught...by." Refer to Structure 5.

40. (B) *Prepositional phrase after noun:* "works of art." Refer to Structure 6.

SECTION 3: VOCABULARY AND READING COMPREHENSION

Steps to the Answers

Words can have different meanings depending on the sentences they are used in. The meanings given here are the closest to the meanings that might make sense in the test sentences.

1. Vincent Van Gogh is <u>renowned</u> for his post-impressionist painting.

   (A) "Regarded" is similar to "respected."
   (B) "Applauded" is similar to "praised."
   (C) "Accomplished" is similar to "successful."
   (D) **Correct:** "Renowned" means "famous."

2. Extreme sunburn can cause small <u>blisters</u> on the skin.

   (A) "Spots" are "small flat marks."
   (B) **Correct:** "Blisters" are "swellings."
   (C) A "wound" is an "injury."
   (D) A "bite" is an "injury from animal teeth or an insect."

3. Natural occurrences such as hurricanes, earthquakes, and tornadoes can have <u>catastrophic</u> effects on people.

   (A) **Correct:** "Catastrophic" means "disastrous."
   (B) "Killing" means "deadly" here.
   (C) "Categorical" means "unconditional."
   (D) "Unimaginable" means "not able to think of."

4. Jane Goodall has written a new <u>comprehensive</u> book on her study of the chimpanzees in Africa.

   (A) **Correct:** "Comprehensive" means "complete."
   (B) "Factual" means "true."
   (C) "Festive" means "joyous."
   (D) "Illustrated" means "full of pictures."

5. The earthworm is a <u>segmented</u> worm found in almost all parts of the world.

   (A) "Plated" means "coated" or having hard sections like armor.
   (B) "Round" means "circular."
   (C) "Long" means "extended."
   (D) **Correct:** "Segmented" means "having several pieces together."

6. Ammonia is a chemical with a penetrating <u>odor.</u>

    (A) **Correct:** An "odor" is a "smell."
    (B) A "flavor" is a "taste."
    (C) A "sting" is a "kind of pain."
    (D) A "burn" is an "injury caused by fire."

7. After the American Civil War, the Southern armies were <u>granted amnesty.</u>

    (A) "Punished" means "caused to suffer."
    (B) "Frightened" means "afraid".
    (C) **Correct:** "Granted amnesty" means "pardoned; being freed from a crime."
    (D) "Separated" means "divided."

8. Amphibians, like frogs and toads, have <u>moist</u> skin.

    (A) **Correct:** "Moist" means "a little wet."
    (B) "Slimy" means "wet and slippery."
    (C) "Sticky" means "tending to cling together." (My fingers were sticky after touching the honey.)
    (D) "Tough" means "hard."

9. The Bay of Pigs invasion in 1961 resulted in <u>severe</u> criticism of President Kennedy by the American people.

    (A) "Deep" here means "serious."
    (B) "Special" means "particular to one event."
    (C) "Tight" means "difficult" here.
    (D) **Correct:** "Severe" means "harsh."

10. Coral is made by a small <u>sedentary</u> animal that lives in the ocean.

    (A) "Secluded" means "alone."
    (B) "Hard-working" means "working well."
    (C) **Correct:** "Sedentary" actually means "sitting down"; in this case, it means "immobile."
    (D) "Lively" means "active," the opposite of "sedentary."

11. Charles Darwin <u>formulated</u> his famous theory of evolution during his five-year cruise on the "Beagle."

    (A) "Expanded" means "enlarged."
    (B) **Correct:** "Formulated" means "developed."
    (C) "Critiqued" means "evaluated."
    (D) "Finished" means "completed."

12. By the end of the Crimean War, the name of Florence Nightingale was legendary.

   (A) "Imaginary" means "not true."
   (B) "Novel" means "unique" or "new."
   (C) "Gratifying" means "satisfying."
   (D) **Correct:** "Legendary" refers to a "story that has become well known by everyone," therefore, "famous."

13. The most devastating earthquake in North America occurred in Alaska in 1964.

   (A) **Correct:** "Devastating" here means "damaging."
   (B) "Divisive" means "causing a disagreement."
   (C) "Crushing" means that "something is pressing down on something else."
   (D) "Shocking" can mean "disturbing" in this sentence.

14. In many coastal areas of the U.S. there is a deficiency of sand, causing an erosion problem.

   (A) "Quality" means "excellence."
   (B) "Propagation" can means "increase" here.
   (C) "Movement" means "changing position."
   (D) **Correct:** "Deficiency" means "a lack of something; not having enough."

15. The increase in world population was negligible until around 1800.

   (A) **Correct:** "Negligible" means "a very small amount," therefore, "unimportant."
   (B) "Needless" means "unnecessary."
   (C) "Average" is a mathematical term; it can also mean "standard."
   (D) "Misleading" means "causing the wrong impression."

16. A credit card allows the user to receive credit at the time of a purchase.

   (A) "Donate" means "to give away."
   (B) "Arbitrate" means "to help settle a dispute."
   (C) "Reject" is "to throw something away; discard."
   (D) **Correct:** "To receive credit" is "to get credit; obtain credit."

17. Credit card holders can postpone payment on their purchases by accepting a monthly interest charge.

   (A) "Provide" means "supply."
   (B) "Decrease" means "to become less."

(C) "To mail" means "to send by mail."

(D) **Correct:** "To postpone payment" is "to arrange to pay at a later time; to defer payment."

18. William Faulkner, a <u>brilliant</u> American novelist, was awarded the 1949 Nobel Prize in literature.

(A) **Correct:** "Brilliant" means "very intelligent or clever."

(B) "Starry" means "shining like stars."

(C) A "captive" is a "prisoner."

(D) "Well-known" means "famous."

19. When frost appears on a window, it often has a delicate and <u>curious</u> pattern.

(A) "Special" means "uncommon" or "unique" here.

(B) **Correct:** "Curious" means "strange" in this sentence.

(C) "Fine" means "very good."

(D) "Cute" means "pretty" or "nice-looking."

20. The American Dental Association cautions people not to <u>neglect</u> their teeth during their growing years.

(A) "Abuse" means "to be cruel" or "to do something to cause harm."

(B) "Damage" means "to injure."

(C) "Disrupt" means "to disturb."

(D) **Correct:** "Neglect" means "to disregard or not take care of something; not pay attention to something."

21. When the earth turns, the moon <u>appears</u> to rise in the east and set in the west.

(A) "To refer to" means "to look at for information." (You can refer to your dictionary for the meaning of a new word.)

(B) **Correct:** "Appears to" means "seems to."

(C) "Is likely to" means "is expected to."

(D) "Is supposed to" means "should."

22. One goal of a physical fitness program is to <u>maximize</u> a person's strength and endurance.

(A) "Split" means "to divide."

(B) "Distinguish" means "to separate and classify."

(C) **Correct:** "Maximize" here means "to increase."

(D) "Combine" means "to put together."

23. Among the dangers of drilling for oil in the ocean is the problem of potential leaks.

    (A) "Serious" means "important."
    (B) "Dangerous" means "unsafe."
    (C) "Imminent" means that "something is likely to happen soon."
    (D) **Correct:** "Potential" means "future possibility."

24. Kangaroos give birth to babies that develop within their mothers' pouches.

    (A) **Correct:** "Pouches" means "sacks."
    (B) "Bodies" refers to "the main part of a person or animal."
    (C) "Egg" in this sentence would be "an embryo."
    (D) A "nest" is "a place a bird builds for its eggs."

25. Unicorns, dragons, and centaurs are all imaginary animals.

    (A) "Magic" here could mean "supernatural."
    (B) "Unimportant" means "not necessary."
    (C) "Pictorial" means that something is "expressed in pictures."
    (D) **Correct:** "Imaginary" means "unreal."

26. The Milky Way consists of about a hundred billion stars.

    (A) "Is conscious of" means "is aware of."
    (B) "Surrounds" means that something is "all around something else; on all sides."
    (C) **Correct:** "Consists of" means "contains."
    (D) "Makes" means "produces."

27. Blizzards in high mountains can be dangerous for hikers and skiers.

    (A) **Correct:** "Blizzards" are "terrible snow storms."
    (B) "High winds" means that "the winds are very strong."
    (C) "Avalanches" are "falling hills of snow or rock."
    (D) "Slippery ice" means that "the ice is very smooth and hard to walk on without falling down."

28. To produce raisins, the ripened grapes are usually picked by hand, placed on trays, and set in the sun for several days.

    (A) "Dried" means that "the moisture has been taken out."
    (B) "Cleaned" means that "the dirt has been taken out."
    (C) "Crushed" means that "something has been pressed or flattened."
    (D) **Correct:** "Ripened" means that "the fruit is mature and ready to eat."

29. Of the Olympic ski events, ski jumping is the most <u>spectacular</u>.

(A) **Correct:** "Spectacular" means "striking" in this sentence.
(B) "Dangerous" means "unsafe."
(C) "Appealing" means "attractive" or "desirable."
(D) "Difficult" means "hard" or "not easy."

30. The central states in the U.S. are <u>noted for</u> their production of wheat and corn.

(A) "Applauded for" is similar to "approved of."
(B) "Informed of" means "knowledgeable about."
(C) **Correct:** "Noted for" is the same as "known for."
(D) "Described by" is similar to "pictured in words" or "talked about." There is no feeling of being famous, as there is in the correct word.

SECTION 4: READING COMPREHENSION

> ### N O T E
>
> Some people can find the answers faster if they briefly read the questions before reading the paragraphs. The focus of the questions can give you a general idea of what to remember when you read. If this strategy helps you, then read very quickly, and note the focus of the questions. If, however, you are a person who likes to read the whole paragraph quickly first, then begin your reading strategy with Step 2 below.

FIRST PARAGRAPH, QUESTIONS 31–34

STEP 1—Briefly look at the questions below the paragraph. Note the general focus.

31. Focus: title (main idea)
32. Focus: description of dome
33. Focus: shape of dome
34. Focus: Fuller's books

STEP 2—Read the paragraph.

The American architect and engineer, Buckminster Fuller, was born [1]
in 1895 in Massachusetts. He devoted his life to the invention of [2]
revolutionary technological designs to solve problems of modern living. [3]
He is best known for his development of the geodesic dome, which is [4]
an extremely light and yet enormously strong spherical structure com- [5]
posed of triangular pieces. The geodesic dome is an application of his [6]
principle of deriving maximum output from a minimum input of [7]
material and energy. In the 1950s many of these domes were built for [8]
military and industrial uses. A considerable number of homes have [9]
also been built using geodesic dome structures. Fuller was also a con- [10]
troversial writer. Among his many books are *Nine Chains to the* [11]
Moon (1938), *Ideas and Integrities* (1963—an autobiography), *Utopia* [12]
or Oblivion (1970), and *Earth, Inc.* (1973). [13]

STEP 3—Briefly summarize the main points:

1. Buckminster Fuller was an American architect.
2. He was famous for designing the dome.
3. He was also a writer.

STEP 4—Read each question; answer it. (Look back in the paragraph for information if necessary.)

31. (A) Too narrow; it doesn't refer to Fuller.
    (B) **Correct:** (line 1).
    (C) Too general; the paragraph only discusses one type of architectural style.
    (D) Too narrow; the paragraph is only about one revolutionary design.

HINT

When choosing an answer, be sure to compare all the answer choices in order to choose the *best answer*. For instance, in the above question, the title "An American Architect" is the best. If, however, another title was more complete (i.e., "Fuller: An Architect and Engineer"), then the first choice would not be correct.

---

32. (A) "Uses a lot of material" is incorrect; "mimimum input" (line 7) means that it "uses only a little material."

(B) The dome's size was not mentioned.

(C) The idea of spaciousness was not mentioned.

(D) **Correct:** restatement and inference (line 7).

33. (A) The length is never mentioned.

(B) There is no comparison to a box.

(C) **Correct** (inference; line 5): "Spherical" means "ball-shaped."

(D) The structure is made of triangular-shaped pieces, but that is not the shape of the completed dome.

34. (A) **Correct:** restatement (lines 11, 12).

(B) This book was mentioned, but it is not his autobiography.

(C) See (B).

(D) See (B).

SECOND PARAGRAPH, QUESTIONS 35–40

STEP 1—Briefly look at the questions. Note the general focus.

35. Focus: how clouds are formed

36. Focus: how water returns to the earth

37. Focus: what is groundwater?

38. Focus: how much groundwater?

39. Focus: why groundwater is low

40. Focus: title (main idea)

STEP 2—Read the paragraphs.

Water on the earth is being continuously recycled in a process   1
known as the hydrologic cycle. The first step of the cycle is the   2
evaporation of water in the oceans. Evaporation is the process of   3
water turning into vapor, which then forms clouds in the sky. The second   4
step is the water returning to the earth in the form of precipitation,   5
either rain, snow, or ice. When the water reaches the earth's surface, it   6
runs off into the rivers, lakes, and the ocean, where the cycle begins   7
again.   8
    Not all water, however, stays on the surface of the earth in the   9
hydrologic cycle. Some of it seeps into the ground through infiltration   10
and collects under the earth's surface as groundwater. This ground-   11
water is extremely important to life on earth since 95% of the earth's   12
water is in the oceans, and is too salty for humans or plants. Of the   13
5% on land, only .05% is above ground in rivers or lakes. The rest is   14
underground water. This groundwater is plentiful and dependable, as   15
it doesn't depend on seasonal rain or snow. It is the major source of   16
water for many cities. But as the population increases and the need for   17

water also increases, the groundwater in some areas is getting danger-   **18**
ously low. Added to this problem is an increasing amount of pollution   **19**
that seeps into the groundwater. In the future, with an increasing   **20**
population and more toxic waste, the hydrologic cycle we depend on   **21**
could become dangerously imbalanced.   **22**

STEP 3—Briefly summarize the main points:

    1. The hydrologic cycle is recycled water.
    2. Groundwater is important to life.
    3. Groundwater is getting low as population and pollution increase.

STEP 4—Read and answer the questions. Reread the paragraph as necessary.

35. (A) **Correct:** restatement (lines 3, 4).
    (B) Evaporation is a process. You could say that clouds are formed from evaporated water, but not from evaporation.
    (C) This answer is too general.
    (D) There is no mention of clouds and groundwater together.

36. (A) Infiltration occurs after the water is on the land (see lines 10–11).
    (B) Pollution goes into groundwater. You should be able to eliminate this with common knowledge.
    (C) **Correct:** restatement (line 5).
    (D) Evaporation is the opposite of water returning to the earth (see lines 3, 4).

37. (A) Just the opposite; groundwater does not depend on seasonal rain (line 16).
    (B) Toxic waste can go into groundwater, but groundwater does not come from toxic waste.
    (C) .05% is above ground (line 14), not below ground.
    (D) **Correct:** restatement (lines 10–11).

38. (A) 95% is in the oceans (lines 12, 13).
    (B) **Correct:** restatement/computation (lines 12–14).
    (C) Impossible: groundwater is not above ground.
    (D) See (C).

> ### HINT
>
> With computation questions, be sure to think about the general question, and use your common sense. You may be able to guess the answer based on your background knowledge if you can't do the computation quickly.

39. (A) Conservation increases a supply of water, rather than decreasing it.
    (B) Toxic waste is a possible answer, but it is an additional problem, not the main reason for a low supply of groundwater.
    (C) Pollution is also an additional problem; a possible answer, but not the best answer.
    (D) **Correct:** restatement (lines 16–19).

40. (A) Too narrow: does not mention the hydrologic cycle.
    (B) **Correct:** mentioned in both first and last sentences.
    (C) Too narrow: (see A).
    (D) Too narrow (see A).

THIRD PARAGRAPH, QUESTIONS 41–47

STEP 1 — Briefly look at the questions below the paragraph. Note the general focus.

    41. Focus: what is happening?
    42. Focus: what are libraries stopping?
    43. Focus: time phrase
    44. Focus: main inference
    45. Focus: what are many countries doing?
    46. Focus: what new technique?
    47. Focus: title (main idea)

STEP 2 — Read the paragraph.

The Library of Congress in Washington, D.C., which houses the	1
largest collection of books in the world, is fighting a battle against	2
paper deterioration. The pages of old books, often yellowed and torn,	3
sometimes crumble when they are touched. The main culprit in the	4
battle is the acidic paper which has been used for making books since	5
the nineteenth century. Air pollution and moisture have added to the	6
problem. Strangely, the books that are in most danger of destruction	7
are not the oldest books. The paper in books made before the last cen-	8

tury was made from cotton and linen rags, which are naturally low in   **9**
acid. And the Gutenberg Bible, printed five centuries ago, was made   **10**
of thin calfskin, and is in remarkably good shape. But in the nine-   **11**
teenth century, with widespread literacy bringing a demand for a   **12**
cheaper and more plentiful supply of paper, the industry began using   **13**
chemically treated wood pulp for making paper. It is the chemical in   **14**
this paper that is causing today's problem.   **15**

    This problem of paper deterioration is one of global concern.   **16**
France, Canada, and Austria are all doing research into new methods   **17**
of deacidification. A new technology has recently been developed, in   **18**
fact, that allows for mass deacidification of thousands of books at the   **19**
same time. It costs less than microfilming, and still preserves books in   **20**
their original form. It is hoped there will soon be treatment facilities   **21**
all over the world to preserve and deacidify library book collections.   **22**

STEP 3—Briefly summarize the main points:

    1. There is a big problem of paper deteriorating in the world.
    2. The acid used in making paper since the nineteenth century is caus-
       ing the problem.
    3. Countries all over the world are trying to figure out how to save old
       books.
    4. A new method of taking the acid out of old paper has been
       developed.

STEP 4—Read each questions; answer it. (Look back in the paragraph for
information, if necessary.)

41. (A) Books are headed for destruction (line 6).
    (B) **Correct:** restatement (lines 1–3).
    (C) Chemical acid is causing paper deterioration (lines 4, 5, 12–14).
    (D) There is no mention of who is implementing new techniques.

42. (A) Too narrow: no mention of natural deterioration.
    (B) Too narrow: yellowing of pages is only part of the problem.
    (C) Too narrow: only an additional point.
    (D) **Correct** (restatement; lines 2 and 3): "Fighting a battle" means
        "trying to stop."

43. (A) The crumbling has been happening since the nineteenth century,
        not before (lines 5, 6).
    (B) The industry has used wood pulp since the nineteenth century,
        not before (lines 11–14).
    (C) **Correct:** inference (lines 5, 6).
    (D) Deacidification is a new process.

44. (A) We can infer the opposite: cotton and linen are good for making paper (lines 8, 9, 10).
    (B) **Correct** (inference; lines 10, 11): the Gutenberg Bible, made of calfskin, is still in good shape.
    (C) The paragraph states the opposite: woodpulp is cheaper (lines 12, 13, 14).
    (D) Inference: microfilming is an expensive way to preserve books, not an inexpensive way (line 20).

45. (A) Many countries are doing research (lines 17, 18).
    (B) This happened before the nineteenth century (lines 8, 9, 10).
    (C) **Correct** (inference; lines 17, 18): "deacidification" = "preservation."
    (D) There are not many treatment centers yet (lines 21, 22).

46. (A) Microfilming may be a new technique, but it is not a method of deacidification (lines 19, 20).
    (B) The Gutenberg Bible does not need to be saved (lines 10, 11).
    (C) Chemically treated wood pulp is causing today's problem (lines 14, 15).
    (D) **Correct**: restatement (lines 18, 19, 20).

47. (A) **Correct**: topic mentioned in first sentence of both paragraphs.
    (B) Too narrow: does not refer to the problem of paper deterioration.
    (C) Too narrow: see (B).
    (D) Too general: does not specifically mention the problems with paper.

FOURTH PARAGRAPH, QUESTIONS 48–53

STEP 1—Briefly look at the questions below the paragraph. Note the general focus.

48. Focus: beginning impressionists wanted what?
49. Focus: first impressionists did what?
50. Focus: early impressionists painted what?
51. Focus: Monet and Sisley painted what?
52. Focus: what is typical?
53. Focus: did not like when?

STEP 2—Read the paragraph.

Impressionism, in painting, developed in the late nineteenth century 1
in France. It began with a loosely structured group of painters who got 2
together mainly to exhibit their paintings. Their art was characterized 3
by the attempt to depict light and movement by using pure broken col- 4

or. The movement began with four friends who met in a café: Monet,   **5**
Renoir, Sisley, and Bazille. They were reacting against the academic   **6**
standards of their time, and the romantic emphasis on emotion as a   **7**
subject matter. They rejected the role of imagination in art. Instead,   **8**
they observed nature closely, painting with a scientific interest in   **9**
visual phenomenon. Their subject matter was as diverse as their per-   **10**
sonalities. Monet and Sisley painted landscapes with changing effects   **11**
of light, while Renoir painted idealized women and children. The   **12**
works of impressionists were received with hostility until the 1920s.   **13**
By the 1930s impressionism had a large cult following, and by the   **14**
1950s even the least important works by people associated with the   **15**
movement commanded enormous prices.   **16**

STEP 3—Briefly summarize the main points.

1. Impressionism began with four friends.
2. They didn't want to emphasize emotion in painting.
3. They looked scientifically at nature.
4. Their work was not appreciated in the beginning.

STEP 4—Read each question; answer it. Look back in the paragraph for information if necessary.

48. (A) "Light" is used as a noun: "effects of light," not as an adjective (lines 11, 12).
  (B) They were reacting against the academic standards, not fighting the government.
  (C) They had a scientific interest, not a desire to be scientists.
  (D) **Correct** (restatement; lines 2, 3): "exhibit" means "show."

49. (A) Just the opposite (lines 6, 7); they were reacting against the standards.
  (B) This is not mentioned.
  (C) **Correct** (inference; lines 6, 7): They were reacting against the standards because they did not like them.
  (D) They developed new standards, but not official standards.

50. (A) Just the opposite: they rejected imagination (line 8).
  (B) **Correct** (restatement; line 10): Their subject matter was diverse.
  (C) Only Monet and Sisley painted landscapes (line 11).
  (D) They had diverse personalities; they didn't paint diverse personalities (line 10).

51. (A) **Correct** (restatement; line 11): "Country scenes" = "landscapes."
  (B) Renoir painted portraits, not Monet and Sisley (line 12).

    (C) Not mentioned, also common knowledge: There were no skyscrapers in the nineteenth century.

    (D) Not mentioned: "landscape" means "natural scenery" (trees, flowers, mountains) rather than animals.

52. (A) Just the opposite: they reacted against romantic emphasis.

    (B) **Correct** (inference; (lines 8, 9): They rejected the role of imagination. They painted with scientific interest.

    (C) Not mentioned (could be inferred, but (B) is a better answer).

    (D) Renoir painted idealized women: There is no mention of idealizing life.

53. (A) **Correct** (inference; line 13): "Hostility" here means "didn't like."

    (B) If they "had a large cult following," they were liked.

    (C) If they "commanded enormous prices," they were liked.

    (D) This time period is not mentioned.

FIFTH PARAGRAPH, QUESTIONS 54–60

STEP 1—Briefly look at the questions below the paragraph. Note the general focus.

    54. Focus: what is tissue transplant?

    55. Focus: date: 600 B.C.

    56. Focus: where is the cornea?

    57. Focus: common problem

    58. Focus: date: when performed?

    59. Focus: first heart transplant

    60. Focus: title (main idea)

STEP 2—Read the paragraph.

    Tissue transplants and organ transplants are both used in the treatment of disease. Tissue transplants include the transplanting of skin, bones, and the cornea of the eye; whereas organ transplanting includes replacing the kidney, heart, lung, and liver. Skin and cornea transplants are very common and successful, and have been performed for hundreds of years. In fact, there is evidence that skin transplants were done as early as 600 B.C. in India. Organ transplants, on the other hand, are quite recent. They are also more difficult to perform. Moreover, it is not always easy to find a suitable donor. And even if a healthy organ is found, the receiver's body may reject it. This is the major reason for problems with organ transplants.

    The first heart transplant was performed by Dr. Christiaan Barnard

in 1967 in South Africa. Many successful heart transplant operations　**13**
have been performed since then. In 1982, Dr. Barney Clark was the　**14**
first to receive an artificial heart. Research into organ transplants con-　**15**
tinues all the time. Doctors are continuing to find new ways to combat　**16**
the problems, and make transplants safer and more available to needy　**17**
people.　**18**

STEP 3—Briefly summarize the main points.

1. Tissue transplants and organ transplants are different
2. Tissue: skin, bones, cornea
3. Organ: kidney, heart, lung, liver
4. Tissue transplants: old; organ transplants: recent
5. First heart transplant: 1967
6. Research continues

STEP 4—Read each question; answer it. Look back in the paragraph
for information if necessary.

54. (A) Liver is an organ transplant (line 4).
    (B) A lung is an organ (line 4).
    (C) **Correct:** restatement (lines 2, 3).
    (D) A kidney is an organ (line 4).

55. (A) Organ transplants were performed later (lines 7, 8).
    (B) **Correct:** restatement (lines 6, 7).
    (C) Specific dates not mentioned for cornea transplant.
    (D) Artificial hearts were first developed in 1982 (lines 14, 15).

56. (A) Not mentioned directly, but it says "cornea of the eye" (line 3).
    (B) See (A).
    (C) See (A).
    (D) **Correct** (inference; line 3): "the cornea of the eye."

57. (A) **Correct** (inference; lines 9, 10, 11): "This is the major reason for
        problems" refers to "rejection."
    (B) A problem, but not the major problem stated in this paragraph.
    (C) See (B).
    (D) Replacement is not mentioned.

58. (A) 600 B.C. is the date for skin transplants, not heart transplants.
    (B) **Correct** (restatement; lines 13, 14): "then" means "since 1967."
    (C) 1982 was the date for the first artificial heart.
    (D) This date is never mentioned.

59. (A) It was performed by him.
    (B) He received the first artificial heart.
    (C) **Correct:** restatement (lines 12, 13).
    (D) The artificial heart was later than the first heart transplant.

60. (A) Too general: paragraph doesn't discuss disease.
    (B) Too specific: doesn't mention other transplants.
    (C) Too specific: doesn't mention tissue transplants.
    (D) **Correct:** Covers all main points.

LISTENING COMPREHENSION TAPESCRIPTS

EXERCISE WORKBOOK

Here are the tapescripts for Exercises 2 through 9. These exercises can be heard on the tape that accompanies this book. If you do not have the tape, then ask a native speaker of English to read this script to you while you do the exercises.

TO THE READER: Read each element (sentence, word group) one time only at a normal speed. Pause five seconds between elements to allow the test-taker to fill in the answer sheet. Give a slight stress to words set in *italic*, as in Exercise 3.

EXERCISE 2   PAGE 34

Discrimination between Similar-Sounding Words

DIRECTIONS: On the tape, you will hear a sentence spoken just one time. As you listen to the speaker, read the sentences below. The sentences you hear will not be the same as the ones you read, but one sentence will have a similar meaning. Put a check by the sentence that is closest in meaning to the one you hear. When you are finished, check your answers in the answer key on page 163. Now listen to the first sentence as an example:

On the tape you hear: It was Thursday.

In the book you read:

_____ The speaker is talking about a day.

_____ The speaker is talking about drinking.

You should have checked, "The speaker is talking about a day." If you checked, "The speaker is talking about drinking," it probably means that you heard the word "thirsty" instead of "Thursday." Now continue with the examples as you listen to the tape.

1. He resigned yesterday.
2. The crew was wonderful.
3. The fog disturbed him.
4. The company funded that school.
5. He made them eat steak.
6. I don't like the prize.
7. Did they go?
8. Where is Sue?
9. He did fifty questions.
10. Are you washing now?

EXERCISE 3 — PAGE 36

Synonyms

The exercise is on the tape. In Part A of the Listening Comprehension section of the TOEFL, you will hear single, unrelated sentences similar to the ones below. In order to choose the correct restatement, you will have to understand many idioms and other vocabulary words. This exercise contains sentences similar to those on TOEFL Listening Comprehension tests.

DIRECTIONS: In Exercise 3, you will hear sentences spoken just one time. After you listen to each sentence, turn off the tape and write another sentence that means the same thing, but uses some different words. When you have finished, check your sentences with the answer key on page 163. Remember that the answer key has only sample sentences. There may be more than one correct restatement of each sentence that you hear.

EXAMPLE: I can't stand it.
Now write a sentence that means the same thing as "I can't stand it."
   Continue writing restatements for each sentence you hear.

1. *I'd rather* stay home.
2. *Let me know* when you're ready.
3. There's *no need* to hurry.
4. School will be *over* next week.
5. I'd *think twice* about that.
6. The children walked *two by two.*
7. The professor *came up with* a solution to our problem.
8. I know this town *backwards and forwards.*
9. Don't *overdo* it when you exercise.

10. *Nobody has to show me* how to do this.
11. The teacher *made a point* of telling us to arrive early.
12. My mother *no longer* smokes.
13. We had *barely enough* water for the wash.
14. It's *well worth your time* to see the show.
15. I'm *willing* to work now.

EXERCISE 4 PAGE 38

Determining Testing Points

In Exercise 4, you will hear several sentences. After you listen to each sentence, stop the tape and write the answers to the questions about that sentence. When you have finished, check your answers in the answer key on page 164.

    A. This book is very up-to-date.
    B. She glanced at him through the door.
    C. Be careful that you don't overcook the pudding.
    D. The rent here is rather high, don't you think?
    E. He broke the world's record for high jumping.
    F. Be sure not to take more than you can eat.
    G. I'll never forget how much Jim did for me.
    H. The delivery man left when no one answered the door.

EXERCISE 5 PAGE 42

Word Groups

DIRECTIONS: For Exercise 5, you will hear groups of words on the tape that belong in categories. The words in each group represent one place. After you hear each category, stop the tape and write the name of the place where you would most likely to hear the words spoken. The answers are in the answer key, page 164.

Group one

a check
a deposit slip
an account
a checking account
a savings account
to be overdrawn
balance
interest

Group two

caps and gowns
robes
ceremony
a valedictorian
doctoral candidate
degree

Group three

"open wide"
"say 'ah'"
a cavity
a filling

Group four

to take a bow
to clap
Please hold your applause.
The curtain rises at 8.

Group five

a bride
a groom
a reception
to take vows
a honeymoon
a minister, a priest, a rabbi
to toast

Group six

a pill
a tablet
a prescription
to fill a prescription
a druggist

Group seven

a washer
a dryer
wash and wear
to spin dry
dry clean

Group eight

cut and set
curl
wave

rollers
permanent (perm)
wash and set
dryer

Group nine

a dormitory
a roommate
a cafeteria
a course schedule
units
credits
grades
exams
finals
a semester
a quarter
a term
a lecture
a lab
a counselor
a dean
a professor
a doctorate degree
a Ph.D. candidate

Group ten

Are you ready to order?
a menu
à la carte
cocktails
salad dressing
oil and vinegar
thousand island
blue cheese
roquefort
a waitress
a waiter
a tip
decaffeinated

Word Categories

DIRECTIONS: This exercise uses the same word groups as Exercise 5. For this exercise, you will hear several words spoken on the tape. Each time you hear a word, write it next to the correct place listed below. The words are not given in order. When you are finished, you will have more than one word on some lines. Do not stop the tape for this exercise. Work as fast as you can. The first word is written for you. Check your answers in the answer key, page 165. Here are the words.

TO THE READER: Pause for eight seconds between words.

curl . . . curtain . . . cavity . . . checking account . . . honeymoon . . . overdrawn . . . degree . . . wave . . . prescription . . . clap . . . credits . . . roquefort . . . lab . . . spin dry . . . cap and gown . . . toast . . . quarter

Place and Speaker (Inference)

DIRECTIONS: In Part B of the TOEFL exam, you can figure out the answer more easily if you know where the conversation takes place and the relationship between the speakers. In Exercise 7 you will hear sentences from situations that might be used in TOEFL exams. As you listen to the tape, imagine where each sentence would most likely be spoken. Write the name of the place and the possible speaker on the lines in your book. When you have finished, check your answers in the answer key, page 165. There may be other possible answers.

In what place would you probably hear the following sentences? Who would probably say them?

TO THE READER: Pause for thirty seconds after each sentence.

1. "Could you please help me with my class schedule?"
2. "How much are these a pound?"
3. "I'd like to buy some travelers' checks."
4. "You can't keep a cat in your dorm room."
5. "Are you ready to order?"
6. "There will be a supervisors' meeting at 4 P.M."
7. "Check your luggage at the counter."
8. "Do you have an appointment with Dr. Marcus?"
9. "The court will recess for lunch at 12:30."
10. "The children have a 20 minute recess at 10:30."

EXERCISE 8

Using Logical Skills: Guess the Question

No tapescript is needed for this exercise.

Practice for the Mini-Talk: Guess the Answer

DIRECTIONS: As you listen to the following talk, look at the answer choices on pages 46–47. You see five sets of answer choices. You do not know the questions, only the possible answers. First, look briefly at the groups of answers to get an idea of what types of questions might be asked. (For instance, the question for number 1 might be, "Who is talking?") Second, as you listen to the tape, mark the answers that you think will answer the questions. Then read the actual questions, listed in the answer key on page 166, and choose your answers again. You should have been able to eliminate one or two of the answer choices before you even read the questions.

Hi. My name is John. I'm your TA for chemistry 1A, Professor Smith's class. Let me explain a little about this lab section. It's a required meeting, once a week. I expect you to do all the experiments and keep the results in your lab notebook. I'll collect the notebooks every two weeks. You'll be graded on your lab notebooks, your attendance, and quizzes. But the most important information I want to give you today is about the safety procedures.

First of all, you must wear shoes that cover your feet in the lab. You can't wear thongs or sandals. Tennis shoes are okay. Also, don't wear clothes that have loose baggy parts, like long-neck scarves or big necklaces and loose belts. They could get caught in something or fall into a liquid.

Another important safety precaution is cleaning up. Be sure to put the waste in the correct containers. We can't mix liquid with paper. This is extremely important. I don't want any fires in this room.

You are responsible for washing out your own lab equipment and putting it away. If you don't do this, I will deduct points from your grades. I'm not going to clean up after you.

Okay. That's about all for this meeting. Next week we'll begin the first experiment. Be sure to get a lab notebook before then. Also, let Professor Smith know that you are attending this section.

PRACTICE TEST 1

SECTION 1, PART A, LISTENING COMPREHENSION

TO THE READER: Pause thirteen seconds after each sentence.

EXAMPLE 1: Would you mind opening the door for me?

EXAMPLE 2: There is so much fog that I can barely see the cars on the road.

1. I'd rather go early than late.
2. Unless you go to the party, I won't go.
3. It looks like rain.
4. I ran into my old friend in town yesterday.
5. Unlike her brother, Ann is open-minded.
6. Come in a minute so I can give you a run-down on the class.
7. Not once has she missed a class this semester!
8. The telephone is disconnected; Bill must have forgotten to pay the bill.
9. Whatever she knows, she's not telling anyone.
10. It takes a long time, but in the long run, it's well worth it.
11. This tape is out-of-date.
12. Having a car is by no means cheap.
13. Although he's eighteen, he doesn't act very grown-up.
14. Randy prefers pizza to tacos.
15. Jim used to smoke a lot more.
16. Exercise is a good remedy for depression.
17. They are the same books except for their covers.
18. Mary had the salesman wrap the present.
19. Never have I been so angry!
20. Jenny is smaller than her younger sister, Jane.

SECTION 1, PART B

TO THE READER: Read the sentences below. Pause thirteen seconds after each question.

EXAMPLE:

Woman: Oh dear. We're out of milk.
Man: No problem. I'll pick some up on my way home from work.

What does the man say he will do?

21. MAN: Can you go to the beach with me tomorrow?
    WOMAN: I wish I could, but I have to catch up on last week's work.

    What does the woman mean?

22. WOMAN: How's your class going?
    MAN: Terrible. It seems like the more the professor talks, the less I understand.

    How does the man feel about the class?

23. MAN: Shall we eat lunch out today?
    WOMAN: Only if we split the bill.

    What does the woman want to do?

24. MAN: I have a sore throat.
    WOMAN: You'd better take some Vitamin C.

    What does the man mean?

25. MAN: Hi, Mary. How're you doing?
    WOMAN: Oh, it's been a long day!

    What does the woman mean?

26. WOMAN: Jack, would you please check my mailbox while I'm gone?
    MAN: Sure, no problem.

    What does the woman want Jack to do?

27. MAN: If you don't like it, you don't have to take it.
    WOMAN: Thanks, but I like it.

    What will the woman probably do?

28. MAN: Would you like to have a piece of cake?
    WOMAN: No, thanks. I'm on a diet.

    What does the woman mean?

29. WOMAN: What kind of dressing would you like?
    MAN: Italian, please.

    Where does this conversation probably take place?

30. WOMAN: The deadline for computer registration is tomorrow.
    MAN: But I haven't decided which course to take yet.

    What are they talking about?

31. WOMAN: Will you accept a collect call from Lisa?
    MAN: Yes, I will.

    What will the man do?

32. MAN: Hello. I'm interested in the rates for Triple S insurance.
    WOMAN: Okay. Have you had any tickets or accidents in the last three years?

    What are they talking about?

33. MAN: Dr. Smith, could you let me audit your class?
WOMAN: Sure, officially or unofficially?

What does the man want to do?

34. MAN: You're wearing your glasses again!
WOMAN: I couldn't find my contact lenses.

What does the woman mean?

35. WOMAN: It's not important how well you do something.
MAN: No, it's important that you do the right thing.

What do they mean?

SECTION 1, PART C

Sample Talk

On Friday, November 14, there will be an International Festival from 7:00 to 10:00 P.M. at the Student Center. Everybody is invited to come. The program will include performances by the Scottish Country Dance Group and the University International Dancers. Also included will be folk songs from Spain and an international student costume show. There will be also be dancing for everyone. You're encouraged to wear the costume of your heritage. Refreshments will be served, and admission is free. Please come!

EXAMPLE 1: Who is this announcement probably given to?

EXAMPLE 2: What will most people be able to do at the Festival?

Questions 36 through 40 are based on the following dialogue:

PROFESSOR: Good afternoon. In today's class, I want to discuss and
(WOMAN) demonstrate one of the principles of relaxation exercise. This might be different from other ways you've been taught to exercise. What I want you to do is this: stretch your body to the point where you feel a little pull. Then stop stretching, but keep the same posture and exhale deeply. By doing this, you will allow your body to release the stress and reduce the resistance. Then you will be able to stretch further, and relax, and have no pain.

STUDENT: But Mrs. Jones, I've done exercises all my life, and I know
(MAN) that it always hurts to stretch. In fact, if you don't feel any

pain, it means that you're not stretching enough. You know the old saying, "No pain, no gain!"

PROFESSOR: Oh yes, I'm well aware of that saying, and, in fact, I agree with it. But let's look at this saying in another way. "No pain, no gain." It can be painful to gain a new concept. Sometimes, it's even more painful to change your ideas than it is to have a tooth pulled. Now let's apply this idea to your exercises for today.

TO THE READER: Pause thirteen seconds after each question.

36. Where does this conversation probably take place?
37. What does the woman mainly want to explain?
38. According to the man, what is painful?
39. Which statement would both speakers probably agree to?
40. What will probably happen next?

Questions 41 through 45 are based on the following personal account:

In the United States, social security numbers are used to identify people for work, for school, and for other official business. You need to know your social security number when you apply for a job, when you fill out tax forms, and when you register for school. Basically, you need a social security number in order to survive in American society.

When I first came to the United States, I was told that I should apply for my social security number. So I took the bus down to the social security office. The office was busy, with several people waiting in line. When it was my turn, the officer gave me a long form and told me to fill it out and return it to him. I took my form, found a seat, and sat down to fill it out.

I read over the form, but to my frustration, even after reading it over several times, I still could not make any sense out of it. I felt terrible, and began to doubt my ability to survive in America. "Oh dear," I thought. "If this is so difficult for me, how will I ever get through school?" After trying again and again to read and understand the form, I finally said to myself, "Even with all the years I've studied English, I haven't learned enough vocabulary to fill out a basic form. But I must apply for a social security number. There is no way around it. I will have to get help." So I reluctantly approached the officer for help. "Excuse me, sir. Could you help me with this form? I'm a newcomer here, and I can't understand it." The officer looked over the form, and said in surprise, "Oh, no. I've made a mistake. This form is in Spanish. Here, take a new form." Was I embarrassed! He gave me the new form, and I filled it out in a few minutes. Two weeks later, I received notice of my social security number. I have been in the United States for two years now, but I still can't forget that embarrassing situation of my first visit to the social security office.

TO THE READER: Pause thirteen seconds after each question.

41. What is a social security number?
42. Who said he made a mistake?
43. Why couldn't the newcomer fill out the form?
44. Why was the newcomer embarrassed?
45. Did the newcomer get a social security number?

Questions 46 through 50 are based on the following reading:

Today I'd like to begin a discussion on the problem of the heating up of the earth. First we'll touch on the relationship between fluorocarbons and the ozone layer. You probably remember that the ozone layer is the protective shield around the earth. It is important to all life because it filters out harmful ultraviolet light from the sun. Ozone itself, a form of oxygen, is regularly made by the action of the sun in the upper atmosphere. It is also regularly destroyed by natural chemical processes. The problem now is that too much of the ozone layer is being destroyed. Scientists suspect that certain chemicals, such as fluorocarbons, are contributing to this depletion of the ozone layer. And how do we use fluorocarbons? The most common uses are in spray cans and automobile cooling systems. The chemical pollution from these fluorocarbons can account for some of the ozone losses that have been reported. There are, however, new studies linking the sun itself to the depletion of the ozone layer. We'll go into that new study more next time.

TO THE READER: Pause thirteen seconds after each question.

46. Who is the speaker probably addressing?
47. What is the speaker's main topic?
48. What is the most important purpose of the ozone layer?
49. What is the ozone layer made of?
50. What will the speaker probably discuss next?

PRACTICE TEST 2

SECTION 1, PART A

EXAMPLE I: Would you mind opening the door for me?

EXAMPLE 2: There is so much fog that I can barely see the cars on the road.

TO THE READER: Pause thirteen seconds after each sentence.

1. You'll miss the train unless you hurry.
2. We all think Grandma should take it easy after her fall.
3. By the time John gets to the party, the director will have already gone.
4. Sandra finished the work in no time at all.
5. The door for the handicapped is in the rear.
6. One student presented a project which was discussed by the entire group.
7. Jenny once dreamed of being an Olympic gold medal winner in gymnastics.
8. You're on the right track.
9. Mr. Wilson is wealthy enough to retire.
10. Black clothes are not as fit to wear in summer as white ones.
11. The design was complete, but the work had just begun.
12. They were large enough to be called small planets.
13. If you do this part, I'll take care of the rest.
14. His determination to do what seemed impossible was the key to his success.
15. Computer science is becoming an overcrowded field.
16. Whatever it costs, I want it.
17. My uncle is a well-known lecturer on speech.
18. George dropped the class due to a schedule conflict.
19. We couldn't have gone to the beach on a better day.
20. I'm working as fast as I can.

SECTION 1, PART B

EXAMPLE:

> *Woman:* Oh dear. We're out of milk.
> *Man:* No problem. I'll pick some up on my way home from work.

What does the man say he will do?

TO THE READER: Read the sentences below. Pause thirteen seconds after each sentence.

21. MAN: What do you think the boss will do when we tell him the bad news?
WOMAN: Oh, you can never tell with him!

What does the woman mean?

22. MAN: Well, I'll be leaving now.
WOMAN: Must you go so soon?

How does the woman feel?

23. WOMAN: Would you like this gift-wrapped?
MAN: Thanks, I would.

Where does this conversation take place?

24. MAN: How long do you think it will take to finish this job?
WOMAN: Off-hand, I'd say 3 hours.

How long will it take?

25. WOMAN: I'm sorry. The class is full.
MAN: Well, could I be put on the waiting list?

What does the man mean?

26. MAN: What time do we have to check out tomorrow?
WOMAN: I'm not sure. Let's check at the front desk.

Where does this conversation take place?

27. MAN: Would you like to go have some coffee?
WOMAN: Thanks, but I have some work I have to catch up on.

What does the woman mean?

28. WOMAN: How much is a dorm room?
MAN: It's $500 a month for room and board.

What do you get for $500?

29. WOMAN: May I try these on?
MAN: Yes, but no more than three items are allowed in the dressing room.

Where does this conversation take place?

30. WOMAN: I'm really angry at John. He never listens to me.
MAN: Take it easy, Ellen. Things will work out.

What does the man want Ellen to do?

31. MAN: Would you like a chocolate or butter brickle cone?
WOMAN: I don't care. I like them both.

Where does this conversation most likely take place?

32. MAN: Did you hear that Ann got laid off?
WOMAN: No, that's terrible.

What happened to Ann?

33. WOMAN: Have you called Pete yet?
MAN: I'll call him as soon as I get home.

What does the man mean?

34. MAN: Which kind of pie do you want?
WOMAN: I don't know. I like pumpkin as well as apple.

What does the woman mean?

35. WOMAN: How much was
the bill?
MAN: All in all, it came
to $54.00.

What does the man mean?

SECTION 1, PART C

Sample Talk

On Friday, November 14, there will be an International Festival from 7:00 to 10:00 P.M. at the Student Center. Everybody is invited to come. The program will include performances by the Scottish Country Dance Group and the University International Dancers. Also included will be folk songs from Spain and an international student costume show. There will also be dancing for everyone. You're encouraged to wear the costume of your heritage. Refreshments will be served, and admission is free. Please come!

EXAMPLE QUESTION 1: Who is this announcement probably given to?

EXAMPLE QUESTION 2: What will most people be able to do at the Festival?

Questions 36–43

Now that I've extracted your tooth, I want to give you some words of advice. Remember that this is surgery. You need to go home and rest for the rest of the day. You shouldn't do your regular work. Since you're an adult, it might take you longer to heal than if you were a child. The numbness will wear off after a few hours, and if it's painful after that, you should take two aspirins.

Now the most important thing to remember is to apply ice to your cheek immediately when you get home. This will keep the swelling down. You can use an ice bag or put chopped ice in a towel. Hold it on your cheek over the extraction area for twenty minutes and then take it off for twenty minutes. Keep this up for four or five hours.

Secondly, don't rinse your mouth today. Tomorrow you should rinse your mouth gently every three or four hours with salt water. Put about a quarter of a teaspoon of salt in a glass of warm water. Continue this rinsing for several days.

Don't be alarmed if there is some bleeding this morning. A little bleeding is normal following an extraction. I've put gauze pads over the extraction and I will give you some to take home. Change the pads about a half hour after you get home.

That's all you need to do. Call me anytime if you have a lot of bleeding or pain. And remember to apply ice right away.

TO THE READER: Pause thirteen seconds after each question.

36. Who is probably speaking?
37. When is the man speaking?
38. How long will the person's mouth be numb?
39. What does he say is the most important thing to do?
40. When does he say to rinse with salt water?
41. What do the gauze pads do?
42. What does the speaker say about bleeding?
43. What kind of person does the speaker seem to be?

Questions 44–50

Welcome, everyone, to this workshop on student housing. I'll go through the information about types of housing available for the fall and the procedure for application. Then, if you have any questions, feel free to ask me.

There are three main types of housing here for you to choose from: the student dorms, the married student apartments, and the international houses. As of now, there is some space available in each type, but they are filling up fast. You should get your application in as soon as possible. Let me explain some of the main features of each type of housing.

The student dorms are for any student. We have men's dorms, women's dorms, and co-ed dorms. In the co-ed dorms there is one large bathroom and shower area for both sexes to use. Most of the rooms have two beds, two closets, and two desks. We also have a few triples, and a few single suites, but I think the suites are already taken. There are no cooking facilities in the dorms, but you can buy a meal ticket for the cafeteria.

The married student apartments are for married students only. Each apartment has a kitchen, a living-dining area and either one or two bedrooms. Children are allowed in the apartments.

The international houses are a group of apartments for both foreign students and resident students. They are organized into language and culture themes, and some of them have rules about speaking only a certain language during meal times. It's been a good way for students to learn about other cultures and languages. I think that Spanish House is full, but there are rooms available in all the other houses.

That's the main information. I'll pass out these applications now and answer your individual questions.

TO THE READER: Pause thirteen seconds after each question.

44. Who is the speaker probably addressing?
45. Which are not a regular part of the student dorms?
46. What do the married student apartments not allow?
47. Which students are the international houses for?
48. Which of the following is most likely required in Spanish House during some periods?
49. Which type of housing has no more room for students?
50. What will the audience probably do next?

PRACTICE TEST ANSWER SHEET A

Section 1: Listening Comprehension

1	2	3	4	5	6	7	8	9	10	11	12	13	14	15	16	17	18	19	20	21	22	23	24	25	26	27	28	29	30	31	32	33	34	35	36	37	38	39	40	41	42	43	44	45	46	47	48	49	50
Ⓐ	Ⓐ	Ⓐ	Ⓐ	Ⓐ	Ⓐ	Ⓐ	Ⓐ	Ⓐ	Ⓐ	Ⓐ	Ⓐ	Ⓐ	Ⓐ	Ⓐ	Ⓐ	Ⓐ	Ⓐ	Ⓐ	Ⓐ	Ⓐ	Ⓐ	Ⓐ	Ⓐ	Ⓐ	Ⓐ	Ⓐ	Ⓐ	Ⓐ	Ⓐ	Ⓐ	Ⓐ	Ⓐ	Ⓐ	Ⓐ	Ⓐ	Ⓐ	Ⓐ	Ⓐ	Ⓐ	Ⓐ	Ⓐ	Ⓐ	Ⓐ	Ⓐ	Ⓐ	Ⓐ	Ⓐ	Ⓐ	Ⓐ
Ⓑ	Ⓑ	Ⓑ	Ⓑ	Ⓑ	Ⓑ	Ⓑ	Ⓑ	Ⓑ	Ⓑ	Ⓑ	Ⓑ	Ⓑ	Ⓑ	Ⓑ	Ⓑ	Ⓑ	Ⓑ	Ⓑ	Ⓑ	Ⓑ	Ⓑ	Ⓑ	Ⓑ	Ⓑ	Ⓑ	Ⓑ	Ⓑ	Ⓑ	Ⓑ	Ⓑ	Ⓑ	Ⓑ	Ⓑ	Ⓑ	Ⓑ	Ⓑ	Ⓑ	Ⓑ	Ⓑ	Ⓑ	Ⓑ	Ⓑ	Ⓑ	Ⓑ	Ⓑ	Ⓑ	Ⓑ	Ⓑ	Ⓑ
Ⓒ	Ⓒ	Ⓒ	Ⓒ	Ⓒ	Ⓒ	Ⓒ	Ⓒ	Ⓒ	Ⓒ	Ⓒ	Ⓒ	Ⓒ	Ⓒ	Ⓒ	Ⓒ	Ⓒ	Ⓒ	Ⓒ	Ⓒ	Ⓒ	Ⓒ	Ⓒ	Ⓒ	Ⓒ	Ⓒ	Ⓒ	Ⓒ	Ⓒ	Ⓒ	Ⓒ	Ⓒ	Ⓒ	Ⓒ	Ⓒ	Ⓒ	Ⓒ	Ⓒ	Ⓒ	Ⓒ	Ⓒ	Ⓒ	Ⓒ	Ⓒ	Ⓒ	Ⓒ	Ⓒ	Ⓒ	Ⓒ	Ⓒ
Ⓓ	Ⓓ	Ⓓ	Ⓓ	Ⓓ	Ⓓ	Ⓓ	Ⓓ	Ⓓ	Ⓓ	Ⓓ	Ⓓ	Ⓓ	Ⓓ	Ⓓ	Ⓓ	Ⓓ	Ⓓ	Ⓓ	Ⓓ	Ⓓ	Ⓓ	Ⓓ	Ⓓ	Ⓓ	Ⓓ	Ⓓ	Ⓓ	Ⓓ	Ⓓ	Ⓓ	Ⓓ	Ⓓ	Ⓓ	Ⓓ	Ⓓ	Ⓓ	Ⓓ	Ⓓ	Ⓓ	Ⓓ	Ⓓ	Ⓓ	Ⓓ	Ⓓ	Ⓓ	Ⓓ	Ⓓ	Ⓓ	Ⓓ

Section 2: Structure and Written Expression

1	2	3	4	5	6	7	8	9	10	11	12	13	14	15	16	17	18	19	20	21	22	23	24	25	26	27	28	29	30	31	32	33	34	35	36	37	38	39	40
Ⓐ	Ⓐ	Ⓐ	Ⓐ	Ⓐ	Ⓐ	Ⓐ	Ⓐ	Ⓐ	Ⓐ	Ⓐ	Ⓐ	Ⓐ	Ⓐ	Ⓐ	Ⓐ	Ⓐ	Ⓐ	Ⓐ	Ⓐ	Ⓐ	Ⓐ	Ⓐ	Ⓐ	Ⓐ	Ⓐ	Ⓐ	Ⓐ	Ⓐ	Ⓐ	Ⓐ	Ⓐ	Ⓐ	Ⓐ	Ⓐ	Ⓐ	Ⓐ	Ⓐ	Ⓐ	Ⓐ
Ⓑ	Ⓑ	Ⓑ	Ⓑ	Ⓑ	Ⓑ	Ⓑ	Ⓑ	Ⓑ	Ⓑ	Ⓑ	Ⓑ	Ⓑ	Ⓑ	Ⓑ	Ⓑ	Ⓑ	Ⓑ	Ⓑ	Ⓑ	Ⓑ	Ⓑ	Ⓑ	Ⓑ	Ⓑ	Ⓑ	Ⓑ	Ⓑ	Ⓑ	Ⓑ	Ⓑ	Ⓑ	Ⓑ	Ⓑ	Ⓑ	Ⓑ	Ⓑ	Ⓑ	Ⓑ	Ⓑ
Ⓒ	Ⓒ	Ⓒ	Ⓒ	Ⓒ	Ⓒ	Ⓒ	Ⓒ	Ⓒ	Ⓒ	Ⓒ	Ⓒ	Ⓒ	Ⓒ	Ⓒ	Ⓒ	Ⓒ	Ⓒ	Ⓒ	Ⓒ	Ⓒ	Ⓒ	Ⓒ	Ⓒ	Ⓒ	Ⓒ	Ⓒ	Ⓒ	Ⓒ	Ⓒ	Ⓒ	Ⓒ	Ⓒ	Ⓒ	Ⓒ	Ⓒ	Ⓒ	Ⓒ	Ⓒ	Ⓒ
Ⓓ	Ⓓ	Ⓓ	Ⓓ	Ⓓ	Ⓓ	Ⓓ	Ⓓ	Ⓓ	Ⓓ	Ⓓ	Ⓓ	Ⓓ	Ⓓ	Ⓓ	Ⓓ	Ⓓ	Ⓓ	Ⓓ	Ⓓ	Ⓓ	Ⓓ	Ⓓ	Ⓓ	Ⓓ	Ⓓ	Ⓓ	Ⓓ	Ⓓ	Ⓓ	Ⓓ	Ⓓ	Ⓓ	Ⓓ	Ⓓ	Ⓓ	Ⓓ	Ⓓ	Ⓓ	Ⓓ

Section 3: Vocabulary and Reading Comprehension

1	2	3	4	5	6	7	8	9	10	11	12	13	14	15	16	17	18	19	20	21	22	23	24	25	26	27	28	29	30	31	32	33	34	35	36	37	38	39	40	41	42	43	44	45	46	47	48	49	50
Ⓐ	Ⓐ	Ⓐ	Ⓐ	Ⓐ	Ⓐ	Ⓐ	Ⓐ	Ⓐ	Ⓐ	Ⓐ	Ⓐ	Ⓐ	Ⓐ	Ⓐ	Ⓐ	Ⓐ	Ⓐ	Ⓐ	Ⓐ	Ⓐ	Ⓐ	Ⓐ	Ⓐ	Ⓐ	Ⓐ	Ⓐ	Ⓐ	Ⓐ	Ⓐ	Ⓐ	Ⓐ	Ⓐ	Ⓐ	Ⓐ	Ⓐ	Ⓐ	Ⓐ	Ⓐ	Ⓐ	Ⓐ	Ⓐ	Ⓐ	Ⓐ	Ⓐ	Ⓐ	Ⓐ	Ⓐ	Ⓐ	Ⓐ
Ⓑ	Ⓑ	Ⓑ	Ⓑ	Ⓑ	Ⓑ	Ⓑ	Ⓑ	Ⓑ	Ⓑ	Ⓑ	Ⓑ	Ⓑ	Ⓑ	Ⓑ	Ⓑ	Ⓑ	Ⓑ	Ⓑ	Ⓑ	Ⓑ	Ⓑ	Ⓑ	Ⓑ	Ⓑ	Ⓑ	Ⓑ	Ⓑ	Ⓑ	Ⓑ	Ⓑ	Ⓑ	Ⓑ	Ⓑ	Ⓑ	Ⓑ	Ⓑ	Ⓑ	Ⓑ	Ⓑ	Ⓑ	Ⓑ	Ⓑ	Ⓑ	Ⓑ	Ⓑ	Ⓑ	Ⓑ	Ⓑ	Ⓑ
Ⓒ	Ⓒ	Ⓒ	Ⓒ	Ⓒ	Ⓒ	Ⓒ	Ⓒ	Ⓒ	Ⓒ	Ⓒ	Ⓒ	Ⓒ	Ⓒ	Ⓒ	Ⓒ	Ⓒ	Ⓒ	Ⓒ	Ⓒ	Ⓒ	Ⓒ	Ⓒ	Ⓒ	Ⓒ	Ⓒ	Ⓒ	Ⓒ	Ⓒ	Ⓒ	Ⓒ	Ⓒ	Ⓒ	Ⓒ	Ⓒ	Ⓒ	Ⓒ	Ⓒ	Ⓒ	Ⓒ	Ⓒ	Ⓒ	Ⓒ	Ⓒ	Ⓒ	Ⓒ	Ⓒ	Ⓒ	Ⓒ	Ⓒ
Ⓓ	Ⓓ	Ⓓ	Ⓓ	Ⓓ	Ⓓ	Ⓓ	Ⓓ	Ⓓ	Ⓓ	Ⓓ	Ⓓ	Ⓓ	Ⓓ	Ⓓ	Ⓓ	Ⓓ	Ⓓ	Ⓓ	Ⓓ	Ⓓ	Ⓓ	Ⓓ	Ⓓ	Ⓓ	Ⓓ	Ⓓ	Ⓓ	Ⓓ	Ⓓ	Ⓓ	Ⓓ	Ⓓ	Ⓓ	Ⓓ	Ⓓ	Ⓓ	Ⓓ	Ⓓ	Ⓓ	Ⓓ	Ⓓ	Ⓓ	Ⓓ	Ⓓ	Ⓓ	Ⓓ	Ⓓ	Ⓓ	Ⓓ

51	52	53	54	55	56	57	58	59	60
Ⓐ	Ⓐ	Ⓐ	Ⓐ	Ⓐ	Ⓐ	Ⓐ	Ⓐ	Ⓐ	Ⓐ
Ⓑ	Ⓑ	Ⓑ	Ⓑ	Ⓑ	Ⓑ	Ⓑ	Ⓑ	Ⓑ	Ⓑ
Ⓒ	Ⓒ	Ⓒ	Ⓒ	Ⓒ	Ⓒ	Ⓒ	Ⓒ	Ⓒ	Ⓒ
Ⓓ	Ⓓ	Ⓓ	Ⓓ	Ⓓ	Ⓓ	Ⓓ	Ⓓ	Ⓓ	Ⓓ

Date Taken _____

Number Correct _____

PRACTICE TEST ANSWER SHEET B

Section 1: Listening Comprehension

1 Ⓐ Ⓑ Ⓒ Ⓓ	14 Ⓐ Ⓑ Ⓒ Ⓓ	27 Ⓐ Ⓑ Ⓒ Ⓓ	40 Ⓐ Ⓑ Ⓒ Ⓓ
2 Ⓐ Ⓑ Ⓒ Ⓓ	15 Ⓐ Ⓑ Ⓒ Ⓓ	28 Ⓐ Ⓑ Ⓒ Ⓓ	41 Ⓐ Ⓑ Ⓒ Ⓓ
3 Ⓐ Ⓑ Ⓒ Ⓓ	16 Ⓐ Ⓑ Ⓒ Ⓓ	29 Ⓐ Ⓑ Ⓒ Ⓓ	42 Ⓐ Ⓑ Ⓒ Ⓓ
4 Ⓐ Ⓑ Ⓒ Ⓓ	17 Ⓐ Ⓑ Ⓒ Ⓓ	30 Ⓐ Ⓑ Ⓒ Ⓓ	43 Ⓐ Ⓑ Ⓒ Ⓓ
5 Ⓐ Ⓑ Ⓒ Ⓓ	18 Ⓐ Ⓑ Ⓒ Ⓓ	31 Ⓐ Ⓑ Ⓒ Ⓓ	44 Ⓐ Ⓑ Ⓒ Ⓓ
6 Ⓐ Ⓑ Ⓒ Ⓓ	19 Ⓐ Ⓑ Ⓒ Ⓓ	32 Ⓐ Ⓑ Ⓒ Ⓓ	45 Ⓐ Ⓑ Ⓒ Ⓓ
7 Ⓐ Ⓑ Ⓒ Ⓓ	20 Ⓐ Ⓑ Ⓒ Ⓓ	33 Ⓐ Ⓑ Ⓒ Ⓓ	46 Ⓐ Ⓑ Ⓒ Ⓓ
8 Ⓐ Ⓑ Ⓒ Ⓓ	21 Ⓐ Ⓑ Ⓒ Ⓓ	34 Ⓐ Ⓑ Ⓒ Ⓓ	47 Ⓐ Ⓑ Ⓒ Ⓓ
9 Ⓐ Ⓑ Ⓒ Ⓓ	22 Ⓐ Ⓑ Ⓒ Ⓓ	35 Ⓐ Ⓑ Ⓒ Ⓓ	48 Ⓐ Ⓑ Ⓒ Ⓓ
10 Ⓐ Ⓑ Ⓒ Ⓓ	23 Ⓐ Ⓑ Ⓒ Ⓓ	36 Ⓐ Ⓑ Ⓒ Ⓓ	49 Ⓐ Ⓑ Ⓒ Ⓓ
11 Ⓐ Ⓑ Ⓒ Ⓓ	24 Ⓐ Ⓑ Ⓒ Ⓓ	37 Ⓐ Ⓑ Ⓒ Ⓓ	50 Ⓐ Ⓑ Ⓒ Ⓓ
12 Ⓐ Ⓑ Ⓒ Ⓓ	25 Ⓐ Ⓑ Ⓒ Ⓓ	38 Ⓐ Ⓑ Ⓒ Ⓓ	
13 Ⓐ Ⓑ Ⓒ Ⓓ	26 Ⓐ Ⓑ Ⓒ Ⓓ	39 Ⓐ Ⓑ Ⓒ Ⓓ	

Section 2: Structure and Written Expression

1 Ⓐ Ⓑ Ⓒ Ⓓ	11 Ⓐ Ⓑ Ⓒ Ⓓ	21 Ⓐ Ⓑ Ⓒ Ⓓ	31 Ⓐ Ⓑ Ⓒ Ⓓ
2 Ⓐ Ⓑ Ⓒ Ⓓ	12 Ⓐ Ⓑ Ⓒ Ⓓ	22 Ⓐ Ⓑ Ⓒ Ⓓ	32 Ⓐ Ⓑ Ⓒ Ⓓ
3 Ⓐ Ⓑ Ⓒ Ⓓ	13 Ⓐ Ⓑ Ⓒ Ⓓ	23 Ⓐ Ⓑ Ⓒ Ⓓ	33 Ⓐ Ⓑ Ⓒ Ⓓ
4 Ⓐ Ⓑ Ⓒ Ⓓ	14 Ⓐ Ⓑ Ⓒ Ⓓ	24 Ⓐ Ⓑ Ⓒ Ⓓ	34 Ⓐ Ⓑ Ⓒ Ⓓ
5 Ⓐ Ⓑ Ⓒ Ⓓ	15 Ⓐ Ⓑ Ⓒ Ⓓ	25 Ⓐ Ⓑ Ⓒ Ⓓ	35 Ⓐ Ⓑ Ⓒ Ⓓ
6 Ⓐ Ⓑ Ⓒ Ⓓ	16 Ⓐ Ⓑ Ⓒ Ⓓ	26 Ⓐ Ⓑ Ⓒ Ⓓ	36 Ⓐ Ⓑ Ⓒ Ⓓ
7 Ⓐ Ⓑ Ⓒ Ⓓ	17 Ⓐ Ⓑ Ⓒ Ⓓ	27 Ⓐ Ⓑ Ⓒ Ⓓ	37 Ⓐ Ⓑ Ⓒ Ⓓ
8 Ⓐ Ⓑ Ⓒ Ⓓ	18 Ⓐ Ⓑ Ⓒ Ⓓ	28 Ⓐ Ⓑ Ⓒ Ⓓ	38 Ⓐ Ⓑ Ⓒ Ⓓ
9 Ⓐ Ⓑ Ⓒ Ⓓ	19 Ⓐ Ⓑ Ⓒ Ⓓ	29 Ⓐ Ⓑ Ⓒ Ⓓ	39 Ⓐ Ⓑ Ⓒ Ⓓ
10 Ⓐ Ⓑ Ⓒ Ⓓ	20 Ⓐ Ⓑ Ⓒ Ⓓ	30 Ⓐ Ⓑ Ⓒ Ⓓ	40 Ⓐ Ⓑ Ⓒ Ⓓ

Section 3: Vocabulary and Reading Comprehension

1 Ⓐ Ⓑ Ⓒ Ⓓ	16 Ⓐ Ⓑ Ⓒ Ⓓ	31 Ⓐ Ⓑ Ⓒ Ⓓ	46 Ⓐ Ⓑ Ⓒ Ⓓ
2 Ⓐ Ⓑ Ⓒ Ⓓ	17 Ⓐ Ⓑ Ⓒ Ⓓ	32 Ⓐ Ⓑ Ⓒ Ⓓ	47 Ⓐ Ⓑ Ⓒ Ⓓ
3 Ⓐ Ⓑ Ⓒ Ⓓ	18 Ⓐ Ⓑ Ⓒ Ⓓ	33 Ⓐ Ⓑ Ⓒ Ⓓ	48 Ⓐ Ⓑ Ⓒ Ⓓ
4 Ⓐ Ⓑ Ⓒ Ⓓ	19 Ⓐ Ⓑ Ⓒ Ⓓ	34 Ⓐ Ⓑ Ⓒ Ⓓ	49 Ⓐ Ⓑ Ⓒ Ⓓ
5 Ⓐ Ⓑ Ⓒ Ⓓ	20 Ⓐ Ⓑ Ⓒ Ⓓ	35 Ⓐ Ⓑ Ⓒ Ⓓ	50 Ⓐ Ⓑ Ⓒ Ⓓ
6 Ⓐ Ⓑ Ⓒ Ⓓ	21 Ⓐ Ⓑ Ⓒ Ⓓ	36 Ⓐ Ⓑ Ⓒ Ⓓ	51 Ⓐ Ⓑ Ⓒ Ⓓ
7 Ⓐ Ⓑ Ⓒ Ⓓ	22 Ⓐ Ⓑ Ⓒ Ⓓ	37 Ⓐ Ⓑ Ⓒ Ⓓ	52 Ⓐ Ⓑ Ⓒ Ⓓ
8 Ⓐ Ⓑ Ⓒ Ⓓ	23 Ⓐ Ⓑ Ⓒ Ⓓ	38 Ⓐ Ⓑ Ⓒ Ⓓ	53 Ⓐ Ⓑ Ⓒ Ⓓ
9 Ⓐ Ⓑ Ⓒ Ⓓ	24 Ⓐ Ⓑ Ⓒ Ⓓ	39 Ⓐ Ⓑ Ⓒ Ⓓ	54 Ⓐ Ⓑ Ⓒ Ⓓ
10 Ⓐ Ⓑ Ⓒ Ⓓ	25 Ⓐ Ⓑ Ⓒ Ⓓ	40 Ⓐ Ⓑ Ⓒ Ⓓ	55 Ⓐ Ⓑ Ⓒ Ⓓ
11 Ⓐ Ⓑ Ⓒ Ⓓ	26 Ⓐ Ⓑ Ⓒ Ⓓ	41 Ⓐ Ⓑ Ⓒ Ⓓ	56 Ⓐ Ⓑ Ⓒ Ⓓ
12 Ⓐ Ⓑ Ⓒ Ⓓ	27 Ⓐ Ⓑ Ⓒ Ⓓ	42 Ⓐ Ⓑ Ⓒ Ⓓ	57 Ⓐ Ⓑ Ⓒ Ⓓ
13 Ⓐ Ⓑ Ⓒ Ⓓ	28 Ⓐ Ⓑ Ⓒ Ⓓ	43 Ⓐ Ⓑ Ⓒ Ⓓ	58 Ⓐ Ⓑ Ⓒ Ⓓ
14 Ⓐ Ⓑ Ⓒ Ⓓ	29 Ⓐ Ⓑ Ⓒ Ⓓ	44 Ⓐ Ⓑ Ⓒ Ⓓ	59 Ⓐ Ⓑ Ⓒ Ⓓ
15 Ⓐ Ⓑ Ⓒ Ⓓ	30 Ⓐ Ⓑ Ⓒ Ⓓ	45 Ⓐ Ⓑ Ⓒ Ⓓ	60 Ⓐ Ⓑ Ⓒ Ⓓ

Date Taken _____   Number Correct _____

PRACTICE TEST ANSWER SHEET A

Section 1: Listening Comprehension

1	2	3	4	5	6	7	8	9	10	11	12	13	14	15	16	17	18	19	20	21	22	23	24	25	26	27	28	29	30	31	32	33	34	35	36	37	38	39	40	41	42	43	44	45	46	47	48	49	50
Ⓐ	Ⓐ	Ⓐ	Ⓐ	Ⓐ	Ⓐ	Ⓐ	Ⓐ	Ⓐ	Ⓐ	Ⓐ	Ⓐ	Ⓐ	Ⓐ	Ⓐ	Ⓐ	Ⓐ	Ⓐ	Ⓐ	Ⓐ	Ⓐ	Ⓐ	Ⓐ	Ⓐ	Ⓐ	Ⓐ	Ⓐ	Ⓐ	Ⓐ	Ⓐ	Ⓐ	Ⓐ	Ⓐ	Ⓐ	Ⓐ	Ⓐ	Ⓐ	Ⓐ	Ⓐ	Ⓐ	Ⓐ	Ⓐ	Ⓐ	Ⓐ	Ⓐ	Ⓐ	Ⓐ	Ⓐ	Ⓐ	Ⓐ
Ⓑ	Ⓑ	Ⓑ	Ⓑ	Ⓑ	Ⓑ	Ⓑ	Ⓑ	Ⓑ	Ⓑ	Ⓑ	Ⓑ	Ⓑ	Ⓑ	Ⓑ	Ⓑ	Ⓑ	Ⓑ	Ⓑ	Ⓑ	Ⓑ	Ⓑ	Ⓑ	Ⓑ	Ⓑ	Ⓑ	Ⓑ	Ⓑ	Ⓑ	Ⓑ	Ⓑ	Ⓑ	Ⓑ	Ⓑ	Ⓑ	Ⓑ	Ⓑ	Ⓑ	Ⓑ	Ⓑ	Ⓑ	Ⓑ	Ⓑ	Ⓑ	Ⓑ	Ⓑ	Ⓑ	Ⓑ	Ⓑ	Ⓑ
Ⓒ	Ⓒ	Ⓒ	Ⓒ	Ⓒ	Ⓒ	Ⓒ	Ⓒ	Ⓒ	Ⓒ	Ⓒ	Ⓒ	Ⓒ	Ⓒ	Ⓒ	Ⓒ	Ⓒ	Ⓒ	Ⓒ	Ⓒ	Ⓒ	Ⓒ	Ⓒ	Ⓒ	Ⓒ	Ⓒ	Ⓒ	Ⓒ	Ⓒ	Ⓒ	Ⓒ	Ⓒ	Ⓒ	Ⓒ	Ⓒ	Ⓒ	Ⓒ	Ⓒ	Ⓒ	Ⓒ	Ⓒ	Ⓒ	Ⓒ	Ⓒ	Ⓒ	Ⓒ	Ⓒ	Ⓒ	Ⓒ	Ⓒ
Ⓓ	Ⓓ	Ⓓ	Ⓓ	Ⓓ	Ⓓ	Ⓓ	Ⓓ	Ⓓ	Ⓓ	Ⓓ	Ⓓ	Ⓓ	Ⓓ	Ⓓ	Ⓓ	Ⓓ	Ⓓ	Ⓓ	Ⓓ	Ⓓ	Ⓓ	Ⓓ	Ⓓ	Ⓓ	Ⓓ	Ⓓ	Ⓓ	Ⓓ	Ⓓ	Ⓓ	Ⓓ	Ⓓ	Ⓓ	Ⓓ	Ⓓ	Ⓓ	Ⓓ	Ⓓ	Ⓓ	Ⓓ	Ⓓ	Ⓓ	Ⓓ	Ⓓ	Ⓓ	Ⓓ	Ⓓ	Ⓓ	Ⓓ

Section 2: Structure and Written Expression

1	2	3	4	5	6	7	8	9	10	11	12	13	14	15	16	17	18	19	20	21	22	23	24	25	26	27	28	29	30	31	32	33	34	35	36	37	38	39	40
Ⓐ	Ⓐ	Ⓐ	Ⓐ	Ⓐ	Ⓐ	Ⓐ	Ⓐ	Ⓐ	Ⓐ	Ⓐ	Ⓐ	Ⓐ	Ⓐ	Ⓐ	Ⓐ	Ⓐ	Ⓐ	Ⓐ	Ⓐ	Ⓐ	Ⓐ	Ⓐ	Ⓐ	Ⓐ	Ⓐ	Ⓐ	Ⓐ	Ⓐ	Ⓐ	Ⓐ	Ⓐ	Ⓐ	Ⓐ	Ⓐ	Ⓐ	Ⓐ	Ⓐ	Ⓐ	Ⓐ
Ⓑ	Ⓑ	Ⓑ	Ⓑ	Ⓑ	Ⓑ	Ⓑ	Ⓑ	Ⓑ	Ⓑ	Ⓑ	Ⓑ	Ⓑ	Ⓑ	Ⓑ	Ⓑ	Ⓑ	Ⓑ	Ⓑ	Ⓑ	Ⓑ	Ⓑ	Ⓑ	Ⓑ	Ⓑ	Ⓑ	Ⓑ	Ⓑ	Ⓑ	Ⓑ	Ⓑ	Ⓑ	Ⓑ	Ⓑ	Ⓑ	Ⓑ	Ⓑ	Ⓑ	Ⓑ	Ⓑ
Ⓒ	Ⓒ	Ⓒ	Ⓒ	Ⓒ	Ⓒ	Ⓒ	Ⓒ	Ⓒ	Ⓒ	Ⓒ	Ⓒ	Ⓒ	Ⓒ	Ⓒ	Ⓒ	Ⓒ	Ⓒ	Ⓒ	Ⓒ	Ⓒ	Ⓒ	Ⓒ	Ⓒ	Ⓒ	Ⓒ	Ⓒ	Ⓒ	Ⓒ	Ⓒ	Ⓒ	Ⓒ	Ⓒ	Ⓒ	Ⓒ	Ⓒ	Ⓒ	Ⓒ	Ⓒ	Ⓒ
Ⓓ	Ⓓ	Ⓓ	Ⓓ	Ⓓ	Ⓓ	Ⓓ	Ⓓ	Ⓓ	Ⓓ	Ⓓ	Ⓓ	Ⓓ	Ⓓ	Ⓓ	Ⓓ	Ⓓ	Ⓓ	Ⓓ	Ⓓ	Ⓓ	Ⓓ	Ⓓ	Ⓓ	Ⓓ	Ⓓ	Ⓓ	Ⓓ	Ⓓ	Ⓓ	Ⓓ	Ⓓ	Ⓓ	Ⓓ	Ⓓ	Ⓓ	Ⓓ	Ⓓ	Ⓓ	Ⓓ

Section 3: Vocabulary and Reading Comprehension

1	2	3	4	5	6	7	8	9	10	11	12	13	14	15	16	17	18	19	20	21	22	23	24	25	26	27	28	29	30	31	32	33	34	35	36	37	38	39	40	41	42	43	44	45	46	47	48	49	50
Ⓐ	Ⓐ	Ⓐ	Ⓐ	Ⓐ	Ⓐ	Ⓐ	Ⓐ	Ⓐ	Ⓐ	Ⓐ	Ⓐ	Ⓐ	Ⓐ	Ⓐ	Ⓐ	Ⓐ	Ⓐ	Ⓐ	Ⓐ	Ⓐ	Ⓐ	Ⓐ	Ⓐ	Ⓐ	Ⓐ	Ⓐ	Ⓐ	Ⓐ	Ⓐ	Ⓐ	Ⓐ	Ⓐ	Ⓐ	Ⓐ	Ⓐ	Ⓐ	Ⓐ	Ⓐ	Ⓐ	Ⓐ	Ⓐ	Ⓐ	Ⓐ	Ⓐ	Ⓐ	Ⓐ	Ⓐ	Ⓐ	Ⓐ
Ⓑ	Ⓑ	Ⓑ	Ⓑ	Ⓑ	Ⓑ	Ⓑ	Ⓑ	Ⓑ	Ⓑ	Ⓑ	Ⓑ	Ⓑ	Ⓑ	Ⓑ	Ⓑ	Ⓑ	Ⓑ	Ⓑ	Ⓑ	Ⓑ	Ⓑ	Ⓑ	Ⓑ	Ⓑ	Ⓑ	Ⓑ	Ⓑ	Ⓑ	Ⓑ	Ⓑ	Ⓑ	Ⓑ	Ⓑ	Ⓑ	Ⓑ	Ⓑ	Ⓑ	Ⓑ	Ⓑ	Ⓑ	Ⓑ	Ⓑ	Ⓑ	Ⓑ	Ⓑ	Ⓑ	Ⓑ	Ⓑ	Ⓑ
Ⓒ	Ⓒ	Ⓒ	Ⓒ	Ⓒ	Ⓒ	Ⓒ	Ⓒ	Ⓒ	Ⓒ	Ⓒ	Ⓒ	Ⓒ	Ⓒ	Ⓒ	Ⓒ	Ⓒ	Ⓒ	Ⓒ	Ⓒ	Ⓒ	Ⓒ	Ⓒ	Ⓒ	Ⓒ	Ⓒ	Ⓒ	Ⓒ	Ⓒ	Ⓒ	Ⓒ	Ⓒ	Ⓒ	Ⓒ	Ⓒ	Ⓒ	Ⓒ	Ⓒ	Ⓒ	Ⓒ	Ⓒ	Ⓒ	Ⓒ	Ⓒ	Ⓒ	Ⓒ	Ⓒ	Ⓒ	Ⓒ	Ⓒ
Ⓓ	Ⓓ	Ⓓ	Ⓓ	Ⓓ	Ⓓ	Ⓓ	Ⓓ	Ⓓ	Ⓓ	Ⓓ	Ⓓ	Ⓓ	Ⓓ	Ⓓ	Ⓓ	Ⓓ	Ⓓ	Ⓓ	Ⓓ	Ⓓ	Ⓓ	Ⓓ	Ⓓ	Ⓓ	Ⓓ	Ⓓ	Ⓓ	Ⓓ	Ⓓ	Ⓓ	Ⓓ	Ⓓ	Ⓓ	Ⓓ	Ⓓ	Ⓓ	Ⓓ	Ⓓ	Ⓓ	Ⓓ	Ⓓ	Ⓓ	Ⓓ	Ⓓ	Ⓓ	Ⓓ	Ⓓ	Ⓓ	Ⓓ

51	52	53	54	55	56	57	58	59	60
Ⓐ	Ⓐ	Ⓐ	Ⓐ	Ⓐ	Ⓐ	Ⓐ	Ⓐ	Ⓐ	Ⓐ
Ⓑ	Ⓑ	Ⓑ	Ⓑ	Ⓑ	Ⓑ	Ⓑ	Ⓑ	Ⓑ	Ⓑ
Ⓒ	Ⓒ	Ⓒ	Ⓒ	Ⓒ	Ⓒ	Ⓒ	Ⓒ	Ⓒ	Ⓒ
Ⓓ	Ⓓ	Ⓓ	Ⓓ	Ⓓ	Ⓓ	Ⓓ	Ⓓ	Ⓓ	Ⓓ

Date Taken _____

Number Correct _____

251

PRACTICE TEST ANSWER SHEET B

Section 1: Listening Comprehension

1 Ⓐ Ⓑ Ⓒ Ⓓ	14 Ⓐ Ⓑ Ⓒ Ⓓ	27 Ⓐ Ⓑ Ⓒ Ⓓ	40 Ⓐ Ⓑ Ⓒ Ⓓ
2 Ⓐ Ⓑ Ⓒ Ⓓ	15 Ⓐ Ⓑ Ⓒ Ⓓ	28 Ⓐ Ⓑ Ⓒ Ⓓ	41 Ⓐ Ⓑ Ⓒ Ⓓ
3 Ⓐ Ⓑ Ⓒ Ⓓ	16 Ⓐ Ⓑ Ⓒ Ⓓ	29 Ⓐ Ⓑ Ⓒ Ⓓ	42 Ⓐ Ⓑ Ⓒ Ⓓ
4 Ⓐ Ⓑ Ⓒ Ⓓ	17 Ⓐ Ⓑ Ⓒ Ⓓ	30 Ⓐ Ⓑ Ⓒ Ⓓ	43 Ⓐ Ⓑ Ⓒ Ⓓ
5 Ⓐ Ⓑ Ⓒ Ⓓ	18 Ⓐ Ⓑ Ⓒ Ⓓ	31 Ⓐ Ⓑ Ⓒ Ⓓ	44 Ⓐ Ⓑ Ⓒ Ⓓ
6 Ⓐ Ⓑ Ⓒ Ⓓ	19 Ⓐ Ⓑ Ⓒ Ⓓ	32 Ⓐ Ⓑ Ⓒ Ⓓ	45 Ⓐ Ⓑ Ⓒ Ⓓ
7 Ⓐ Ⓑ Ⓒ Ⓓ	20 Ⓐ Ⓑ Ⓒ Ⓓ	33 Ⓐ Ⓑ Ⓒ Ⓓ	46 Ⓐ Ⓑ Ⓒ Ⓓ
8 Ⓐ Ⓑ Ⓒ Ⓓ	21 Ⓐ Ⓑ Ⓒ Ⓓ	34 Ⓐ Ⓑ Ⓒ Ⓓ	47 Ⓐ Ⓑ Ⓒ Ⓓ
9 Ⓐ Ⓑ Ⓒ Ⓓ	22 Ⓐ Ⓑ Ⓒ Ⓓ	35 Ⓐ Ⓑ Ⓒ Ⓓ	48 Ⓐ Ⓑ Ⓒ Ⓓ
10 Ⓐ Ⓑ Ⓒ Ⓓ	23 Ⓐ Ⓑ Ⓒ Ⓓ	36 Ⓐ Ⓑ Ⓒ Ⓓ	49 Ⓐ Ⓑ Ⓒ Ⓓ
11 Ⓐ Ⓑ Ⓒ Ⓓ	24 Ⓐ Ⓑ Ⓒ Ⓓ	37 Ⓐ Ⓑ Ⓒ Ⓓ	50 Ⓐ Ⓑ Ⓒ Ⓓ
12 Ⓐ Ⓑ Ⓒ Ⓓ	25 Ⓐ Ⓑ Ⓒ Ⓓ	38 Ⓐ Ⓑ Ⓒ Ⓓ	
13 Ⓐ Ⓑ Ⓒ Ⓓ	26 Ⓐ Ⓑ Ⓒ Ⓓ	39 Ⓐ Ⓑ Ⓒ Ⓓ	

Section 2: Structure and Written Expression

1 Ⓐ Ⓑ Ⓒ Ⓓ	11 Ⓐ Ⓑ Ⓒ Ⓓ	21 Ⓐ Ⓑ Ⓒ Ⓓ	31 Ⓐ Ⓑ Ⓒ Ⓓ
2 Ⓐ Ⓑ Ⓒ Ⓓ	12 Ⓐ Ⓑ Ⓒ Ⓓ	22 Ⓐ Ⓑ Ⓒ Ⓓ	32 Ⓐ Ⓑ Ⓒ Ⓓ
3 Ⓐ Ⓑ Ⓒ Ⓓ	13 Ⓐ Ⓑ Ⓒ Ⓓ	23 Ⓐ Ⓑ Ⓒ Ⓓ	33 Ⓐ Ⓑ Ⓒ Ⓓ
4 Ⓐ Ⓑ Ⓒ Ⓓ	14 Ⓐ Ⓑ Ⓒ Ⓓ	24 Ⓐ Ⓑ Ⓒ Ⓓ	34 Ⓐ Ⓑ Ⓒ Ⓓ
5 Ⓐ Ⓑ Ⓒ Ⓓ	15 Ⓐ Ⓑ Ⓒ Ⓓ	25 Ⓐ Ⓑ Ⓒ Ⓓ	35 Ⓐ Ⓑ Ⓒ Ⓓ
6 Ⓐ Ⓑ Ⓒ Ⓓ	16 Ⓐ Ⓑ Ⓒ Ⓓ	26 Ⓐ Ⓑ Ⓒ Ⓓ	36 Ⓐ Ⓑ Ⓒ Ⓓ
7 Ⓐ Ⓑ Ⓒ Ⓓ	17 Ⓐ Ⓑ Ⓒ Ⓓ	27 Ⓐ Ⓑ Ⓒ Ⓓ	37 Ⓐ Ⓑ Ⓒ Ⓓ
8 Ⓐ Ⓑ Ⓒ Ⓓ	18 Ⓐ Ⓑ Ⓒ Ⓓ	28 Ⓐ Ⓑ Ⓒ Ⓓ	38 Ⓐ Ⓑ Ⓒ Ⓓ
9 Ⓐ Ⓑ Ⓒ Ⓓ	19 Ⓐ Ⓑ Ⓒ Ⓓ	29 Ⓐ Ⓑ Ⓒ Ⓓ	39 Ⓐ Ⓑ Ⓒ Ⓓ
10 Ⓐ Ⓑ Ⓒ Ⓓ	20 Ⓐ Ⓑ Ⓒ Ⓓ	30 Ⓐ Ⓑ Ⓒ Ⓓ	40 Ⓐ Ⓑ Ⓒ Ⓓ

Section 3: Vocabulary and Reading Comprehension

1 Ⓐ Ⓑ Ⓒ Ⓓ	16 Ⓐ Ⓑ Ⓒ Ⓓ	31 Ⓐ Ⓑ Ⓒ Ⓓ	46 Ⓐ Ⓑ Ⓒ Ⓓ
2 Ⓐ Ⓑ Ⓒ Ⓓ	17 Ⓐ Ⓑ Ⓒ Ⓓ	32 Ⓐ Ⓑ Ⓒ Ⓓ	47 Ⓐ Ⓑ Ⓒ Ⓓ
3 Ⓐ Ⓑ Ⓒ Ⓓ	18 Ⓐ Ⓑ Ⓒ Ⓓ	33 Ⓐ Ⓑ Ⓒ Ⓓ	48 Ⓐ Ⓑ Ⓒ Ⓓ
4 Ⓐ Ⓑ Ⓒ Ⓓ	19 Ⓐ Ⓑ Ⓒ Ⓓ	34 Ⓐ Ⓑ Ⓒ Ⓓ	49 Ⓐ Ⓑ Ⓒ Ⓓ
5 Ⓐ Ⓑ Ⓒ Ⓓ	20 Ⓐ Ⓑ Ⓒ Ⓓ	35 Ⓐ Ⓑ Ⓒ Ⓓ	50 Ⓐ Ⓑ Ⓒ Ⓓ
6 Ⓐ Ⓑ Ⓒ Ⓓ	21 Ⓐ Ⓑ Ⓒ Ⓓ	36 Ⓐ Ⓑ Ⓒ Ⓓ	51 Ⓐ Ⓑ Ⓒ Ⓓ
7 Ⓐ Ⓑ Ⓒ Ⓓ	22 Ⓐ Ⓑ Ⓒ Ⓓ	37 Ⓐ Ⓑ Ⓒ Ⓓ	52 Ⓐ Ⓑ Ⓒ Ⓓ
8 Ⓐ Ⓑ Ⓒ Ⓓ	23 Ⓐ Ⓑ Ⓒ Ⓓ	38 Ⓐ Ⓑ Ⓒ Ⓓ	53 Ⓐ Ⓑ Ⓒ Ⓓ
9 Ⓐ Ⓑ Ⓒ Ⓓ	24 Ⓐ Ⓑ Ⓒ Ⓓ	39 Ⓐ Ⓑ Ⓒ Ⓓ	54 Ⓐ Ⓑ Ⓒ Ⓓ
10 Ⓐ Ⓑ Ⓒ Ⓓ	25 Ⓐ Ⓑ Ⓒ Ⓓ	40 Ⓐ Ⓑ Ⓒ Ⓓ	55 Ⓐ Ⓑ Ⓒ Ⓓ
11 Ⓐ Ⓑ Ⓒ Ⓓ	26 Ⓐ Ⓑ Ⓒ Ⓓ	41 Ⓐ Ⓑ Ⓒ Ⓓ	56 Ⓐ Ⓑ Ⓒ Ⓓ
12 Ⓐ Ⓑ Ⓒ Ⓓ	27 Ⓐ Ⓑ Ⓒ Ⓓ	42 Ⓐ Ⓑ Ⓒ Ⓓ	57 Ⓐ Ⓑ Ⓒ Ⓓ
13 Ⓐ Ⓑ Ⓒ Ⓓ	28 Ⓐ Ⓑ Ⓒ Ⓓ	43 Ⓐ Ⓑ Ⓒ Ⓓ	58 Ⓐ Ⓑ Ⓒ Ⓓ
14 Ⓐ Ⓑ Ⓒ Ⓓ	29 Ⓐ Ⓑ Ⓒ Ⓓ	44 Ⓐ Ⓑ Ⓒ Ⓓ	59 Ⓐ Ⓑ Ⓒ Ⓓ
15 Ⓐ Ⓑ Ⓒ Ⓓ	30 Ⓐ Ⓑ Ⓒ Ⓓ	45 Ⓐ Ⓑ Ⓒ Ⓓ	60 Ⓐ Ⓑ Ⓒ Ⓓ

Date Taken _____   Number Correct _____

Improve *YOUR* performance on the *TOEFL listening comprehension section with Arco's TOEFL Skills Listening Comprehension Cassette*

With Arco's TOEFL Skills Listening Comprehension Cassette you can simulate actual test conditions for the TOEFL Listening Comprehension section. The cassette contains the spoken parts of all the practice exercises and the Sample Exams in Arco's *TOEFL Skills for Top Scores*. It will help you to become familiar with spoken English as it will be used on the exam.

To order your TOEFL Skills cassette, use the form below.